PROFESSIONAL NODE.JS®

Continues

PROFESSIONAL

Node.js®

PROFESSIONAL

Node.js®

BUILDING JAVASCRIPT-BASED SCALABLE SOFTWARE

Pedro Teixeira

John Wiley & Sons, Inc.

Professional Node.js®: Building JavaScript-Based Scalable Software

Published by
John Wiley & Sons, Inc.
10475 Crosspoint Boulevard
Indianapolis, IN 46256
www.wiley.com

Published simultaneously in Canada

ISBN: 978-1-118-18546-9
ISBN: 978-1-118-22754-1 (ebk)
ISBN: 978-1-118-24056-4 (ebk)
ISBN: 978-1-118-26518-5 (ebk)

Manufactured in the United States of America

10 9 8 7 6 5 4 3 2 1

For general information on our other products and services please contact our Customer Care Department within the United States at (877) 762-2974, outside the United States at (317) 572-3993 or fax (317) 572-4002.

Wiley publishes in a variety of print and electronic formats and by print-on-demand. Some material included with standard print versions of this book may not be included in e-books or in print-on-demand. If this book refers to media such as a CD or DVD that is not included in the version you purchased, you may download this material at http://booksupport.wiley.com. For more information about Wiley products, visit www.wiley.com.

Library of Congress Control Number: 2012940020

This book is dedicated to my wife, Susana.
Throughout all these years she has always been an
example of strength and persistence.

ABOUT THE AUTHOR

PEDRO TEIXEIRA is a prolific open-source programmer and author of many Node.js modules. After graduating with a degree in Software Engineering more than 14 years ago, he has been a consultant, a programmer, and an active and internationally known Node.js community member.

He is a founding partner of The Node Firm and a Senior Programmer at Nodejitsu Inc., the leading Node.js platform-as-a-service provider. He is also the author of the popular Node Tuts screencasts.

When Pedro was 10 years old, his father taught him how to program a ZX Spectrum, and since then he has never wanted to stop. He taught himself how to program his father's Apple IIc and then entered the PC era. In college he was introduced to the universe of UNIX and open-source, becoming seriously addicted to it. In his professional life he has developed systems and products built with Visual Basic, C, C++, Java, PHP, Ruby, and JavaScript for big telecommunications companies, banks, hotel chains, and others.

He has been a Node.js enthusiast since its initial development, having authored many applications and many well-known modules like Fugue, Alfred.js, Carrier, Nock, and more.

ABOUT THE TECHNICAL EDITOR

MANUEL KIESSLING is a software development and systems administration team lead, using and teaching agile practices in both domains. He runs several open-source projects, is an active blogger, and wrote the freely available Node Beginner Book. He currently lives near Cologne, Germany, with his wife and two children.

He is the co-author of Chapter 22, "Making Universal Real-Time Web Applications Using Socket.IO," and Chapter 23, "Connecting to MySQL Using node-mysql."

CREDITS

ACQUISITIONS EDITOR
Mary James

PROJECT EDITOR
Tora Estep

TECHNICAL EDITOR
Manuel Kiessling

PRODUCTION EDITOR
Daniel Scribner

COPY EDITOR
Kezia Endsley

EDITORIAL MANAGER
Mary Beth Wakefield

FREELANCER EDITORIAL MANAGER
Rosemarie Graham

ASSOCIATE DIRECTOR OF MARKETING
David Mayhew

MARKETING MANAGER
Ashley Zurcher

BUSINESS MANAGER
Amy Knies

PRODUCTION MANAGER
Tim Tate

VICE PRESIDENT AND EXECUTIVE GROUP PUBLISHER
Richard Swadley

VICE PRESIDENT AND EXECUTIVE PUBLISHER
Neil Edde

ASSOCIATE PUBLISHER
Jim Minatel

PROJECT COORDINATOR, COVER
Katie Crocker

PROOFREADER
Nicole Hirschman

INDEXER
Ron Strauss

COVER DESIGNER
Ryan Sneed

COVER IMAGE
© Gregory Olsen/iStockPhoto

ACKNOWLEDGMENTS

FIRST, I WANT TO THANK my wife, Susana, and my kids, Henrique and Beatriz. You have given me courage and persistence by reminding me what is really important in life.

I'd also like to thank my Acquisitions Editor at Wiley, Mary E. James, for having faith in me and signing me up to write this book.

I want to thank my good friend and former colleague, programmer and photographer Pedro Mendes, who persuaded me to start writing a book about Node.js over a few beers in Lisbon.

I also want to thank my good friend Nuno Job, who has been my companion in this open-source and Node.js crusade for these last few years.

A big word of appreciation also goes out to the Node.js community in general. You are the best, most welcoming, appreciative, and fun programming community I have been a part of.

Lastly, I want to thank you, the reader, for buying this book. I hope it helps you in learning about the ins and outs of the wonderful world of programming in Node.js.

CONTENTS

PART III: FILES, PROCESSES, STREAMS, AND NETWORKING

INTRODUCTION

IN 1995, WHEN I WAS IN MY SECOND YEAR IN COLLEGE, I was introduced to UNIX network programming. In C, you could create sockets to open TCP connections to servers and code the servers that accepted these connections. I remember the excitement I felt the first time I created a TCP server: I could accept connections and receive and send messages on them.

If I wanted my server to accept many concurrent connections, the common solution was to use threads, and soon I had created my first multi-threaded TCP server. This server accessed a shared data structure, which needed to synchronize the access to all the client threads that had been spawned. Getting the synchronization fine-grained (to maximize resources and time) and right (to avoid deadlocks) proved to be more difficult than anticipated.

A couple of years later, I entered the working world to become a consultant, programming and leading teams of programmers to implement various client projects. At first I continued to work within the UNIX world, but soon I was diverted to Java and all its enterprise flavors and finally landed on the fertile plains of web development, using scripting languages like PHP and Ruby. Doing web development, I slowly became familiar with JavaScript and the event-driven programming model, never realizing it would later connect me back to the world of UNIX.

Fast-forwarding to early 2010, a good friend of mine talked to me about Node.js. It was fast, he said, and you can program it in JavaScript. It transported the event-driven browser programming into the UNIX network programming world.

Curious, I went to take a look at the API documents and was immediately hooked. The ease with which you could create highly scalable servers without using threads and mix-and-match client and server code made me take a deep dive into Node's source code and surrounding modules. Node.js connected the ease of a scripting language with all the power of UNIX network programming, and I felt like I was finally home.

WHO THIS BOOK IS FOR

This book was written for the developer who is familiar with JavaScript, either browser or server-side programming. The reader should be familiar with some introductory concepts of how TCP and HTTP works. For the later chapters on web application development, it also helps if the reader is familiar with classic development for the web (HTML, CSS, and JavaScript).

If you already have Node.js installed, you may skip to Chapter 2, "Introducing Node."

If you already know the basics of how Node.js works internally and know about server-side event programming in JavaScript, you may skip to Chapter 3, "Loading Modules."

After introducing core Node.js concepts and API subsets, I go into application building starting in Chapter 17 ("Testing Modules and Applications") and cover debugging (Chapter 18, "Debugging Modules and Applications"), and I present some tips on controlling asynchronous flow (Chapter 19, "Controlling the Callback Flow").

Next, I address the necessary parts of building web applications, starting in Chapter 20, "Building and Using HTTP Middleware," passing through Express.js (Chapter 21), and creating real-time web allocations using Socket.IO (Chapter 22).

Finally, I also address how to access and use databases from Node.js, including MySQL (Chapter 23), CouchDB (Chapter 24), and MongoDB (Chapter 25).

WHAT THIS BOOK COVERS

This book covers Node.js v0.8, Express.js v2.5, Socket.io 0.9, Node-mysql v0.9, Nano v3.1, and Mongoose v2.7.

HOW THIS BOOK IS STRUCTURED

The book starts with setting up and introducing Node.js.

It then explains the Node core fundamentals, which include modules, buffers, the Event Emitter pattern, and timers, after which the fundamental Node core specific file and networking APIs are introduced and explained, all complemented with practical examples.

After covering core Node concepts, the book continues with some best practices for developing applications with Node.js, such as testing modules, debugging applications, and maintaining control of the asynchronous callback flow.

Building real-time web applications is one of the main use cases of Node, and this book shows you how to do it using Connect, Express.js, and Socket.IO.

Because most applications need to connect to a database, the book explains how to connect to and use MySQL, CouchDB, and MongoDB from your Node.js application.

WHAT YOU NEED TO USE THIS BOOK

To install and run Node.js applications, you need a PC or Macintosh computer running a recent version of either Windows, Linux, or MacOS.

The source code for the samples is available for download from the Wrox website at: `www.wrox.com/remtitle.cgi?isbn=P010093766`.

CONVENTIONS

To help you get the most from the text and keep track of what's happening, we've used a number of conventions throughout the book.

> **WARNING** *Warnings hold important, not-to-be-forgotten information that is directly relevant to the surrounding text.*

> **NOTE** *Notes indicates notes, tips, hints, tricks, and asides to the current discussion.*

- We *italicize* new terms and important words when we introduce them.
- We show keyboard strokes like this: Ctrl+A.
- We show file names, URLs, and code within the text like so: `persistence.properties`.

We present code in two different ways:

```
We use a monofont type with no highlighting for most code examples.
```

```
We use bold to emphasize code that is particularly important in the present context
or to show changes from a previous code snippet.
```

SOURCE CODE

As you work through the examples in this book, you may choose either to type in the code manually, or to use the source code files that accompany the book. All the source code used in this book is available for download at `www.wrox.com`. Specifically for this book, the code download is on the Download Code tab at: `http://www.wrox.com/WileyCDA/WroxTitle/Professional-Node-js-Building-Javascript-Based-Scalable-Software.productCd-1118185463.html`.

You can also search for the book at `www.wrox.com` by ISBN to find the code. And a complete list of code downloads for all current Wrox books is available at `www.wrox.com/dynamic/books/download.aspx`.

Throughout each chapter, you'll find references to the names of code files as needed in listing titles and text.

Most of the code on `www.wrox.com` is compressed in a .ZIP, .RAR archive, or similar archive format appropriate to the platform. Once you download the code, just decompress it with an appropriate compression tool.

> **NOTE** *Because many books have similar titles, you may find it easiest to search by ISBN; this book's ISBN is 978-1-118-18546-9.*

Once you download the code, just decompress it with your favorite compression tool. Alternately, you can go to the main Wrox code download page at `www.wrox.com/dynamic/books/download.aspx` to see the code available for this book and all other Wrox books.

ERRATA

We make every effort to ensure that there are no errors in the text or in the code. However, no one is perfect, and mistakes do occur. If you find an error in one of our books, like a spelling mistake or faulty piece of code, we would be very grateful for your feedback. By sending in errata, you may save another reader hours of frustration, and at the same time, you will be helping us provide even higher quality information.

To find the errata page for this book, go to `http://www.wrox.com/WileyCDA/WroxTitle/Professional-Node-js-Building-Javascript-Based-Scalable-Software.productCd-1118185463.html` and click the Errata link. On this page you can view all errata that has been submitted for this book and posted by Wrox editors.

If you don't spot "your" error on the Book Errata page, go to `www.wrox.com/contact/techsupport.shtml` and complete the form there to send us the error you have found. We'll check the information and, if appropriate, post a message to the book's errata page and fix the problem in subsequent editions of the book.

P2P.WROX.COM

For author and peer discussion, join the P2P forums at `http://p2p.wrox.com`. The forums are a web-based system for you to post messages relating to Wrox books and related technologies and interact with other readers and technology users. The forums offer a subscription feature to e-mail you topics of interest of your choosing when new posts are made to the forums. Wrox authors, editors, other industry experts, and your fellow readers are present on these forums.

At `http://p2p.wrox.com`, you will find a number of different forums that will help you, not only as you read this book but also as you develop your own applications. To join the forums, just follow these steps:

1. Go to `http://p2p.wrox.com` and click the Register link.
2. Read the terms of use and click Agree.
3. Complete the required information to join, as well as any optional information you wish to provide, and click Submit.

4. You will receive an e-mail with information describing how to verify your account and complete the joining process.

> **NOTE** *You can read messages in the forums without joining P2P, but to post your own messages, you must join.*

Once you join, you can post new messages and respond to messages other users post. You can read messages at any time on the web. If you would like to have new messages from a particular forum e-mailed to you, click the Subscribe to This Forum icon by the forum name in the forum listing.

For more information about how to use the Wrox P2P, be sure to read the P2P FAQs for answers to questions about how the forum software works, as well as many common questions specific to P2P and Wrox books. To read the FAQs, click the FAQ link on any P2P page.

PART I
Introduction and Setup

1

Installing Node

WHAT'S IN THIS CHAPTER?

- Getting Node up and running
- Installing Node Package Manager (NPM)
- Using NPM to install, uninstall, and update packages

At the European JSConf in 2009, Ryan Dahl, a young programmer, presented a project he had been working on. This project was a platform that combined Google's V8 JavaScript engine, an event loop, and a low-level I/O API. This project was not like other server-side JavaScript platforms where all the I/O primitives were event-driven and there was no way around it. By leveraging the power and simplicity of JavaScript, this project turned the difficult task of writing event-driven server-side applications into an easy one. The project received a standing ovation and has since then been met with unprecedented growth, popularity, and adoption.

The project was named Node.js and is now known to developers simply as Node. Node provides a purely event-driven, non-blocking infrastructure for building highly concurrent software.

> **NOTE** *Node allows you to easily construct fast and scalable network services.*

Ever since its introduction, Node has received attention from some of the biggest players in the industry. They have used Node to deploy networked services that are fast and scalable. Node is so attractive for several reasons.

One reason is JavaScript. JavaScript is the most widely used programming language on the planet. Most web programmers are used to writing JavaScript in the browser, and the server is a natural extension of that.

The other reason is Node's simplicity. Node's core functionalities are kept to a minimum and all the existing APIs are quite elegant, exposing the minimum amount of complexity to the programmers. When you want to build something more complex, you can easily pick, install, and use several of the available third-party modules.

Another reason Node is attractive is because of how easy it is to get started using it. You can download and install it very easily and then get it up and running in a matter of minutes.

The typical way to install Node on your development machine is by following the steps on the `http://nodejs.org` website. Node installs out of the box on Windows, Linux, Macintosh, and Solaris.

INSTALLING NODE ON WINDOWS

Node supports the Windows operating system since version 0.6.0. To install Node on Windows, point your browser to `http://nodejs.org/#download` and download the node-v*.msi Windows installer by clicking on the link. You should then be prompted with a security dialog box, as shown in Figure 1-1.

Click on the Run button, and you will be prompted with another security dialog box asking for confirmation. If you agree, the Node install wizard begins (see Figure 1-2).

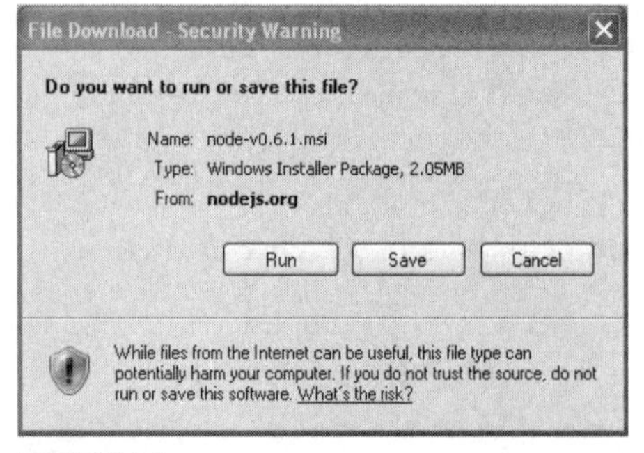

FIGURE 1-1

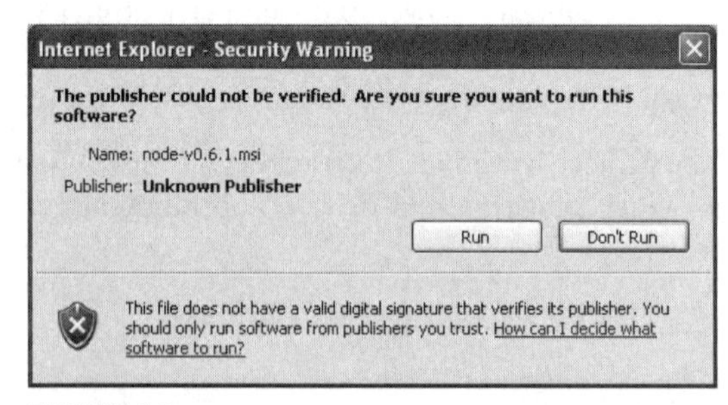

FIGURE 1-2

When you click Run, the Installation Wizard starts (see Figure 1-3).

Click on the Next button and Node will start installing. A few moments later you will get the confirmation that Node was installed (see Figure 1-4).

FIGURE 1-3

FIGURE 1-4

INSTALLING ON MAC OS X

If you use Mac OS X you can install Node using an Install Wizard. To start, head to `http://nodejs.org/#download` and download the node-v*.pkg Macintosh installer by clicking on the link. Once the download is finished, click on the downloaded file to run it. You will then get the first wizard dialog box, as seen in Figure 1-5.

Choose to continue and install. The wizard will then ask you for the system user password, after which the installation will start. A few seconds later you'll get the confirmation window stating that Node is installed on your system (see Figure 1-6).

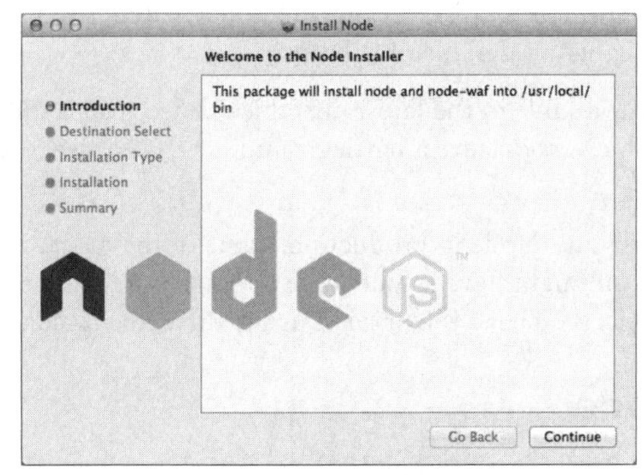

FIGURE 1-5

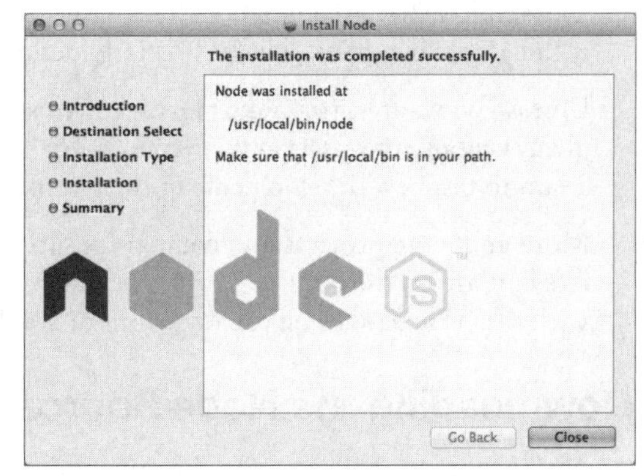

FIGURE 1-6

INSTALLING NODE USING THE SOURCE CODE

If you have a UNIX system, you can install Node by compiling the source code. First you need to select which version of Node you will be installing, then you will download the source code and build, install, and run Node.

> **NOTE** *Node depends on several third-party code libraries, but fortunately most of them are already distributed along with the program. If you are building from source code, you should need only two things:*
>
> - *python (version 2.4 or higher) — The build tools distributed with Node run on python.*
> - *libssl-dev — If you plan to use SSL/TLS encryption in your networking, you'll need this. libssl is the library used in the openssl tool. On Linux and UNIX systems it can usually be installed with your favorite package manager. The libssl library comes pre-installed on Mac OS X.*

Choosing the Node Version

Two different versions of Node are usually available for download on the `nodejs.org` website: the latest stable and the latest unstable.

In Node, the minor version numbering denotes the stability of the version. Stable versions have an even minor version (0.2, 0.4, 0.6), and unstable versions have an odd minor version (0.1, 0.3, 0.5, 0.7).

Not only might an unstable version be functionally unstable, but the API might also be mutating. The stable versions should not change the public API. For each stable branch, a new patch should include only bug fixes, whereas APIs sometimes change in the unstable branch.

Unless you want to test a new feature that is only available in the latest unstable release, you should always choose the latest stable version. The unstable versions are a battleground for the Node Core Team to test new developments in the platform.

More and more projects and companies successfully use Node in production (some of the most relevant are on the `nodejs.org` home page), but you might have to put some effort into keeping up with the API changes on each new minor stable release. That's the price of using a new technology.

Downloading the Node Source Code

After you choose a version to download, copy the source code *tarball* URL from the `http://nodejs.org` website and download it. If you're running in a UNIX system, you probably have *wget* installed, which means that you can download it by using a shell prompt and typing the following:

```
$ wget http://nodejs.org/dist/v0.6.1/node-v0.6.12.tar.gz
```

If you don't have *wget* installed, you may also use the *curl* utility:

```
$ curl -O http://nodejs.org/dist/v0.6.1/node-v0.6.12.tar.gz
```

If you don't have either of these tools installed, you have to find another way to download the *tarball* file into your local directory — such as by using a browser or transferring it via the local network.

(The examples in this book use the latest stable version at the time of writing, which is 0.6.12.)

Building Node

Now that you have the source code in your computer, you can build the Node executable. First you need to unpack the source files like this:

```
$ tar xfz node-v0.6.12.tar.gz
```

Then step into the source directory:

```
$ cd node-v0.6.12
```

Configure it:

```
$ ./configure
```

You should get a successful output like this:

```
'configure' finished successfully (9.278s)
```

Then you are ready to compile it:

```
$ make
```

You should get a successful output like this:

```
'build' finished successfully (0.734s)
```

Installing Node

When you have built Node, you can install it by running the following command:

```
$ make install
```

This will copy the Node executable into `/usr/local/bin/node`.

If you have a permissions problem when issuing this command, run it as the root user or using sudo:

```
$ sudo make install
```

Running Node

Now you are ready to start using Node. First you can simply experiment running Node as a *command-line interface* (CLI). For that you need only to call the Node executable with no arguments like this:

```
$ node
```

This will start the CLI, which will then wait for you to input an expression. Just to test the installation and see Node actually doing something, you can type:

```
> console.log('Hello World!');
Hello World!
> undefined
```

You can also run a JavaScript script from a file. For instance, if you create a file with this content:

```
console.log('Hello World!');
```

Name the file `hello_world.js`. Then run the file by passing the file path as first argument to the *Node* executable while inside a shell prompt. For example:

```
$ node hello_world.js
Hello World!
```

You can quit the CLI by typing Ctrl+D or Ctrl+C.

SETTING UP AND USING NODE PACKAGE MANAGER

You can only get so far using the language features and the core functions. That's why most programming platforms have a system in place that allows you to download, install, and manage third-party modules. In Node, you have *Node Package Manager* (NPM).

NPM is three things — a third-party package repository, a way to manage packages installed in your computer, and a standard to define dependencies on other packages. NPM provides a public registry service that contains all the packages that programmers publish in NPM. NPM also provides a command-line tool to download, install, and manage these packages. You can also use the standard package descriptor format to specify which third-party modules your module or application depends on.

You don't need to know about NPM to start using Node, but it will become necessary once you want to use third-party modules. Because Node provides only low-level APIs, including third-party modules is almost always necessary to fulfill any complex application without having to do it all yourself. As you will see, NPM allows you to download and play with modules without installing packages globally, which makes it ideal for playing around and trying things.

NPM and Node once required separate installs, but since Node version 0.6.0, NPM is already included.

Using NPM to Install, Update, and Uninstall Packages

NPM is a powerful package manager and can be used in many ways. NPM maintains a centralized repository of public modules, which you can browse at `http://search.npmjs.org`. A Node opensource module author may choose, as most do, to publish the module to NPM, and in the installation instructions should be the NPM module name you can use to remotely download and install it.

This section covers the most typical uses of NPM, which are installing and removing packages. This should be just enough for you to start managing your application dependencies on third-party modules published on NPM. However, first you need to understand the differences between global and local modes of operation and how these affect module lookups.

Using the Global versus the Local Mode

NPM has two main modes of operation: global and local. These two modes change target directories for storing packages and have deep implications for how Node loads modules.

The local mode is the default mode of operation in NPM. In this mode, NPM works on the local directory level, never making system-wide changes. This mode is ideal for installing the modules your application depends on without affecting other applications you might also have installed locally.

The global mode is more suited for installing modules that should always be available globally, like the ones that provide command-line utilities and that are not directly used by applications.

Always use the default local mode if you are in doubt. If module authors intend for one specific module to be installed globally, generally they will tell you so in the installation instructions.

The Global Mode

If you installed Node using the default directory, while in the global mode, NPM installs packages into `/usr/local/lib/node_modules`. If you type the following in the shell, NPM will search for, download, and install the latest version of the package named `sax` inside the directory `/usr/local/lib/node_modules/sax`:

```
$  npm install -g sax
```

> **NOTE** *If your current shell user doesn't have enough permissions, you will need to login as the root user or run this command within sudo:*
>
> ```
> $ sudo npm install -g sax
> ```

If you then have the requirement for this package in any Node script:

```
var sax = require('sax');
```

Node will pick up this module in this directory (unless you have it installed locally, in which case Node prefers the local version).

The local mode is the default mode, and you have to explicitly activate the global mode in NPM by using the -g flag.

The Local Mode

The local mode is the default mode of operation in NPM and the recommended dependency resolution mechanism. In this mode NPM installs everything inside the current directory — which can be your application root directory — and never touches any global settings. This way you can choose, application by application, which modules and which versions to include without polluting global module space. This means that you can have two applications that depend on different versions of the same module without them conflicting.

In this mode, NPM works with the node_modules directory under the current working directory. If you are inside /home/user/apps/my_app, NPM will use /home/user/apps/my_app/node_modules as file storage for the modules.

If you run a Node application installed in the directory /home/user/apps/my_app, Node will search this /home/user/apps/my_app/node_modules directory first (before trying the parent directories and finally searching for it inside the global one). This means that, when Node is resolving a module dependency, a module installed using the local mode will always take precedence over a module installed globally.

Installing a Module

Using the following command, you can download and install the latest version of a package:

```
$ npm install <package name>
```

For example, to download and install the latest version of the sax package, you should first change your current directory to your application root directory and then type:

```
$ npm install sax
```

This will create the node_modules directory if it doesn't already exist and install the sax module under it.

You can also choose which version of a specific module to install by specifying it like this:

```
$ npm install <package name>@<version spec>
```

You can use a specific version number in the <version spec> placeholder. For instance, if you want to install version 0.2.5 of the sax module, you need to type:

```
$ npm install sax@0.2.5
```

Under <version spec> you can also specify a version range. For instance, if you want to install the latest release of the 0.2 branch, you can type:

```
$ npm install sax@0.2.x
```

If you want to install the latest version before 0.3 you should type:

```
$ npm install sax@"<0.3"
```

You can get more sophisticated and combine version specifications like this:

```
$ npm install sax@">=0.1.0 <0.3.1"
```

Uninstalling a Module

When you use the following command, NPM will try to find and uninstall the package with the specified name.

```
$ npm uninstall <package name>
```

If you want to remove a globally installed package, you should use:

```
$ npm uninstall -g <package name>
```

Updating a Module

You can also update an installed module by using the following command:

```
$ npm update <package name>
```

This command will fetch the latest version of the package and update it. If the package does not exist, it will install it.

You can also use the global switch (`-g`) to update a globally installed module like this:

```
$ npm update -g <package name>
```

Using the Executable Files

It's possible that a module includes one or more executable files. If you choose to install a module globally and you used the default installation directory settings, NPM installs the executables inside `/usr/local/bin`. This path is usually included in the default executable `PATH` environment variable.

If you installed a package locally, NPM installs any executables inside the `./node_modules/.bin` directory.

Resolving Dependencies

NPM not only installs the packages you request but also installs the packages that those packages depend on. For instance, if you request to install package A and this package depends on package B and C, Node will fetch packages B and C and install them inside `./node_modules/A/node_modules`.

For instance, if you locally installed the *nano* package like this:

```
$ npm install nano
```

NPM outputs something like:

```
nano@0.9.3 ./node_modules/nano
├── underscore@1.1.7
└── request@2.1.1
```

This shows that the *nano* package depends on the *underscore* and *request* packages and indicates which versions of these packages were installed. If you peek inside the `./node_modules/nano/node_modules` directory, you'll see these packages installed there:

```
$ ls node_modules/nano/node_modules
request  underscore
```

Using *package.json* to Define Dependencies

When coding a Node application, you can also include a `package.json` file at the root. The `package.json` file is where you can define some of your application metadata, such as the name, authors, repository, contacts, and so on. This is also where you should specify extraneous dependencies.

You don't need to use it to publish the application to NPM — you may want to keep that application private — but you can still use `package.json` to specify the application dependencies.

The `package.json` is a JSON-formatted file that can contain a series of attributes, but for the purposes of declaring the dependencies you only need one: `dependencies`. An application that depends on the *sax*, *nano*, and *request* packages could have a `package.json` file like this:

```
{
  "name" : "MyApp",
  "version" : "1.0.0",
  "dependencies" : {
    "sax" : "0.3.x",
    "nano" : "*",
    "request" : ">0.2.0"
  }
}
```

Here you are specifying that your application or module depends on *sax* version 0.3, on any version of *nano*, and on any version of *request* greater than 0.2.0.

> **NOTE** *You may also find that if you omit the* `name` *and* `version` *fields, NPM will not work. This happens because NPM was initially conceived to describe public packages, not private applications.*

Then, on the application root, type:

```
$ npm install
```

NPM will then analyze the dependencies and your `node_modules` directory and automatically download and install any missing packages.

You can also update all the locally installed packages to the latest version that meets your dependency specifications, like this:

```
$ npm update
```

In fact you can always use this last command, because it will also make NPM fetch any missing packages.

SUMMARY

You've learned how to install *Node* and the *Node Package Manager*. You can now use NPM to install, uninstall, and remove third-party packages. You can also use the `package.json` file together with NPM to manage the third-party packages you depend on.

Now that you have Node and NPM installed, you are ready to experiment with them. But first you need some background on Node and the event-driven programming style.

2

Introducing Node

WHAT'S IN THIS CHAPTER?

- What is the event-driven programming style and what are the advantages of using it
- How Node.js and JavaScript make event-driven programming easy

Traditional programming does I/O the same way as it does local function calls: Processing cannot continue until an operation finishes. This programming model of blocking when doing I/O operations derives from the early days of time-sharing systems in which each process corresponded to one human user. The purpose was to isolate users from one another. In those systems, a user would typically need to finish one operation before deciding what the next operation would be. But with widespread use of computer networks and the Internet, this model of "one user, one process" did not scale well. Managing many processes places a big burden on the operating system — in memory and context switching costs — and the performance of these tasks starts to decay after a certain number is reached.

Multi-threading is one alternative to this programming model. A thread is a kind of light-weight process that shares memory with every other thread within the same process. Threads were created as an ad hoc extension of the previous model to accommodate several concurrent threads of execution. When one thread is waiting for an I/O operation, another thread can take over the CPU. When the I/O operation finishes, that thread can wake up, which means the thread that was running can be interrupted and eventually be resumed later. Furthermore, some systems allow threads to execute in parallel in different CPU cores.

This means that programmers do not know what set of threads is executing at any given time, so they must be careful with concurrent access to the shared memory state. They have to use synchronization primitives like locks and semaphores to synchronize access to some data structures, forcing them to foresee every possible way threads can be scheduled to execute to try to prevent problems. If the application relies heavily on a shared state between threads, this type of programming can easily lead to strange bugs that happen at random and are usually difficult to find.

An alternative to having the operating system scheduling the thread execution for you is to use cooperative multi-threading. In this scheme you are responsible for explicitly relinquishing the CPU to give time for another thread to execute. Because you are now responsible for thread scheduling, this can relax the synchronization requirements. However, this approach can become complex and error-prone for the same reasons as regular multi-threading.

INTRODUCING THE EVENT-DRIVEN PROGRAMMING STYLE

Event-driven programming is a programming style whereby the flow of execution is determined by events. Events are handled by event handlers or event callbacks. An *event callback* is a function that is invoked when something significant happens — such as when the result of a database query is available or when the user clicks on a button.

Consider how a query to a database is completed in typical blocking I/O programming:

```
result = query('SELECT * FROM posts WHERE id = 1');
do_something_with(result);
```

This query requires that the current thread or process wait until the database layer finishes processing it.

In event-driven systems, this query would be performed in this way:

```
query_finished = function(result) {
  do_something_with(result);
}
query('SELECT * FROM posts WHERE id = 1', query_finished);
```

Here you are first defining what will happen when the query is finished and storing that in a function named `query_finished`. Then you are passing that function as an argument to the query. When it's finished, the query will invoke the `query_finished` function, instead of simply returning the result.

This style of programming — whereby instead of using a return value you define functions that are called by the system when interesting events occur — is called *event-driven* or *asynchronous* programming. This is one of the defining features of Node. This style of programming means the current process will not block when it is doing I/O. Therefore, several I/O operations can occur in parallel, and each respective callback function will be invoked when the operation finishes.

The event-driven programming style is accompanied by an *event loop*. An event loop is a construct that mainly performs two functions in a continuous loop — event detection and event handler triggering. In any run of the loop, it has to detect which events just happened. Then, when an event happens, the event loop must determine the event callback and invoke it.

This event loop is just one thread running inside one process, which means that, when an event happens, the event handler can run without interruption. This means the following:

- There is at most one event handler running at any given time.
- Any event handler will run to completion without being interrupted.

This allows the programmer to relax the synchronization requirements and not have to worry about concurrent threads of execution changing the shared memory state.

A WELL-KNOWN SECRET

For quite some time, the systems-programming community has known that event-driven programming is the best way to create a service that can handle many concurrent connections. It has been known to be more efficient regarding memory because there is less context to store, and more efficient regarding time because there is less context switching.

This knowledge has infiltrated other platforms and communities; some of the most well-known event loop implementations are Ruby's *Event Machine,* Perl's *AnyEvent*, and Python's *Twisted*. There are also others for these and other languages.

Implementing an application using one of these frameworks requires framework-specific knowledge and framework-specific libraries. For example, when using Event Machine, you should avoid using synchronous libraries. To gain the benefit of not blocking, you are limited to using asynchronous libraries built specifically for Event Machine. If you use any blocking library (like most of the ones in the Ruby standard library), your server will not be able to scale optimally because the event loop will be constantly blocking, which prevents timely processing of I/O events.

Node was devised as a non-blocking I/O server platform from day one, so generally you should expect everything built on top of it to be non-blocking. Because JavaScript itself is very minimal and does not impose any way of doing I/O (it does not have a standard I/O library), Node has a clean slate to build upon.

HOW NODE AND JAVASCRIPT MAKE WRITING ASYNCHRONOUS APPLICATIONS EASIER

Ryan Dahl, the author of Node, began his project building a C platform, but maintaining the context between function calls was too complicated and led to complex code. He then turned to Lua, but Lua already had several blocking I/O libraries. This mix of blocking and non-blocking could confuse developers and prevent many of them from building scalable applications, thus Lua was not ideal either.

Dahl then turned to JavaScript. JavaScript has closures and first-class functions, which makes it a powerful match for event-driven programming. The power of JavaScript is one of the main reasons Node has become so popular.

What Are Closures?

Closures are functions that inherit variables from their enclosing environment. When you pass a function callback as an argument to another function that will do I/O, this callback function will be invoked later, and this function will — almost magically — remember the context in which it was declared, along with all the variables available in that context and any parent contexts. This powerful feature is at the heart of Node's success.

The following example shows how a closure works when programming JavaScript in the web browser. For instance, if you want to listen for an event — a button click, for instance — you can do something like:

```
var clickCount = 0;
document.getElementById('myButton').onclick = function() {
  clickCount += 1;
  alert("clicked " + clickCount + " times.");
};
```

Or, using jQuery:

```
var clickCount = 0;
$('button#mybutton').click(function() {
  clickedCount ++;
  alert('Clicked ' + clickCount + ' times.');
});
```

In JavaScript, functions are first-class objects, which means you can pass functions as arguments to other functions. In both examples you assigned or passed a function as an argument to be executed later. The click handling function — your callback function — has every variable in scope at the point where the function was declared, which means that, in this case, it has access to the `clickCount` variable declared in the parent closure.

The variable `clickCount` stores the number of times that the user has clicked on the button. This variable is stored in the global scope (the outermost scope you can get to in JavaScript). Storing variables in the global scope is generally bad practice because they can easily collide with other code; you should keep variables in a scope that is local to the functions that need to use them. Most of the time you can easily avoid global scope pollution by wrapping all of your code inside another function to create an additional closure, as in the next example:

```
(function() {
  var clickCount = 0;
  $('button#mybutton').click(function() {
    clickCount ++;
    alert('Clicked ' + clickCount + ' times.');
  });
}());
```

NOTE *Line 7 invokes a function immediately after defining it. This is a common JavaScript pattern where you create a function just to create a new scope.*

How Closures Help When Programming Asynchronously

In event-driven programming you start by defining the code that will be executed when an event occurs, then put that code inside a function, and finally pass that function as an argument to be called later.

In JavaScript, a function operates not by working in isolation but by remembering the context where it was declared, which enables manipulation of any variable present in that or any parent context.

When you pass a callback function as an argument, that function will be invoked some time later, but it can manipulate any variable present in that or in the parent scope, even if these scopes have already returned. In the last example, the callback function was able to access and manipulate the `clickCount` variable, even though it was invoked from within the jQuery `click()` function.

This shows that by using the closure pattern, you can have the best of both worlds: You can do event-driven programming without having to maintain the state by passing it around to functions. A JavaScript closure keeps the state for you.

SUMMARY

Event-driven programming is a programming style whereby the flow is determined by the occurrence of events. Programmers register callbacks to be used as event handlers for events they are interested in, and the system invokes these handlers when those events occur. This model of programming has some advantages over the traditional blocking paradigm where, to scale, you have to use multiple processes or threads.

JavaScript is a powerful language, which is well suited for this style of programming, mainly because it has first-class functions and closures.

PART II
Node Core API Basics

3

Loading Modules

WHAT'S IN THIS CHAPTER?

- Loading modules
- Creating modules
- Using the `node_modules` folder

JavaScript is one of the most frequently deployed programming languages in the world; it's the web's *lingua franca*, used by all the browsers. The core of the language was created quickly back in the Netscape days, in a rush to beat Microsoft during the heat of the browser wars. The language was released prematurely, which inevitably meant it came out with some bad features.

Despite its short development time, JavaScript also shipped with some really powerful features. The sharing of a global namespace among scripts is not one of them, though.

Once you load JavaScript code into a web page, it is injected into the global namespace, which is a common addressing space shared by all other scripts that have been loaded. This can lead to security issues, conflicts, and general bugs that are hard to trace and solve.

Thankfully, Node brings some order in this regard to server-side JavaScript and implements the CommonJS modules standard. In this standard each module has its own context, separated from the other modules. This means that modules cannot pollute a global scope — because there is none — and cannot interfere with other modules.

In this chapter, you will learn about different types of modules and how to load them into your application.

Dividing your code into a series of well-defined modules can help you keep your code under control. You will also see how you can create and use your own modules.

UNDERSTANDING HOW NODE LOADS MODULES

In Node, modules are referenced either by file path or by name. A module that is referenced by a name will eventually map into a file path unless the module is a core module. Node's core modules expose some Node core functions to the programmer, and they are preloaded when a Node process starts.

Other modules include third-party modules that you installed using NPM (Node Package Manager) or local modules that you or your colleagues have created.

Each module of any type exposes a public API that the programmer can use after the module is imported into the current script. To use a module of any type, you have to use the `require` function like this:

```
var module = require('module_name');
```

This will import a core module or a module installed by NPM. The *`require`* function returns an object that represents the JavaScript API exposed by the module. Depending on the module, that object can be any JavaScript value — a function, an object with some properties that can be functions, an array, or any other type of JavaScript object.

EXPORTING A MODULE

The CommonJS module system is the only way you can share objects or functions among files in Node. For a sufficiently complex application you should divide some of the classes, objects, or functions into reusable well-defined modules. To the module user, a module exposes exactly what you specify it to.

In Node, files and modules are in one-to-one correspondence, which you can see in the following example. Start by creating a file named `circle.js`, which just exports the `Circle` constructor:

```
function Circle(x, y, r) {

  function r_squared() {
    return Math.pow(r, 2);
  }

  function area() {
    return Math.PI * r_squared();
  }

  return {
    area: area
  };
}

module.exports = Circle;
```

The important bit here lies on the last line, where you define what is to be exported by the module. `module` is a variable that represents the module you are currently in. `module.exports` is the object that the module will export to other scripts that require this module. You can export any object. In this case, you are just exporting the `Circle` constructor function, which a module user can use to create fully functional `Circle` instances.

You can also export more complex objects. `module.exports` is initialized with an empty object, which you can populate with the attributes you want to export. For instance, you can devise a module that exports a set of functions:

```
function printA() {
  console.log('A');
}

function printB() {
  console.log('B');
}

function printC() {
  console.log('C');
}

module.exports.printA = printA;
module.exports.printB = printB;
module.exports.pi = Math.PI;
```

This module exports two functions (`printA` and `printB`) and a number (`pi`). A client of this module would look something like this:

```
var myModule2 = require('./myModule2');
myModule2.printA(); // -> A
myModule2.printB(); // -> B
console.log(myModule2.pi); // -> 3.141592653589793
```

Loading a Module

As explained previously, you can use the `require` function to load a module. Having a `require` function call in your code does not change the state of the global namespaces, because there is no such thing in Node. If the module is found and doesn't contain a syntax or initialization error, calling `require()` simply returns the module object, which you can then assign to any local variable you choose.

There are several ways to reference modules, depending on which kind of module it is — a core module, a third-party module installed via NPM, or a local module. Let's take a look at the different methods.

Loading a Core Module

Node has several modules compiled into its binary distribution. These are called the *core modules*, are referred to solely by the module name — not the path — and are preferentially loaded even if a third-party module exists with the same name.

For instance, if you wanted to load and use the `http` core module, you would do the following:

```
var http = require('http');
```

This returns the `http` module object that implements the API described in the Node API documentation.

Loading a File Module

You can also load a non-core module from the file system by providing the absolute path like this:

```
var myModule = require('/home/pedro/my_modules/my_module');
```

Or you can provide a path relative to the current file:

```
var myModule = require('../my_modules/my_module');
var myModule2 = require('./lib/my_module_2');
```

Notice here that you can omit the `.js` file termination. When it fails to find such a file, Node will look for the path by adding the `.js` extension. So, if the file `my_module.js` exists inside the current directory, the two following lines are equivalent:

```
var myModule = require('./my_module');
var myModule = require('./my_module.js');
```

Loading a Folder Module

You can use the path for a folder to load a module like this:

```
var myModule = require('./myModuleDir');
```

If you do so, Node will search inside that folder. Node will presume this folder is a package and will try to look for a package definition. That package definition should be a file named `package.json`.

If that folder does not contain a package definition file named `package.json`, the package entry point will assume the default value of `index.js`, and Node will look, in this case, for a file under the path `./myModuleDir/index.js`.

However, if you place a file named `package.json` inside the module directory, Node will try to parse that file and look for and use the `main` attribute as a relative path for the entry point. For instance, if your `./myModuleDir/package.json` file looks something like the following, Node will try to load the file with the path`./myModuleDir/lib/myModule.js`:

```
{
  "name" : "myModule",
  "main" : "./lib/myModule.js"
}
```

Loading from the node_modules Folder

If the module name is not relative and is not a core module, Node will try to find it inside the `node_modules` folder in the current directory.

For instance, if you do the following, Node will try to look for the file `./node_modules/myModule.js`:

```
var myModule = require('myModule.js');
```

If Node fails to find the file, it will look inside the parent folder called `../node_modules/myModule.js`. If it fails again, it will try the parent folder and keep descending until it reaches the root or finds the required module.

You can use this feature to manage the contents of the `node_modules` directory or, preferentially, you can leave it up to NPM (see Chapter 1) to manage the modules for you. This local `node_modules` directory is the default place where NPM installs modules, and this functionality is what ties Node and NPM together. Typically, as a programmer, you won't care much about this feature. You can simply use NPM to install, update, and remove packages, and it will manage the `node_modules` directory for you.

Caching Modules

Modules are cached the first time they are loaded, which means that every call to `require('myModule')` returns exactly the same module if the module name resolves to the exact same filename.

For instance, say you have the following module inside the file called `my_module.js`:

```
console.log('module my_module initializing...');
module.exports = function() {
  console.log('Hi!');
};
console.log('my_module initialized.');
```

If the following script loads the script once:

```
var myModuleInstance1 = require('./my_module');
```

It will print the following:

```
module my_module initializing...
my_module initialized
```

If you require the module two times:

```
var myModuleInstance1 = require('./my_module');
var myModuleInstance2 = require('./my_module');
```

You will notice that the output is still the same:

```
module my_module initializing...
my_module initialized
```

This means that the module initialization runs only once, which may be important to know when you are building a module that produces some side effects when being initialized.

SUMMARY

Node sets aside JavaScript's default global namespace and uses CommonJS modules instead. This enables you to better organize your code, thus avoiding security issues and bugs. You can use `require()` to load a core module, a third-party module, or your own module from a file or a folder.

You can load non-core modules using relative or absolute file paths. You can also load your modules by name if you place them inside the `node_modules` folder or install them using NPM.

You can create your own modules by authoring a JavaScript file that exports the objects that represent the module API.

Using Buffers to Manipulate, Encode, and Decode Binary Data

WHAT'S IN THIS CHAPTER?

- Understanding why you need buffers in Node
- Creating a buffer from a string
- Converting a buffer to a string
- Manipulating the bytes in a buffer
- Slicing and copying a buffer

JavaScript is good at handling strings, but because it was initially designed to manipulate HTML documents, it is not very good at handling binary data. JavaScript doesn't have a *byte* type — it just has numbers — or structured types, or even byte arrays: It just has strings.

Because Node is based on JavaScript, Node can handle text protocols like HTTP, but you can also use it to talk to databases, manipulate images, and handle file uploads. As you can imagine, doing this using only strings is very difficult. In the early days, Node handled binary data by encoding each byte inside a text character, but that proved to be wasteful, slow, unreliable, and hard to manipulate.

To make these types of binary-handling tasks easier, Node includes a binary buffer implementation, which is exposed as a JavaScript API under the `Buffer` pseudo-class. A buffer length is specified in bytes, and you can randomly set and get bytes from a buffer.

> **NOTE** *Another thing that is special about this buffer class is that the memory where the data sits is allocated outside of the JavaScript VM memory heap. This means that these objects will not be moved around by the garbage-collection algorithm: It will sit in this permanent memory address without changing, which saves CPU cycles that would be wasted making memory copies of the buffer contents.*

CREATING A BUFFER

You can create a buffer from a UTF-8-encoded string like this:

```
var buf = new Buffer('Hello World!');
```

You can also create a buffer from strings with other encodings as long as you specify the encoding on the second argument of the constructor:

```
var buf = new Buffer('8b76fde713ce', 'base64');
```

Accepted encodings and their identifiers are:

- `ascii`—ASCII. This encoding is limited to the ASCII character set.
- `utf8`—UTF-8. This is a variable width encoding that can represent every character in the Unicode character set. It has become the dominant encoding on the web. This is the default encoding if you don't specify one.
- `base64`—Base64. This encoding is used to represent binary data in an ASCII string format by translating it into a radix-64 representation. Base64 is commonly used to embed binary data into textual documents in a way that ensures that the data remains intact during transport.

If you don't have the initial content for a buffer and you need to create a buffer with a certain capacity to hold data in the future, you can create a new buffer by specifying its length like this:

```
var buf = new Buffer(1024); // creating a 1024 byte buffer
```

GETTING AND SETTING BYTES IN A BUFFER

After you create or receive a buffer, you might want to inspect and change its contents. You can access the byte value on any position of a buffer by using the `[]` operator like this:

```
var buf = new Buffer('my buffer content');
// accessing the 10th position of buf
console.log(buf[10]); // -> 99
```

> **NOTE** *When you create an initialized buffer, keep in mind that it will contain random bytes, not zeros.*
>
> ```
> var buf = new Buffer(1024);
> console.log(buf[100]); // -> 5 (some random number)
> ```

You can also manipulate the content of any position:

```
buf[99] = 125; // set the 100th byte to 125
```

> **NOTE** *In certain cases, some buffer operations will not yield an error. For instance:*
>
> - *If you set any position of the buffer to a number greater than 255, that position will be assigned the 256 modulo value.*
> - *If you assign the number 256 to a buffer position, you will actually be assigning the value 0.*
> - *If you assign a fractional number like 100.7 to a buffer position, the buffer position will store the integer part — 100 in this case.*
> - *If you try to assign a position that is out of bounds, the assignment will fail and the buffer will remain unaltered.*

You can obtain a buffer length by inquiring the `length` property like this:

```
var buf = new Buffer(100);
console.log(buf.length); // -> 100
```

You can then use a buffer length to iterate over the buffer content and set or get each individual byte value:

```
var buf = new Buffer(100);

for(var i = 0; i < buf.length; i++) {
  buf[i] = i;
}
```

Here, you create a new buffer with the capacity of 100 bytes and then set each byte with a value starting from 0 to 99.

SLICING A BUFFER

Once you have created or received a buffer, you may want to extract a part from it. You can slice a buffer to create another smaller buffer, specifying the starting and ending positions like this:

```
var buffer = new Buffer("this is the content of my buffer");
var smallerBuffer = buffer.slice(8, 19);
console.log(smallerBuffer.toString()); // -> "the content"
```

Notice that when you slice a buffer no new memory is allocated and nothing is copied. The new buffer uses the parent buffer memory and just references different start and/or end positions. This has some implications.

First, if your program changes the parent buffer and any of that change touches any of the bytes of the child buffer, the child buffer will change. Because the parent and the child buffer are different JavaScript objects, this may not be obvious to you and can introduce some bugs.

Second, when you create a smaller buffer from a parent buffer this way, the parent buffer has to be kept around after the operation and not be reclaimed by the garbage collector, which can easily introduce a memory if you're not careful.

> **NOTE** *If you are concerned that you will leak memory by keeping an old buffer around, you should use the* `copy` *method instead, covered in the next section.*

COPYING A BUFFER

You can also copy part of a buffer into another buffer by using the `copy` method like this:

```
var buffer1 = new Buffer("this is the content of my buffer");
var buffer2 = new Buffer(11);

var targetStart = 0;
var sourceStart = 8;
var sourceEnd = 19;

buffer1.copy(buffer2, targetStart, sourceStart, sourceEnd);
console.log(buffer2.toString()); // -> "the content"
```

Here, you are copying position 8 to 19 of the `source` buffer into position 0 of the `target` buffer.

DECODING A BUFFER

A buffer can be converted into a UTF-8-encoded string like this:

```
var str = buf.toString();
```

If you specify an encoding you can convert the buffer to another encoding. For instance, if you want to convert a buffer to a base64-encoded string, you can do so this way:

```
var b64Str = buf.toString("base64");
```

Using the `toString` method you can, for instance, transcode a UTF-8 string into base64 like this:

```
var utf8String = 'my string';
var buf = new Buffer(utf8String);
var base64String = buf.toString('base64')
```

SUMMARY

Sometimes you have to deal with binary data, but native JavaScript does not provide a clean way to do that.

The Node `Buffer` class encapsulates access to a continuous memory chunk. You can manipulate the bytes in that memory, obtain slices of it, and then copy that memory between two buffers.

You can also transform a buffer into an encoded string representation or go the other way around: transform a string into a buffer to access or manipulate the individual bits.

5

Using the Event Emitter Pattern to Simplify Event Binding

WHAT'S IN THIS CHAPTER?

- Introducing the event emitter pattern
- Binding and unbinding event listeners
- Creating your own event emitter

In Node many objects emit events. For instance, a TCP server can emit a "connect" event every time a new client connects, or a file stream can emit a "data" event every time a new chunk of data is read. These objects are, in Node nomenclature, *event emitters*. Event emitters allow programmers to subscribe to events they are interested in. The programmer attaches a callback function that will be invoked every time a relevant event in that event emitter occurs. This publisher/subscriber pattern is very similar to the typical GUI pattern, whereby a program gets notified that a certain button was clicked. By using this pattern, a server-side program can react when, for instance, a client connects to the server, data is available on a socket, or a file gets closed.

You can also create your own event emitters. In fact, Node supplies an `EventEmitter` pseudo-class that can work as a base for creating your own event emitters.

UNDERSTANDING THE STANDARD CALLBACK PATTERN

Asynchronous programming does not use function return values to denote that a function is finished. Instead it uses the *continuation-passing style* (CPS):

> *Continuation-passing style (CPS) is a style of programming in which control is passed explicitly in the form of a continuation. (...)*
>
> *A function written in continuation-passing style takes as an extra argument an explicit "continuation," that is, a function of one argument. When the CPS function has computed its result value, it "returns" it by calling the continuation function with this value as the argument.*
>
> WIKIPEDIA — HTTP://EN.WIKIPEDIA.ORG/WIKI/CONTINUATION-PASSING_STYLE

This is a style in which a function invokes a callback after the operation is complete so that your program can continue. As you will see, JavaScript lends itself to this type of programming. Here is an example in Node that involves loading a file into memory:

```
var fs = require('fs');
fs.readFile('/etc/passwd', function(err, fileContent) {
  if (err) {
    throw err;
  }
  console.log('file content', fileContent.toString());
});
```

Here, you are passing an anonymous inline function as the second argument of the `fs.readFile` function, and you're making use of the CPS, because you are continuing the execution of the program inside that function.

As you can see here, the first argument to the callback function is an error object, which will have an instance of the `Error` class if an error occurs. This is a common pattern in Node when using CPS.

UNDERSTANDING THE EVENT EMITTER PATTERN

The standard callback pattern — whereby you pass a callback function as an argument of the function you are executing — works well when you want the client to be notified when a function completes. But if several events take place during execution, or if they happen several times, this style doesn't work as well. For instance, if you are interested in being notified every time data is available on a socket, the standard callback pattern is not very helpful. This is when the event emitter pattern can help. You can use a standard interface to clearly separate the event emitter and the event listener.

When you use an event emitter pattern, two or more objects are involved — the event emitter and one or more event listeners.

An event emitter is an object that — as the name says — emits events. An event listener is a part of the code that binds to the event emitter and listens for certain types of events, like in this example:

```
var req = http.request(options, function(response) {
  response.on("data", function(data) {
    console.log("some data from the response", data);
  });
  response.on("end", function() {
    console.log("response ended");
  });
});
req.end();
```

Here, you are looking at some of the steps required to make an HTTP request to a remote HTTP server using the Node `http.request` API (which is covered later). Line 1 uses the continuation-passing style, passing in an inline function that will be executed once the response is available. The HTTP request API uses the CPS here because the program continues to execute after the `http.request` function completes.

When complete, the `http.request` function invokes the callback, passing a response object. This response object is an event emitter and, according to the Node documentation, can emit, among others, the `data` and `end` events. You are then registering callback functions that will be invoked every time any of these events happen.

As a rule of thumb, use CPS when you want to regain control after the requested operation completes and use the event emitter pattern when an event can happen multiple times.

UNDERSTANDING EVENT TYPES

Notice that emitted events always have a type, which is represented by a string. In this example you have the "data" and "end" event types. These are arbitrary strings dictated by the event emitter; by convention, event types are usually lowercase words with no spaces.

You cannot infer programmatically what types of events a given event emitter emits: The event emitter API provides no such introspection mechanism. The API you are using should document which event types it is emitting.

The event emitter will invoke the listener once a relevant event occurs, and it will pass in any relevant data. In the previous `http.request` example, the "data" event callback function received the data object as its first and sole argument, whereas the "end" event didn't receive any. These are also arbitrary arguments that are part of the specific API contract. The callback argument signature should be documented in the API specification of each event emitter.

Event emitter is a generic interface that serves any type of event, but there is a special case in the Node implementation, and that's the "error" event. Most event emitter implementations in Node will emit an "error" event every time there is an error. If the programmer chooses to not listen to that event type and an event with the "error" type occurs, the event emitter will notice it and raise that error as an uncaught exception.

You can test that effect by running the following code in the Node REPL, which simulates an event emitter emitting two types of events:

```
var em = new (require('events').EventEmitter)();
em.emit('event1');
em.emit('error', new Error('My mistake'));
```

You will see the following output:

```
> var em = new (require('events').EventEmitter)();
undefined
> em.emit('event1');
false
> em.emit('error', new Error('My mistake'));
Error: My mistake
    at repl:1:18
    at REPLServer.eval (repl.js:80:21)
    at repl.js:190:20
    at REPLServer.eval (repl.js:87:5)
    at Interface.<anonymous> (repl.js:182:12)
    at Interface.emit (events.js:67:17)
    at Interface._onLine (readline.js:162:10)
    at Interface._line (readline.js:426:8)
    at Interface._ttyWrite (readline.js:603:14)
    at ReadStream.<anonymous> (readline.js:82:12)
>
```

Emitting an arbitrary `event1` event did not have any effect, but when you emitted the "error" event, that error was thrown down the stack. If this program were running outside of a REPL, it would have halted because of the uncaught error.

As a rule of thumb, you should always listen to error events and handle them appropriately.

USING THE EVENT EMITTER API

Any object that implements the event emitter pattern (like a TCP Socket, an HTTP request, and many others) implements a set of methods:

- `.addListener` and `.on` — To add an event listener to an event type
- `.once` — To attach an event listener to a given event type that will be called at most once
- `.removeEventListener` — To remove a specific event listener of a given event
- `.removeAllEventListeners` — To remove all event listeners of a given event type

Let's take a closer look at them.

Binding Callbacks Using .addListener() or .on()

By specifying an event type and a callback function, you can register to be called when one of these events occur. For instance, a file read stream may emit a "data" event when some data chunk is available. Here is how you can be informed of that by passing in a callback function:

```
function receiveData(data) {
  console.log("got data from file read stream: %j", data);
}
readStream.addListener("data", receiveData);
```

Instead of using the .addListener function, you can use .on, which is simply a shortcut. The following code is equivalent:

```
function receiveData(data) {
  console.log("got data from file read stream: %j", data);
}
readStream.on("data", receiveData);
```

Here, you are using a named function that you declare in advance, but instead you can use an inline anonymous function to be more succinct:

```
readStream.on("data", function(data) {
  console.log("got data from file read stream: %j", data);
});
```

As pointed out before, the arguments that are passed into the callback depend on the specific event emitter object and event type and are not standardized. A "data" event might emit the data buffer, an "error" event might emit the error object, and the stream "end" event might not emit any value to the event listener.

Binding Multiple Event Listeners

The event emitter pattern allows multiple event listeners to listen to the same event type on the same event emitter. For instance:

```
readStream.on("data", function(data) {
    console.log('I have some data here.');
});
readStream.on("data", function(data) {
    console.log('I have some data here too.');
});
```

In this example you bind two functions to the readStream "data" event type. Every time the readStream object emits the "data" event, you will see printed out:

```
I have some data here.
I have some data here too.
```

The event emitter is then responsible for calling all the registered listeners for a given event type, and it will call them in the order in which they were registered. This means two things:

- An event listener might not be called immediately after the event is emitted. There might be other event listeners called before it.
- Throwing exceptions into the stack is not normal behavior, but it might be caused by a bug in your code. When an event is emitted, if one of the event listeners throws an error when invoked, some event listeners might never be called. In that case, the event emitter will catch the error and may handle it.

As an example, consider this:

```
readStream.on("data", function(data) {
    throw new Error("Something wrong has happened");
});
readStream.on("data", function(data) {
    console.log('I have some data here too.');
});
```

In this example, the second listener will not be invoked because the first one throws an error.

Removing an Event Listener from an Event Emitter Using .removeListener()

If and when you no longer want to be informed of a specific event on a specific object, you can unregister by specifying the event type and the callback function like this:

```
function receiveData(data) {
  console.log("got data from file read stream: %j", data);
}
readStream.on("data", receiveData);
// ...
readStream.removeListener("data", receiveData);
```

In this last example, the last line where you are removing the event listener may happen at any time in the future, as a reaction to another event.

Removing a specific event listener forces you to name your callback function because it will be used in at least two places — when adding the listener and when removing it.

Getting a Callback Executed at Most Once Using .once()

If you are listening for an event that will happen at most once, or even if you are only interested in listening to the first occurrence of any given event type, you can use .once().

This method adds the event listener and removes it right after the first event occurs.

```
function receiveData(data) {
  console.log("got data from file read stream: %j", data);
}
readStream.once("data", receiveData);
```

Here, the `receiveData` function will be called only once. If a data event is emitted on the `readStream` object, the `receiveData` callback will be triggered only once.

This is a convenience method, because you could easily implement it like this:

```
var EventEmitter = require("events").EventEmitter;

EventEmitter.prototype.once = function(type, callback) {
  var that = this;
```

```
    this.on(type, function listener() {
      that.removeListener(type, listener);
      callback.apply(that, arguments);
    });
  };
```

Here, you are redefining the `EventEmitter.prototype.once` function, which redefines the once method for every object that inherits from EventEmitter. You are simply using the `.on()` method and, once you get the event, you use `.removeEventListener()` to unregister the callback and call the original callback.

> **NOTE** *Here you use the* `function.apply()` *method, which takes an object to be used as the implicit variable* `this` *and an array of arguments. In this case, you are passing in the unmodified arguments array, allowing for transparent handover of all arguments originally passed to the callback by the event emitter.*

Removing All Event Listeners from an Event Emitter Using .removeAllListeners()

You can remove all registered listeners for a particular event type from an event emitter like this:

```
emitter.removeAllListeners(type);
```

For instance, if you want to remove all event listeners for the process interruption signal, you could do this:

```
process.removeAllListeners("SIGTERM");
```

> **NOTE** *As a rule of thumb, I recommend you use this function only if you know exactly what you are removing. Otherwise, you might remove event listeners set by other parts of the application. Instead, those parts of the application should themselves be responsible for removing them. However, there could be some rare cases when this function would be useful, such as when you're orderly shutting down an event emitter or even the whole process.*

CREATING AN EVENT EMITTER

The event emitter provides a great way of making a programming interface more generic. When you use a common understood pattern, clients bind to events instead of invoking functions, making your program more flexible.

Also, by using the event emitter, you get some features for free, like having multiple independent listeners for the same events.

Inheriting from Node Event Emitter

If you are interested in using Node's event emitter pattern throughout your application, you can. You can create a pseudo-class and make it inherit from `EventEmitter` like this:

```
util = require('util');
var EventEmitter = require('events').EventEmitter;

// Here is the MyClass constructor:
var MyClass = function() {
}

util.inherits(MyClass, EventEmitter);
```

> **NOTE** `util.inherits` *sets up the prototype chain so that you get the* `EventEmitter` *prototype methods available to your* `MyClass` *instances.*

Emitting Events

By creating a class that inherits from EventEmitter, instances of `MyClass` can emit events:

```
MyClass.prototype.someMethod = function() {
  this.emit("custom event", "argument 1", "argument 2");
};
```

Here, when the `someMethod` method is called on an instance of `MyClass`, the example emits an event named `custom event`. The event also emits some data, in this case two strings: `"argument 1"` and `"argument 2"`. This data will be passed along as arguments to the event listeners.

Clients of `MyClass` instances can listen to the event named `custom event` like this:

```
var myInstance = new MyClass();
myInstance.on('custom event', function(str1, str2) {
  console.log('got a custom event with the str1 %s and str2 %s!', str1, str2);
});
```

For example, you could build a pseudo-class named `Ticker` that emits a "tick" event every second:

```
var util = require('util'),
EventEmitter = require('events').EventEmitter;

var Ticker = function() {
  var self = this;
```

```
    setInterval(function() {
      self.emit('tick');
    }, 1000);
  };
  util.inherits(Ticker, EventEmitter);
```

Clients of this class could instantiate this `Ticker` class and listen for the "tick" events like so:

```
  var ticker = new Ticker();
  ticker.on("tick", function() {
    console.log("tick");
  });
```

SUMMARY

The event emitter pattern is a recurrent pattern in Node. You can use it to decouple event emitter objects from the code interested in certain events.

You can use `event_emitter.on()` to register listeners for certain types of events and `event_emitter.removeListener()` to unregister them.

You can create your own event emitters by inheriting from the `EventEmitter` class and simply using the `.emit()` function.

Scheduling the Execution of Functions Using Timers

WHAT'S IN THIS CHAPTER?

- Deferring the execution of a function
- Canceling a scheduled execution
- Scheduling a periodic execution of a function
- Deferring the execution of a function until the next event loop tick

If you are accustomed to programming in browser JavaScript, you probably use the `setTimeout` and `setInterval` functions. These functions allow for the deferred execution of a function after a given period of time. For example, the following snippet of code, once loaded into a web page, appends the string `"Hello there"` after one second has elapsed:

```
var oneSecond = 1000 * 1; // one second = 1000 x 1 ms
setTimeout(function() {
    document.write('<p>Hello there.</p>');
}, oneSecond);
```

`setInterval` allows for the repetitive execution of a function spaced by a given time interval. If you inject the following snippet into a web page, it will also append the phrase `"Hello there"` to the document and keep doing so every second:

```
var oneSecond = 1000 * 1; // one second = 1000 x 1 ms
setInterval(function() {
    document.write('<p>Hello there.</p>');
}, oneSecond);
```

The need for these functions has arisen because the web has become a platform for building applications instead of static web pages. These scheduling functions help developers build periodic form validation, deferred remote data syncing, and all sorts of user interface interactions that require a delayed reaction. Node implements this exact set of functions. On the server side they can be used for assisting in repetitive or deferred execution of many different procedures that include cache expiration, connection pool cleanup, session timeout, polling, and others.

I will now go over these functions and then discuss some of their limitations.

USING SETTIMEOUT TO DEFER THE EXECUTION OF A FUNCTION

The `setTimeout` function lets you schedule any other function to be executed once in the future. Here is an example:

```
var timeout_ms = 2000; // 2 seconds
var timeout = setTimeout(function() {
  console.log("timed out!");
}, timeout_ms);
```

Exactly as in browser JavaScript, `setTimeout` accepts the deferred function as a first argument and the time after which the function is executed — in milliseconds — as the second argument.

The call to `setTimeout` returns a timeout handler, which is an internal object that cannot be used for anything except canceling the execution using `clearTimeout`.

USING CLEARTIMEOUT TO CANCEL THE EXECUTION OF A FUNCTION

Once you have obtained a timeout handler, you can use it to cancel the scheduled function call using the `clearTimeout` function like this:

```
var timeoutTime = 1000; // one second
var timeout = setTimeout(function() {
  console.log("timed out!");
}, timeoutTime);
clearTimeout(timeout);
```

In this case the timeout will never be fired and `"timed out!"` will never be printed to the console. You can also cancel the scheduled execution at some time in the future. The following code snippet shows an example where this happens:

```
var timeout = setTimeout(function A() {
  console.log("timed out!");
}, 2000);

setTimeout(function B() {
  clearTimeout(timeout);
}, 1000);
```

Here you are scheduling two functions to be executed in the future, A and B. Function A is scheduled to run in two seconds, and function B is scheduled to run in one second. In this case, function A never fires because when function B runs, it unschedules function A.

SCHEDULING AND CANCELING THE REPETITIVE EXECUTION OF A FUNCTION

`setInterval` is similar to `setTimeout`, but instead schedules a function to run every given period of time. You may want to use it to periodically trigger routines that perform some type of cleanup, collection, logging, fetching, polling, or any other procedure you may find useful to run on a repetitive basis.

The following snippet of code outputs `"tick"` to the console every second:

```
var period = 1000; // 1 second
setInterval(function() {
  console.log("tick");
}, period);
```

If you don't want to keep running this process indefinitely or until it ends, you can unschedule it by calling `clearInterval()`.

`setInterval` returns a scheduling handler, which you can provide as an argument to `clearInterval` to unschedule it.

```
var interval = setInterval(function() {
  console.log("tick");
}, 1000);
// …
clearInterval(interval);
```

USING PROCESS.NEXTTICK TO DEFER THE EXECUTION OF A FUNCTION UNTIL THE NEXT EVENT LOOP ITERATION

Sometimes browser JavaScript programmers use `setTimeout(callback, 0)` as a way to defer tasks until the near future. The zero value in the millisecond argument tells the JavaScript runtime that it should execute the callback function as soon as possible after all pending events have been processed. This technique is sometimes used to defer operations that don't need run immediately. For instance, they are sometimes used to start animations or do some computation after the user event has been processed.

In Node, the event loop runs, as the name indicates, in a loop that processes the event queue. Every time the event loop executes, it's called a *tick*.

You can schedule a callback function to be invoked on the next run of the event loop, that is, the next *tick*. Whereas `setTimeout` uses a JavaScript runtime that has its own scheduling queue, the `process.nextTick` function is specific to the Node event loop.

By using `process.nextTick(callback)` instead of `setTimeout(callback, 0)`, your callback runs immediately after all the events in the event queue have been processed, which is much sooner (in the CPU time scale) than when the JavaScript timeout queue is activated.

You can defer the execution of a function until the next event loop *tick* like this:

```
process.nextTick(function() {
  my_expensive_computation_function();
});
```

> **NOTE** *The* `process` *object is one of the few Node global objects.*

BLOCKING THE EVENT LOOP

Node and JavaScript runtimes in general are single-threaded event loops. On each loop, the runtime processes the next event in queue by calling the associated callback function. When that event is done, the event loop fetches and processes the next event; this pattern continues until the queue is empty. If one of these callbacks takes a long time, the event loop won't process pending events in the meantime. This can lead to a slow application or service.

Using memory- or processor-intensive functions when handling events can lead to the event loop becoming slow and the events becoming queued up and unserved or even blocked.

Here is an example of blocking the event loop:

```
process.nextTick(function nextTick1() {
  var a = 0;
  while(true) {
    a ++;
  }
});

process.nextTick(function nextTick2() {
  console.log("next tick");
});

setTimeout(function timeout() {
  console.log("timeout");
}, 1000);
```

In this case, the `nextTick2` and `timeout` functions will never have the chance to run no matter how long you wait because the event loop is blocked by an infinite cycle inside the first `nextTick` function. Even the scheduled timeout function that was supposed to run after one second does not run.

When using `setTimeout`, the callback function goes into a scheduling queue, which, in this case, doesn't even get to be dispatched. This is an extreme case, but you can see how running a processor-intensive task may block or slow down your event loop.

ESCAPING THE EVENT LOOP

By using `process.nextTick`, you can now defer the execution of a non-crucial task to the next *tick*, freeing the event loop to execute other pending events.

As an example, if you need to remove a temporary file you created, but perhaps you don't need to do it before replying to the client, you can defer it like this:

```
stream.on("data", function(data) {
  stream.end("my response");
  process.nextTick(function() {
    fs.unlink("/path/to/file");
  });
});
```

USING SETTIMEOUT INSTEAD OF SETINTERVAL TO FORCE SERIALIZATION

Let's say you want a function that does some I/O — such as parsing a log file — that will periodically be executed. Let's give that function the generic name `my_async_function`. You could start by using `setInterval` like this:

```
var interval = 1000;
setInterval(function() {
  my_async_function(function() {
    console.log('my_async_function finished!');
  });
});
```

However, you must ensure that none of these functions execute at the same time. You really can't guarantee that if you are using `setInterval`. If `my_async_function` takes one millisecond longer than the interval you are using, they would run at the same time.

You need to enforce that the interval between *the end* of one `my_async_function` and *the start* of the next is the desired interval. Here is how you can do this:

```
var interval = 1000; // 1 second

(function schedule() {
  setTimeout(function do_it() {
    my_async_function(function() {
      console.log('async is done!');
      schedule();
    });
  }, interval);
}());
```

Here you are declaring a function named `schedule` (line 3) and invoking it immediately after it is declared (line 10). This `schedule` function schedules the `do_it` function to be executed in one second (the chosen interval). After one second passes, this anonymous function fires, calling `my_async_function` (line 5). When this function finishes, the anonymous callback you passed to it is invoked (line 6), calling the `schedule` function, which will again schedule the `do_it` function to be executed in one second, thus restarting the cycle.

SUMMARY

You can use `setTimeout()` to schedule the future execution of a function, which you can cancel with `clearTimeout()`. You can also schedule the periodic execution of a function by using `setInterval()` and unschedule it by using `clearInterval()`.

If you block the event loop with a processor-intensive operation, your scheduled functions will be delayed or never execute. You learned that you shouldn't perform CPU-intensive operations inside the event loop and that you can defer the execution of a function until the next iteration of the event loop by using `process.nextTick()`.

Using I/O and `setInterval()` does not guarantee that there won't be more than one pending call at any given time. However, you can circumvent this potential issue by using a recursive function and `setTimeout()`.

PART III
Files, Processes, Streams, and Networking

7

Querying, Reading from, and Writing to Files

WHAT'S IN THIS CHAPTER?

- Manipulating file paths
- Extracting information from a file path
- Understanding file descriptors
- Using fs.stat() to capture file statistics
- Opening, reading, writing, and closing files
- Avoiding leaking file descriptors

Node has a streaming API for dealing with files as if they were network streams. It is very convenient, but it only allows you to deal with files in a continuous way. This doesn't work if you need to write in or read from specific positions inside a file. For that, you need to go down a level and deal with the filesystem itself.

This chapter covers file-handling basics, including how to open a file, read specific parts from it, write to it, and close it.

Much of Node's file API is an almost direct translation of the UNIX (POSIX) APIs, such as the way that file descriptors are used. Just like in UNIX, a file descriptor handle in Node is an integer representing the index of an entry on the process file descriptor table.

There are three special file descriptors — 1, 2, and 3. They represent, respectively, the *standard input*, *standard output*, and *standard error* file descriptors. *Standard input* is, as the name indicates, a read-only stream that the process can use to read from the console or from data piped from another process. *Standard output* and *standard error* are output-only file descriptors, and they can be used to output to the console or into another process or file. *Standard error* is reserved for outputting errors, whereas *standard output* is for normal process output.

These file descriptors are available to the process as soon as it starts and do not really represent files. You can write to and read from specific positions within the file. With these file descriptors — much like network streams — you can only read and output continuously. What is written is written and cannot be overridden.

Files are not limited in this way. For instance, in Node you can have append-only files, yet you can also write to a specific position.

Nearly all the code that handles files has to handle and manipulate file paths. This chapter covers these utility functions first and then dives into file reading and content manipulation.

MANIPULATING FILE PATHS

File paths represent files, and these paths come in relative or absolute formats. You can concatenate file paths, extract filename information, and even detect file existence.

In Node you can manipulate file paths by using strings, but that can become difficult, for instance, when you want to join path components. For example, path components can be terminated with /, but they don't have to be, and accounting for those cases can be cumbersome. Path separators also vary according to the OS.

Fortunately, Node has a module named `path` that enables you to normalize, join, and resolve paths, as well as find relative paths between absolute paths, extract components from paths, and determine the existence of paths. In general, the `path` module simply manipulates strings and does not interact with the filesystem to validate the strings (with the exception of the `path.exists()` function).

Normalizing Paths

Normalizing paths before you store or use them is often a good idea. For example, file paths that were input by users or are present in a configuration file, as well as paths that are the result of joining two or more paths, usually need to be normalized. To do so, you can use the `normalize` function present in the `path` module to normalize a path string, thus taking care of `..`, `.`, and `//`. For instance:

```
var path = require('path');
path.normalize('/foo/bar//baz/asdf/quux/..');
// => '/foo/bar/baz/asdf'
```

Joining Paths

By using `path.join()`, you can concatenate path strings. You can concatenate as many as you like, passing all of them as consecutive arguments like so:

```
var path = require('path');
path.join('/foo', 'bar', 'baz/asdf', 'quux', '..');
// => '/foo/bar/baz/asdf'
```

As you can see, `path.join()` also normalizes the path.

Resolving Paths

You can resolve a series of paths into a normalized absolute path by using `path.resolve()`. It works like an iterative `cd` command for every argument, except that it also works on files and it's abstract — it does not tap into the underlying filesystem to try to see if the path exists; it simply manipulates paths.

For instance:

```
var path = require('path');
path.resolve('/foo/bar', './baz');
// => /foo/bar/baz
path.resolve('/foo/bar', '/tmp/file/');
// => /tmp/file
```

If the resulting path is not absolute, `path.resolve` will prepend the current working directory to the path, as in this example:

```
path.resolve('wwwroot', 'static_files/png/', '../gif/image.gif');
// if currently in /home/myself/node, it returns
// => /home/myself/node/wwwroot/static_files/gif/image.gif'
```

Finding the Relative Path Between Two Absolute Paths

By using `path.relative()`, you can also determine how to get from one absolute path to another absolute path. For example:

```
var path = require('path');
path.relative('/data/orandea/test/aaa', '/data/orandea/impl/bbb');
// => ../../impl/bbb
```

Extracting Components of a Path

If you have a file path such as `/foo/bar/myfile.txt`, you may need to retrieve the parent directory contents (the contents of `/foo/bar`) or read another file inside the same directory. For that you have to obtain the directory part of the file path by using `path.dirname(filePath)`. For example:

```
var path = require('path');
path.dirname('/foo/bar/baz/asdf/quux.txt');
// => /foo/bar/baz/asdf
```

In some cases, you might want to extract the filename from the file path, which is the last portion of a path. You can do this by using the `path.basename` function:

```
var path = require('path');
path.basename('/foo/bar/baz/asdf/quux.html')
// => quux.html
```

A file path can also include an extension, which is usually the string in the base name after and including the last `.` character.

You can subtract the file extension from the result by passing in an optional second argument with the expected extension, like this:

```
var path = require('path');
path.basename('/foo/bar/baz/asdf/quux.html', '.html');
// => quux
```

When you use `path.basename` this way, you have to know the extension beforehand. You can determine the extension by using `path.extname()` like so:

```
var path = require('path');
path.extname('/a/b/index.html');
// => '.html'
path.extname('/a/b.c/index');
// => ''
path.extname('/a/b.c/.');
// => ''
path.extname('/a/b.c/d.');
// => '.'
```

Determining the Existence of a Path

All the path manipulations and extractions you have seen so far don't touch the underlying filesystem. However, you might at some point need to determine whether a given path exists. For example, you might need to ensure that a directory or file does not already exist before you create it. You can do that by using `path.exists()`, like so:

```
var path = require('path');
path.exists('/etc/passwd', function(exists) {
  console.log('exists:', exists);
  // => true
});
path.exists('/does_not_exist', function(exists) {
  console.log('exists:', exists);
  // => false
});
```

NOTE *In Node v0.8* `path.exists` *was replaced by* `fs.exists`*, with the exact same semantics.*

To use it you can simply import the "fs" module instead:

```
var fs = require('fs');
fs.exists('/does_not_exist', function(exists) {
  console.log('exists:', exists);
  // => false
});
```

Because the `path.exists()` function does I/O, it is asynchronous, which implies that you have to pass a callback to be informed of the result once it is ready. If you are not inside an I/O callback, you can use the synchronous version `path.existsSync()`, which behaves the same way but returns the result instead of using a callback:

```
var path = require('path');
path.existsSync('/etc/passwd');
// => true
```

INTRODUCING THE FS MODULE

The `fs` module is where all the file query and manipulation functions are stored. With these functions, you can query file statistics, as well as open, read from, write to, and close files.

You can require the `fs` module like this:

```
var fs = require('fs');
```

Querying File Statistics

Sometimes you may need to know some characteristics of a file like its size, creation time, or permissions. You can query some meta-information on a file (or directory) by using the `fs.stat` function like this:

```
var fs = require('fs');
fs.stat('/etc/passwd', function(err, stats) {
  if (err) { throw err;}
  console.log(stats);
});
```

Running this snippet should output something like the following:

```
{ dev: 234881026,
  ino: 95028917,
  mode: 33188,
  nlink: 1,
  uid: 0,
  gid: 0,
  rdev: 0,
  size: 5086,
  blksize: 4096,
  blocks: 0,
  atime: Fri, 18 Nov 2011 22:44:47 GMT,
  mtime: Thu, 08 Sep 2011 23:50:04 GMT,
  ctime: Thu, 08 Sep 2011 23:50:04 GMT }
```

The `fs.stat()` function call passes an instance of the `stats` class into the `callback` function, which you can use to call any of the following:

- `stats.isFile()`—Returns `true` if the file is a standard file and not a directory, a socket, a symbolic link, or a device.
- `stats.isDirectory()`—Returns `true` if the file is a directory.
- `stats.isBlockDevice()`—Returns `true` if the file is a device of the type block; in most UNIX systems this is generally under the `/dev` directory.
- `stats.isCharacterDevice()`—Returns `true` if the file is a device of the character type.
- `stats.isSymbolicLink()`—Returns `true` if the file is a symbolic link to another file.
- `stats.isFifo()`—Returns `true` if the file is a FIFO (a special kind of UNIX named pipe).
- `stats.isSocket()`—Returns `true` if the file is a UNIX domain socket.

OPENING A FILE

Before you can read or manipulate files, you have to open them using the `fs.open` function. Then, a callback function you provide is invoked with the file descriptor, which you can later use to read or write to the opened file.

```
var fs = require('fs');
fs.open('/path/to/file', 'r', function(err, fd) {
  // got fd file descriptor
});
```

The first argument to `fs.open()` is the file path. The second argument contains the flags, which indicate the mode with which the file should open. The flags can be `r`, `r+`, `w`, `w+`, `a`, or `a+`. Here are the semantics of these flags (taken from the `fopen` UNIX manual page):

- `r`—Opens the text file for reading. The stream is positioned at the beginning of the file.
- `r+`—Opens the file for reading and writing. The stream is positioned at the beginning of the file.
- `w`—Truncates the file to zero length or creates a text file for writing. The stream is positioned at the beginning of the file.
- `w+`—Opens the file for reading and writing. The file is created if it does not exist. Otherwise it is truncated. The stream is positioned at the beginning of the file.
- `a`—Opens the file for writing. The file is created if it does not exist. The stream is positioned at the end of the file. Subsequent writes to the file will always end up at the current end of file.
- `a+`—Opens the file for reading and writing. The file is created if it does not exist. The stream is positioned at the end of the file. Subsequent writes to the file will always end up at the current end of file.

READING FROM A FILE

Once a file is open, you can read a part of it, but before you do so, you have to create a buffer that will contain the data. That buffer will be passed to the `fs.read` function to be filled with the file data.

```
var fs = require('fs');
fs.open('./my_file.txt', 'r', function opened(err, fd) {
  if (err) { throw err }
  var readBuffer = new Buffer(1024),
      bufferOffset = 0,
      bufferLength = readBuffer.length,
      filePosition = 100;
  fs.read(fd,
          readBuffer,
          bufferOffset,
          bufferLength,
          filePosition,
          function read(err, readBytes) {
            if (err) { throw err; }
            console.log('just read ' + readBytes + ' bytes');
            if (readBytes > 0) {
              console.log(readBuffer.slice(0, readBytes));
            }
          });
});
```

Here you are opening the file, and when it's opened (calling the `opened` function), you are asking to read a chunk of 1,024 bytes from it, starting at position 100 of the buffer you provided (line 11).

The last argument to the `fs.read()` call is a `callback` function (line 16), which is invoked when one of the following three things happen:

- There is an error.
- Something has been read.
- Nothing could be read.

With the first argument, the callback gets an error object if something went wrong; otherwise, the argument is `null`. If the read succeeds, the second argument (`readBytes`) gets the number of bytes read into the buffer. If the read byte count is zero, the file has reached the end.

> **NOTE** *Once you pass the buffer to* `fs.open()`*, that buffer becomes under the control of the* `read` *command. The control of the buffer will return to you once your callback is invoked. Don't read, write, or use that buffer in another call before that; otherwise, you may read incomplete data, or worse, you may write concurrently into the same buffer.*

Writing to a File

To write into an open file, you can use `fs.write()`, passing in a buffer with data:

```
var fs = require('fs');
fs.open('./my_file.txt', 'a', function opened(err, fd) {
  if (err) { throw err; }
  var writeBuffer = new Buffer('writing this string'),
      bufferPosition = 0,
      bufferLength = writeBuffer.length, filePosition = null;
  fs.write( fd,
            writeBuffer,
            bufferPosition,
            bufferLength,
            filePosition,
            function wrote(err, written) {
              if (err) { throw err; }
              console.log('wrote ' + written + ' bytes');
            });
});
```

In this example, you are opening the file in append mode (a) on line 3, and then writing into it on line 9. You are passing in a buffer with the following information:

- The data you want written to the buffer
- The position inside the buffer where the data should start
- The length of the data you want to write
- The file position you want to start writing from
- A callback function called `wrote` that will be invoked once the operation ends

In this case, you are passing in a file position of `null`, which indicates that the `write` will happen at the current file cursor. Because you are opening the file in append mode, the file cursor is positioned at the end of the file.

Again, as in the `read` operation, you should not use the buffer you provide after the `fs.write` operation has been commanded. Once you pass it in, the buffer is in control of that operation, and you should only reuse it after your callback has been invoked.

Closing a File

With all the examples you've seen so far in this chapter, you might have noticed that the code did not close the files. This is because these are small simple examples destined to be run once. When your Node process exits, the operating system will make sure all the files are closed.

In real applications, however, once you open a file, you will eventually need to close it. For that you just keep track of all the open file descriptors and eventually close them using `fs.close(fd[, callback])` when you no longer need them. It's quite easy to leak file descriptors if you're not careful. Next is an example that provides a function named `openAndWriteToSystemLog` with careful file closing:

```
var fs = require('fs');
function openAndWriteToSystemLog(writeBuffer, callback) {
  fs.open('./my_file', 'a', function opened(err, fd) {
    if (err) { return callback(err); }
    function notifyError(err) {
      fs.close(fd, function() {
        callback(err);
      });
    }
    var bufferOffset = 0,
        bufferLength = writeBuffer.length,
        filePosition = null;
    fs.write( fd, writeBuffer, bufferOffset, bufferLength, filePosition,
      function wrote(err, written) {
        if (err) { return notifyError(err); }
        fs.close(fd, function() {
          callback(err);
        });
      }
    );
  });
}
openAndWriteToSystemLog(
    new Buffer('writing this string'),
    function done(err) {
      if (err) {
        console.log("error while opening and writing:", err.message);
        return;
      }
     console.log('All done with no errors');
    }
);
```

Here, you are providing a function named `openAndWriteToSystemLog` that takes a buffer to write and a callback function to be invoked once the operation is complete or when an error occurs. If an error occurs, it will be passed as the first argument of the callback function.

Note that the `notifyError` internal function takes care of closing the file descriptor and reporting an error.

> **NOTE** *Up to this point, you have learned about low-level file opening, reading, writing, and closing primitives. However, Node has a higher-level set of constructs that allows you to address some files in a simpler way.*
>
> *For example, when you want to append data to a file and you want to do it in a way that is safe to use concurrently, where you may have, at any given time, two or more pending* `write` *operations, you should use a WriteStream.*
>
> *Also, if you want to read a region of one file, consider using a ReadStream.*
>
> *Both these use cases are covered in Chapter 9, "Reading and Writing Streams of Data."*

Summary

When you're working with files, most of the time you have to manipulate and extract parts of the file paths. By using the path module you can join paths, normalize them, calculate differences between them, and resolve relative paths into absolute ones. You can also extract path components like the file extension, the base name, the extension, and the directory path of any given file path.

Node provides a low-level API to the filesystem in the `fs` module. Low-level filesystems use file descriptors to handle their files. You can use `fs.open` to open a file, `fs.write` to write to it, `fs.read` to read from it, and `fs.close` to close it.

In error situations, you should always close your files by handling errors correctly — be sure to close all the file descriptors before calling back.

Creating and Controlling External Processes

WHAT'S IN THIS CHAPTER?

- Launching commands and child processes
- Sending and receiving data from a child process
- Sending signals to and then terminating a child process

Node is designed to handle I/O efficiently, but, as you've seen, some types of programs are not a good fit for this model. For instance, if you were to perform a CPU-intensive task using Node, you would be blocking the event loop, thus limiting your application responsiveness. Instead, CPU-intensive tasks should be assigned to a different process, freeing the event loop. Node allows you to spawn processes that become children of the process that launched them — the parent. In Node, a child process has a two-way channel to communicate with the parent process, and the parent process can monitor and control the child to some degree.

Another instance of when you may want to use a child process is when you want to simply execute an external command from Node and get back the results once the command finishes. For instance, you may want to spawn a UNIX command, a script, or another type of utility that is not directly executable inside Node.

This chapter shows you how to spawn external commands and create, communicate with, and terminate child processes. The point is to enable you to accomplish multiple tasks outside of the Node process.

EXECUTING EXTERNAL COMMANDS

When you need to launch an external shell command or an executable file, you may do so by using the `child_process` module. You can import this module like this:

```
var child_process = require('child_process');
```

You can then use the `exec` function that is defined in this module like this:

```
var exec = child_process.exec;
exec(command, callback);
```

The first argument to the `exec` function is a string with the command as you would launch it from the shell. The second argument is a function callback. This callback will be later called by the `exec` function once the command terminates or an error occurs. You should expect three arguments in this callback: `error, stdout,` and `stderr`. Here is an example:

```
exec('ls', function(err, stdout, stderr) {
  // ...
});
```

If an error occurs, the first argument will be an instance of the `Error` class. If the first argument does not contain an error, the second argument, `stdout`, will contain the command output. The last argument will contain the command error output.

Listing 8-1 shows a more complete example of executing an external command.

LISTING 8-1: Executing an external command. (chapter8/01_external_command.js)

```
// import the exec function defined on the child_process module
var exec = require('child_process').exec;
// launch the command "cat *.js | wc -l"
exec('cat *.js | wc -l', function(err, stdout, stderr) {
    // the command exited or the launching failed
    if (err) {
        // we had an error launching the process
        console.log('child process exited with error code', err.code);
        return;
    }
    console.log(stdout);
});
```

On line 4, you pass in `cat *.js | wc -l` as the command in the first argument to the `exec` invocation. You can use it to launch any other command, written as you would type it inside the shell prompt.

You then pass a callback function as the second argument, which will be invoked if an error occurs or once the child process has terminated.

You can also pass an optional argument containing some configuration options before the callback function, like this:

```
var exec = require('child_process').exec;
var options = {
    timeout: 10000,
    killSignal: 'SIGKILL'
};
exec('cat *.js | wc -l', options, function(err, stdout, stderr) {
    // ...
});
```

The available options are:

- cwd — current working directory. Use this if you want to force the current working directory.
- encoding — the expected encoding for the child output. Defaults to the string uft8, which identifies the UTF-8 encoding. Use this if the process you are executing outputs data in an encoding other than UTF-8. Node supports these encodings:
    - ascii
    - utf8
    - ucs2
    - base64

  If you want more information about the supported Node encodings, refer to Chapter 4, "Using Buffers to Manipulate, Encode, and Decode Binary Data."
- timeout — the timeout in milliseconds for the execution of the command. Defaults to 0, which waits indefinitely for the child process to end.
- maxBuffer — specifies the maximum size in bytes of the output allowed on the stdout or the stderr streams. If exceeded, the child is killed. Defaults to 200 * 1024.
- killSignal — the signal to be sent to the child if it times out or exceeds the output buffers.

  The default value for this is SIGTERM, which sends a termination signal to the process. This is usually the orderly way of ending processes. When using the SIGTERM signal, the process is able to handle and override the default behavior. If the target process expects it, you can send it another signal altogether (like SIGUSR1, for instance). You can also send it a SIGKILL signal, which is handled by the operating system and forces the process to terminate immediately, without a cleanup routine being triggered.

  If you want to handle process termination more closely, you should use the child_process.spawn function instead, which is covered later.
- env — environment variables to be passed into the child process. Defaults to null, which means the child process inherits all the parent environment variables that are defined right before spawning it.

NOTE *With the* `killSignal` *option you can pass a string identifying the name of the signal you want to send to the target process. Signals are identified in Node as strings. Here is a complete list of UNIX signals and their default actions:*

NAME	DEFAULT ACTION	DESCRIPTION
`SIGHUP`	Terminate process	Terminal line hangup
`SIGINT`	Terminate process	Interrupt program
`SIGQUIT`	Create core image	Quit program
`SIGILL`	Create core image	Illegal instruction
`SIGTRAP`	Create core image	Trace trap
`SIGABRT`	Create core image	Abort program
`SIGEMT`	Create core image	Emulate instruction executed
`SIGFPE`	Create core image	Floating-point exception
`SIGKILL`	Terminate process	Kill program
`SIGBUS`	Create core image	Bus error
`SIGSEGV`	Create core image	Segmentation violation
`SIGSYS`	Create core image	Nonexistent system call invoked
`SIGPIPE`	Terminate process	Software termination signal
`SIGALRM`	Terminate process	Real-time timer expired
`SIGTERM`	Terminate process	Software termination signal
`SIGURG`	Discard signal	Urgent condition present on socket
`SIGSTOP`	Stop process	Stop (cannot be caught or ignored)
`SIGTSTP`	Stop process	Stop signal generated from keyboard
`SIGCONT`	Discard signal	Continue after stop
`SIGCHLD`	Discard signal	Child status has changed
`SIGTTIN`	Stop process	Background read attempted from control terminal
`SIGTTOU`	Stop process	Background write attempted to control terminal
`SIGIO`	Discard signal	I/O is possible on a descriptor

NAME	DEFAULT ACTION	DESCRIPTION
SIGXCPU	Terminate process	CPU time limit exceeded
SIGXFSZ	Terminate process	File size limit exceeded
SIGVTALRM	Terminate process	Virtual time alarm
SIGPROF	Terminate process	Profiling timer alarm
SIGWINCH	Discard signal	Window size change
SIGINFO	Discard signal	Status request from keyboard
SIGUSR1	Terminate process	User defined signal 1
SIGUSR2	Terminate process	User defined signal 2

You may want to provide the child process with a set of environment variables that is an extension of the parent ones. If you change the `process.env` object directly, you will change it for every module of your Node process, which is undesirable. Instead, create a new object that is the augmented copy of `process.env`, as seen in Listing 8-2.

LISTING 8-2: Executing a command with augmented environment variables. (chapter8/02_env_vars_augment.js)

```
var env = process.env,
    varName,
    envCopy = {},
    exec = require('child_process').exec;
// Copy process.env into envCopy
for (varName in env) {
  envCopy[varName] = env[varName];
}

// Assign some custom variables
envCopy['CUSTOM ENV VAR'] = 'some value';
envCopy['CUSTOM ENV VAR 2'] = 'some other value';

// Execute some command with process.env and my custom variables
exec('ls -la', { env: envCopy }, function(err, stdout, stderr) {
    if (err) { throw err; }
    console.log('stdout:', stdout);
    console.log('stderr:', stderr);
});
```

Here you are creating an object stored on the variable named `envCopy`, which will initially contain a copy of the contents of the `process.env` object. Then you will add or replace the environment variables you want to see changed. Finally you execute the command, passing in the `envCopy` object as the environment object specification to the `exec` function.

Keep in mind that the environment variables are passed between processes using the operating system, and thus all the values arrive at the child process as strings. For instance, if the parent process passes the number 123 as an environment variable, the child process will receive it as the string `123`.

As an example you'll set up two Node scripts in the same folder. One you can name `parent.js` and the other `child.js`. The first one will launch the second one, so you need the two scripts in place for this to work.

Listing 8-3 shows a quick example of where this happens.

LISTING 8-3: Parent process setting environment variable. (chapter8/03_environment_number_parent.js)

```
var exec = require('child_process').exec;
exec('node child.js', {env: {number: 123}}, function(err, stdout, stderr) {
    if (err) { throw err; }
    console.log('stdout:\n', stdout);
    console.log('stderr:\n', stderr);
});
```

Save this file as `parent.js`. Next is the source code for the child process, which you should place inside a file named `child.js` (see Listing 8-4).

LISTING 8-4: Child process parsing environment variable. (chapter8/04_environment_number_child.js)

```
var number = process.env.number;
console.log(typeof(number)); // → "string"
number = parseInt(number, 10);
console.log(typeof(number)); // → "number"
```

After you have saved this code into a file named `child.js`, you can launch it by using the command line when inside the folder with the source code:

```
$ node parent.js
```

It should output the following:

```
stdout:
 string
number

stderr:
```

Here you can see that, in spite of the parent process passing a number into the name environment variable, the child process receives it as a string (as you can see in line 2 of the output). In line 3 you parse the string into a number.

SPAWNING CHILD PROCESSES

As you have seen, you can use the `child_process.exec()` function to launch external processes. You get your callback invoked when that process ends. This approach is very simple, but it has some drawbacks:

- Except for the command-line arguments and the environment variables, using `exec()` does not allow you to communicate with the child process.
- The child process output is buffered. As a result, you cannot stream it, and it can consume memory.

Fortunately, Node's `child_process` module allows for finer-grained control when launching, stopping, and generally interacting with child processes. You may launch a new process, called the child process, from your application, which is called the parent process. Once you've launched a new child process, Node establishes a two-way communication channel, which both processes can use to send and receive data strings to and from each other. The parent process can also exercise some control over the child, sending it signals and forcing it to terminate.

Creating the Child Process

You can spawn a new child process based on the `child_process.spawn` function, shown in Listing 8-5.

LISTING 8-5: Spawning a child process. (chapter8/05_spawning_child.js)

```
// Import the spawn function defined on child_process module
var spawn = require('child_process').spawn;

// Launch a child process with a "tail -f /var/log/system.log" command
var child = spawn('tail', ['-f', '/var/log/system.log']);
```

Here you spawn a child process to run a `tail` command, passing in arguments `-f` and `/var/log/system.log`. This `tail` command will monitor the file in `/var/log/system.log` — if it exists — and output every new data appended to it into the `stdout` stream. The `spawn` function call returns a `ChildProcess` object, which is a handler object that encapsulates access to the real process. Here you assign this new descriptor to the variable named `child`.

Listening for Data from the Child Process

Any child process handler has a property named `stdout` that represents the child process standard output as a stream. You can then bind to the `data` event on that stream, which is the same as saying "for every data chunk you get from the child output, invoke this callback." Here is an example of that happening:

```
// print child output to the console
child.stdout.on('data', function(data) {
    console.log('tail output: ' + data);
});
```

Every time the child process outputs any data into its standard output, the parent process gets notified and prints it to the console.

Besides the standard output, processes also have another output stream by default named *standard error* stream, which is usually the stream processes use to output error messages.

In this case, if the file `/var/log/system.log` does not exist, the `tail` process will output something like `tail: /var/log/system.log: No such file or directory`. By listening to the `stderr` stream, the parent process can be notified of these errors.

The parent process can also listen for data from that stream using something like this:

```
child.stderr.on('data', function(data) {
    console.log('tail error output:', data);
});
```

The `stderr` property is also a read stream, just like `stdout`. In this example, every time the child process writes to the standard error output, the parent process gets notified and prints out that data.

Sending Data to the Child Process

Besides receiving data from a child process's output streams, the parent process can also send data to the child by writing to the child's standard input stream, represented by the `childProcess.stdin` property.

The child can listen for that data using the `process.stdin` read stream, but note that first you must resume this stream, because it is on a `paused` state by default.

In Listing 8-6 you will build an example with these parts:

- `+1 app`: A simple application that receives integers on its standard input stream, increments them, and outputs the integers incremented by one into the standard output stream. This application serves as an example of a process that does some computation work that a Node process can use to outsource specific work.
- A test client that spawns the +1 app, sends it random integers, and prints the results. This serves as an example of how a Node process can spawn a child process and order it to perform specific tasks.

Create a file named `plus_one.js` with the code in Listing 8-6.

LISTING 8-6: The +1 app example application. (chapter8/06_plus_one.js)

```
// unpause the stdin stream
process.stdin.resume();
process.stdin.on('data', function(data) {
  var number;
  try {
    // parse the input data into a number
    number = parseInt(data.toString(), 10);
```

```
        // increment by one
        number += 1;

        // output the number
        process.stdout.write(number + "\n");
    } catch(err) {
        process.stderr.write(err.message + "\n");
    }
});
```

Here you are waiting for data on the `stdin` stream. Every time you get it, presume it is an integer, parse the data into an integer variable named `number`, increment it, and then output it to the `stdout` stream.

You can run this simple program by calling:

```
$ node plus_one.js
```

Now your application is waiting for input. If you type an integer and press Return, you should get that integer incremented by one back on the screen.

You can quit your application by typing Ctrl-C.

A Test Client

Now you are about to create a Node process that uses the +1 application you created to outsource these calculations.

Start by creating a file named `plus_one_test.js` with Listing 8-7.

LISTING 8-7: Testing the +1 app application. (chapter8/07_plus_one_test.js)

```
var spawn = require('child_process').spawn;

// Spawn the child with a node process executing the plus_one app
var child = spawn('node', ['plus_one.js']);

// Call this function every 1 second (1000 milliseconds):
setInterval(function() {

    // Create a random number smaller than 10.000
    var number = Math.floor(Math.random() * 10000);

    // Send that number to the child process:
    child.stdin.write(number + "\n");

    // Get the response from the child process and print it:
    child.stdout.once('data', function(data) {
        console.log('child replied to ' + number + ' with: ' + data);
    });
}, 1000);
```

continues

LISTING 8-7 *(continued)*

```
child.stderr.on('data', function(data) {
    process.stdout.write(data);
});
```

Here you launch the +1 app as a child process on lines 1 to 4.

Then you use the `setInterval` function to do the following every second:

- Create a random natural number smaller than 10,000.
- Send that number as a string to the child process.
- Wait for the child process to reply with a string.

Because you want to listen for data back from the child only once per number, you will use `child.stdout.once` and not `child.stdout.on`. If you used the latter function, you would register multiple callback functions as time went by. Each callback function would be called every time you got data from on the child `stdout`, which would end up printing the data multiple times and erroneously.

Receiving Notification when the Child Process Exits

When a child process exits, an event is triggered on the parent. Listing 8-8 shows how to listen to this event.

LISTING 8-8: Listening for the child exit event. (chapter8/09_listen_child_exit.js)

```
var spawn = require('child_process').spawn;

// Spawn the child with a "ls -la" command
var child = spawn('ls', ['-la']);

child.stdout.on('data', function(data) {
    console.log('data from child: ' + data);
});

// When child exits:
child.on('exit', function(code) {
    console.log('child process terminated with code ' + code);
});
```

Here, on the last lines in bold, you are listening to the child `exit` event, and, when it occurs, you print that fact to the console. The child process exit code is passed into the callback function as the first argument. Some programs use an exit code other than `0` as a way of signaling failures. For instance, if you try to execute the command `ls -la filename.txt` and there is no file named `filename.txt` on your current working directory, you get an exit code of `1`, as you will if you try running the example in Listing 8-9.

LISTING 8-9: Getting the child process exit code. (chapter8/10_child_exit_code.js)

```
var spawn = require('child_process').spawn;

// Spawn the child with a "ls does_not_exist.txt" command
var child = spawn('ls', ['does_not_exist.txt']);

// When the child process exits:
child.on('exit', function(code) {
    console.log('child process terminated with code ' + code);
});
```

In this case the exit event triggers your callback with the child process exit code as the first argument. If your child process died from a signal and not from an orderly exit, the guilty signal is passed as a string into the second argument of that callback, as in Listing 8-10.

LISTING 8-10: Getting the child process exit signal. (chapter8/11_child_exit_signal.js)

```
var spawn = require('child_process').spawn;

// Spawn the child with a "sleep 10" command
var child = spawn('sleep', ['10']);

setTimeout(function() {
  child.kill();
}, 1000);

child.on('exit', function(code, signal) {
    if (code) {
        console.log('child process terminated with code ' + code);
    } else if (signal) {
        console.log('child process terminated because of signal ' + signal);
    }
});
```

Here you are launching a child that will execute a sleep command for 10 seconds, but before those 10 seconds elapse, you are sending it a `SIGKILL` signal, which makes it print the following:

```
child process terminated because of signal SIGTERM
```

SIGNALING AND KILLING PROCESSES

In this section you will learn how you can control your child process using signals. Signals are a simple way for the parent process to communicate with the child process, or even to kill the child process.

Different signal codes have different meanings, and there are many of them. The most common ones are for killing processes. If a process receives a signal that it doesn't know how to handle, it will terminate. Some signals can be handled by the child process, and some others are solely handled by the operating system.

Generally, you can send a signal to a child process using the `child.kill` method, which by default sends the child a `SIGTERM` signal like this:

```
var spawn = require('child_process').spawn;
var child = spawn('sleep', ['10']);
setTimeout(function() {
  child.kill();
}, 1000);
```

You can also specify which signal to send by passing in a string identifying the signal as the sole argument like this:

```
child.kill('SIGUSR2');
```

Note that even though this method is called `kill`, the signal might not end up killing your process. If the child process handles the signal, the default signal behavior is overridden. A child process written in Node can override a signal by defining a signal handler like this:

```
process.on('SIGUSR2', function() {
    console.log('Got a SIGUSR2 signal');
});
```

Now, when you're defining a signal handler for `SIGUSR2`, your process will not die if it receives such a signal, but should print `Got a SIGUSR2 signal` instead. Using this mechanism, you can devise a simple way of communicating with or even commanding child processes, which is not as rich as when using the input stream, but is much simpler.

`SIGKILL` and `SIGSTOP` are special signals that are handled by the operating system, and the processes cannot override the default behavior. They end up terminating the process, even if you define a signal handler for them.

SUMMARY

In this chapter you executed external commands using the `child_process.exec` function, which allows you to define the environment variables that you pass into the child process without using command-line arguments.

You also learned to spawn child processes that execute external commands by using the `child_process.spawn` method. Doing this allows you to interact with child processes using the input and output streams, and to further communicate with or even kill a child process using signals.

Reading and Writing Streams of Data

WHAT'S IN THIS CHAPTER?

- Introducing the streams interface
- Getting data from a readable stream
- Controlling the flow of a readable stream
- Writing to a writable stream
- Solving the slow client problem
- Using pipe to stitch streams together

Node has a useful abstraction: streams. More specifically, two very useful abstractions: *readable* streams and *writable* streams. They are implemented throughout several Node objects, and they represent inbound (readable stream) or outbound (writable stream) flows of data. An example of a stream is a TCP socket that you read from and write to, or a file that you append or read from sequentially. You have already come across some of them, but this chapter introduces them in a more formal and abstract way, paving the way for some more concrete examples.

> **NOTE** *A stream is an abstract construct that is implemented by several Node objects. The way you create or obtain a stream depends on the type of stream you are using. For instance, you can explicitly create a read or write stream based on a file, but a server-side TCP socket is a stream that is handed to you when a client connects.*
>
> *Besides having the characteristics of a readable or a writable stream, an object can contain other properties or behaviors that are particular to it. For instance, a file readable stream also contains a "path" property that may not be present in other streams.*

USING A READABLE STREAM

A readable stream is like a data faucet. After you have created or obtained one — the method of creating or obtaining one depends on the type of stream — you can control it. You can control the flow by pausing and resuming it, you can get notified when data is available, and you can close it and get notified when the stream ends.

Waiting for Data

Streams can send data in chunks. By listening to the "data" event, you can be notified every time a stream delivers a chunk. You can get the data as a buffer or as a string, depending on your stream-encoding settings.

Data is passed via the event handler function that you bind to the "data" event. Depending on the stream encoding, the data may be delivered in the raw form using a byte buffer or, if you define the stream encoding by using the `stream.setEncoding()` function, be passed in as an encoded string, as in the following examples:

```
var readable stream1 = ...
readable stream1.on('data', function(data) {
  // data is a buffer;
  console.log('got this data:', data);
});

var readable stream2 = ...
readable stream2.setEncoding('utf8');
readable stream2.on('data', function(data) {
  // data is a utf8-encoded string;
  console.log('got this data:', data);
});
```

In the first example, data is passed as a buffer because you didn't specify an encoding. In the second example, data is passed as a UTF-8-encoded string.

> **NOTE** *Because UTF-8 characters can be multibyte, you may receive a character in two separate "data" events when you are expecting UTF-8 characters. If you set the encoding to utf8, the stream takes care of delivering a character only when it is complete.*

Pausing and Resuming a Stream

A readable stream is like a faucet, and you can keep the data from coming by pausing it like this:

```
stream.pause();
```

After you have done this, you will not receive any further "data" events. This feature can help you to avoid implicit buffering, as you will see later.

> **NOTE** *Pausing a stream translates to different behaviors under the hood. For instance, if the stream is a file stream, Node will stop reading from that file. If the stream is a TCP socket, Node will stop reading new data packets, which has the effect of stopping the packet flow from the other end. Other object types implement pause differently.*

When you want to resume a paused stream, you can simply call the `stream.resume()` method. This will reopen the faucet and data will be emitted again — until you pause it again or the stream ends.

Knowing When the Stream Ends

A stream can end. For instance, if you have a readable stream that is streaming file content, when the file ends the stream emits an "end" event. Similarly, if you have an HTTP stream that is delivering the requested body data, when the request ends that stream will also emit the "end" event. You can listen to that event like so:

```
var readable stream = ...
readable stream.on('end', function() {
  console.log('the stream has ended');
});
```

After a readable stream ends, you will receive no more "data" events.

USING WRITABLE STREAMS

A writable stream is an abstraction of something you can send data to. It can be a file or a TCP network connection or even an object that outputs transformed data, such as a zipped file. A writable stream is an object that allows you to write data to it. In this section, you learn to write data to a writable stream and learn about drain events.

Writing Data into a Stream

You can write to a writable stream by passing it a buffer or a string like this:

```
var writable_stream = ...;
writable_stream.write('this is an UTF-8 string');
```

If you are passing in a string as the first argument, you can specify the string encoding by passing it in the second argument. Otherwise, the stream assumes the string is UTF8-encoded.

Here is an example of passing in an alternative encoding:

```
var writable_stream = ...;
writable_stream.write('7e3e4acde5ad240a8ef5e731e644fbd1', 'base64');
```

As stated earlier, you can simply pass in a buffer to write:

```
var writable_stream = ...;
var buffer = new Buffer('this is a buffer with some string');
writable_stream.write(buffer);
```

Once you write to a stream, Node can immediately flush the data to the kernel buffer or, if that's not possible at the time, Node will store it in a queue in memory. You can determine which event occurred by observing the return value of the call to `writable_stream.write()`. The `write` command returns a boolean value that is *`true`* when the buffer was flushed and *`false`* when the buffer was queued. Later in this chapter you'll see how this information can become helpful.

Waiting for a Stream to Drain

Because Node does not block on I/O, it does not block on `read` or `write` commands. As you've seen, on `write` commands you know if the buffer was immediately flushed. If it was not flushed, it's stored in your process memory.

Later, when the stream manages to flush all the pending buffers, it emits a `drain` event that you can listen to:

```
var writable stream = ...;
writable stream.on('drain', function() {
  console.log('drain emitted');
});
```

Later in this chapter you'll see how draining notifications combined with the pause and resume capabilities can come in handy for limiting the memory growth of your Node process.

CONSIDERING SOME STREAM EXAMPLES

So far you've been introduced to the abstract streams interface. Let's look at some examples where Node implements this.

Creating File-System Streams

You can create a readable stream for a file path by doing something like this:

```
var fs = require('fs');
var rs = fs.createReadStream('/path/to/file');
...
```

You can pass a second argument with options to `fs.createReadableStream()`, where you can specify the start and end position on your file, the encoding, the flags, and the buffer size. Here are the `options` arguments:

- `encoding` — The encoding of the strings emitted in "data" events, or `null` if you want raw buffers.
- `fd` — If you already have an open file descriptor, you can pass it in here and the stream will assume it. Defaults to `null`.
- `bufferSize` — The size in bytes of the buffer of each chunk of the file to be read. Defaults to 64KB.
- `start` — The file position of the first byte to be read. Used to read a range of the file instead of the whole file.
- `end` — The file position of the last byte to be read. Used to read a range of the file instead of the whole file.

> **NOTE** *If you already have an open file, you can create a readable stream from it using the fd option:*
>
> ```
> var fs = require('fs');
>
> var path = '/path/to/my/file';
> fs.open(path, 'r', function(err, fd) {
>   fs.createReadStream(null, {fd: fd, encoding: 'utf8'});
>   fs.on('data', console.log);
> });
> ```

Also, if you want to read just a segment of a file, you can use the start and end options. For instance, for the stream to start at byte 10 and continue until the file ends:

```
var fs = require('fs');
var path = '/path/to/my/file'
var readStream = fs.createReadStream(path, {start: 10});
...
```

Or if you want the file stream to stop reading at byte 20:

```
var fs = require('fs');
var path = '/path/to/my/file'
var readStream = fs.createReadStream(path, {end: 20});
...
```

You can also create a file writable stream:

```
var fs = require('fs');
var rs = fs.createWriteStream('/path/to/file', options);
```

`fs.createWriteStream()` also accepts a second argument with an `options` object that has these default values:

```
{ flags: 'w',
  encoding: null,
  mode: 0666 }
```

- The `flags` option contains the flags to be used when opening the file, so all the flags accepted by `fs.open()` are valid here.
- The `mode` option specifies the permission mode the file will be opened with if the file has to be created.

You can also use the `encoding` option to force a specific encoding. For instance, you can use the following to create a file writable stream that assumes UTF-8 encoding:

```
var fs = require('fs');
var rs = fs.createWriteStream('/path/to/file', { encoding: 'utf8' });
```

Understanding Networking Streams

Several kinds of streams are on the networking API of Node. For instance, a client TCP connection is both a writable stream and a readable stream, and also is a server connection.

An HTTP request object is a readable stream. An HTTP response object is a writable stream.

Each of these stream types is covered in later chapters. For now, bear in mind that these stream types have a common interface, which means that you can use some of these objects interchangeably and also that you can abstract some problems and solve them only once. The slow client problem (covered in the next section) is one of these problems.

AVOIDING THE SLOW CLIENT PROBLEM AND SAVING YOUR SERVER

Every time you have a process that reads some data and then has to send that data (or some transformation of it) to another consumer, you have what's usually called the slow client problem.

Understanding the Slow Client Problem

Node does not block while doing I/O. This means that Node does not block on reads or writes — it buffers the data for you if the `write` cannot be flushed into the kernel buffers. Imagine this scenario: You are pumping data into a writable stream (like a TCP connection to a browser), and your source of data is a readable stream (like a file readable stream):

```
require('http').createServer(function(req, res) {
  var rs = fs.createReadStream('/path/to/big/file');

  rs.on('data', function(data) {
    res.write(data);
  });

  rs.on('end', function() {
    res.end();
  });
}).listen(8080);
```

If the file is local, the readable stream should be fast. However, if the network connection to the client is slow, the writable stream will be slow. The readable stream "data" events will happen quickly, and the data will be sent to the writable stream. However, Node will eventually have to start buffering the data because the kernel buffers will fill up.

What happens in practice is that the file will be buffered in memory for each `write` command. Multiply this for every request you have, and soon you will have memory growth problems. Generally, every time you have a data producer and a data consumer and the producer is faster than the consumer, you have to buffer data. That is, unless you can pause the producer until the consumer catches up.

Avoiding the Slow Client Problem

In most cases you can avoid filling up the memory with unflushed buffers by pausing the producer — the readable stream — so that the consumer's data — the writable stream — does not get flushed into the kernel. Fortunately Node readable streams have exactly the required functionality: You can pause and resume them. Here is an example of how you can control the flow:

```
require('http').createServer( function(req, res) {

  var rs = fs.createReadStream('/path/to/big/file');

  rs.on('data', function(data) {
    if (!res.write(data)) {
      rs.pause();
    }
  });

  res.on('drain', function() {
    rs.resume();
  });

  rs.on('end', function() {
    res.end();
  });

}).listen(8080);
```

Here you are creating an HTTP server listening on port 8080 that serves the content of the file `/path/to/big/file` to all HTTP requests.

Line 7 pauses the readable stream if the `write` command cannot flush it to the kernel. Line 11 resumes the readable stream when the writable stream is drained.

Using stream.pipe() to Prevent the Slow Client Problem and Assembling Readable and Writable Streams Using pipe()

This process of pausing the readable stream until the writable stream catches up and then resuming it is a recurring pattern that fortunately has been captured in Node, under the `stream.pipe()` command.

This command is part of the readable stream interface — making the called object the pipe source — and accepts a destination writable stream as first argument.

Here is the previous example using `pipe`:

```
require('http').createServer(function(req, res) {
  var rs = fs.createReadStream('/path/to/big/file');
  rs.pipe(res);
}).listen(8080);
```

By default, `end()` is called on the destination when the readable stream ends. You can prevent that behavior by passing in `end: false` on the second argument `options` object like this:

```
require('http').createServer(function(req, res) {

  var rs = fs.createReadStream('/path/to/big/file');

  rs.pipe(res, { end: false });

  rs.on('end', function() {
    res.write("And that's all, folks!");
    res.end();
  });

}).listen(8080);
```

Here you are pushing the string `"And that's all, folks!"` when the file ends, and then ending the request yourself instead of relying on the `stream.pipe()` method to do it for you.

SUMMARY

A stream is a wonderful abstraction that allows you to leverage Node's architecture to easily implement streaming from any object that implements the API.

The stream interface allows you to control the flow to mitigate the slow client problem, whereby you can pause and resume a readable stream. You can automate this process by using the `stream.pipe()` method, also available in any readable stream instance.

10

Building TCP Servers

WHAT'S IN THIS CHAPTER?

- Creating a TCP server
- Closing server-side TCP connections
- Handling network errors
- Piping data to or from a TCP connection
- Building a TCP chat server

The transmission control protocol (TCP) is one of the fundamental protocols of the Internet. It sits on top of the Internet protocol (IP) and provides a transport mechanism for the application layer. HTTP, for instance, works on top of TCP, as do many other connection-oriented applications such as iRC, SMTP, and IMAP.

Node has a first-class HTTP server implementation in the form of a pseudo-class in `http.Server`, which descends from the TCP server pseudo-class in `net.Server`. This means that everything described in this chapter applies to the Node HTTP server as well.

CREATING A TCP SERVER

You can create a TCP server using the `net` module like this:

```
require('net').createServer(function(socket) {
  // new connection

  socket.on('data', function(data) {
    // got data
  });

  socket.on('end', function(data) {
```

```
    // connection closed
  });

  socket.write('Some string');

}).listen(4001);
```

On line 1 you use the `createServer()` method on the `net` package, which you bind to TCP port 4001 on line 14. You can pass in a callback function to `createServer` to be called every time there is a "connection" event. Inside this callback you will be handed a `socket` object, which you can use to send and receive data to and from the client.

Because the server object is also an event emitter, and you can listen to events during its lifecycle, `net.Server` emits the following events:

- "listening" — When the server is listening on the specified port and address.
- "connection" — When a new connection is established. The callback to this function will receive the corresponding `socket` object. You can also bind to this event by passing a function to `net.createServer()`, like you did in the last example.
- "close" — When the server is closed, that is, it's not bound to that port any more.
- "error" — When an error occurs at the server level. An error event happens, for instance, when you try to bind to an occupied port or to a port you don't have permission to bind to.

Listing 10-1 has an example of outputting the lifecycle of a server.

LISTING 10-1: Lifecycle example of a TCP server.

```
var server = require('net').createServer();

var port = 4001;

server.on('listening', function() {
  console.log('Server is listening on port', port);
});

server.on('connection', function(socket) {
  console.log('Server has a new connection');
  socket.end();
  server.close();
});

server.on('close', function() {
  console.log('Server is now closed');
});

server.on('error', function(err) {
  console.log('Error occurred:', err.message);
});


server.listen(port);
```

You can launch this example and, while the server is running, connect to it by using `telnet` or `nc` like so:

```
$ telnet localhost 4001
```

or

```
$ nc localhost 4001
```

Once you connect, the server will disconnect you (because you told it to in line 11) and then close (in line 12). You should see the following output on the server console:

```
Server is listening on port 4001
Server has a new connection
Server is now closed
```

Using the Socket Object

When you get a "connection" event you are also handed the `socket` object as the first argument of the callback function. This `socket` object is both a read and a write stream, which means that it emits "data" events when it gets a package of data and emits the "end" event when that connection is closed.

Because the `socket` object is also a writable stream, that means you can write buffers or strings to the socket by using `socket.write()`. You can tell the socket that it should terminate the connection after all data has been written by calling `socket.end()`. Listing 10-2 has an example TCP server that simply echoes what you write.

LISTING 10-2: Simple echo TCP server.

```
var server = require('net').createServer(function(socket) {
  console.log('new connection');

  socket.setEncoding('utf8');

  socket.write("Hello! You can start typing. Type 'quit' to exit.\n");

  socket.on('data', function(data) {
    console.log('got:', data.toString())
    if (data.trim().toLowerCase() === 'quit') {
      socket.write('Bye bye!');
      return socket.end();
    }
    socket.write(data);
  });

  socket.on('end', function() {
    console.log('Client connection ended');
  });

}).listen(4001);
```

Again, you can start this server, connect to it using `telnet` or `nc`, as you did before, and play around with it. You can type `quit<enter>` to terminate the connection.

Because the `socket` object is a readable stream, you can control the flow by calling `socket.pause()` and `socket.resume()`, or even pipe it into a writable stream, as shown in Listing 10-3.

LISTING 10-3: Piping out a socket.

```
var ws = require('fs').createWriteStream('mysocketdump.txt');

require('net').createServer(function(socket) {
  socket.pipe(ws);
}).listen(4001);
```

As before, you can test Listing 10-3 by using `telnet` or `nc` like this:

```
$ nc localhost 4001
```

You can type as much as you want, pressing `<enter>` at least once to flush to the server. You can then open the `mysocketdump.txt` file and find the text you typed there.

You can also accomplish the reverse, whereby you pipe a readable stream into the `socket`, as shown in Listing 10-4. For that to work you have to create a file on the local folder named `hello.txt`, fill it with some random text, and then run the Listing 10-4 example.

LISTING 10-4: Piping into a socket.

```
require('net').createServer(function(socket) {
  var rs = require('fs').createReadStream('hello.txt');
  rs.pipe(socket);
}).listen(4001);
```

If you try to connect to the server, you should see the text you inserted in the `hello.txt` file. The connection will also be immediately closed. That's because, as explained in Chapter 9, "Reading and Writing Streams of Data," `pipe` will by default also end the destination when the source ends. If you want to keep the connection open, you should pass `{ end : false }` into the second argument of the `pipe()` command.

Understanding Idle Sockets

By default, when a new connection is set up between two peers, it is kept open until one of them closes it or until the underlying link is lost. However, in Node you can set TCP connections to time out because of inactivity. You can automatically close the connection when no traffic is being sent or received for some time. You can activate and define the timeout by calling `setTimeout(milliseconds)` on the connection. You can also listen for the `timeout` event on the `socket` object.

```
var timeout = 60000; // 1 minute
socket.setTimeout(timeout);
socket.on('timeout', function() {
  socket.write('idle timeout, disconnecting, bye!');
  socket.end();
});
```

Or, you can use this shorter form by passing the event listener in the second argument of `socket.setTimeout()`:

```
socket.setTimeout(60000, function() {
  socket.end('idle timeout, disconnecting, bye!');
});
```

Setting Up Keep-Alive

In Node, a `net.Socket` can implement a keep-alive mechanism to prevent timeouts from occurring on the network or on the peer. Node does that by sending an empty TCP packet with the ACK flag turned on to trigger an empty reply from the other side. This activity will keep the connection alive on both peers.

You can enable the keep-alive functionality by:

```
socket.setKeepAlive(true);
```

You can also specify the delay between the last packet received and the next keep-alive packet. You do so on the second argument to the `socket.keepAlive()` call like this:

```
socket.setKeepAlive(true, 10000); // 10 seconds
```

> **NOTE** *This keep-alive setting is not related to the socket timeout setting discussed earlier. The* `socket.setKeepAlive()` *setting periodically sends an empty packet to keep the connection alive, whereas* `socket.setTimeout()` *is used to define a local inactivity timeout.*

Using Delay or No Delay

The kernel buffers the data before sending the TCP packets, and it uses Nagle's algorithm to determine when to actually send the data. This algorithm is used to reduce the number of packets that are sent across the network when an application sends small chunks of data. Depending on the application, this feature may turn out to be quite useful, but it introduces some delay in sending the data, which may add up to overall latency in your application.

If you want to turn this off and force data to be sent immediately after each `write` command, use this:

```
socket.setNoDelay(true);
```

Of course, you can always revert this setting like this:

```
socket.setNoDelay(false);
```

Listening for Client Connections

As you saw, after the server is created, you can bind it to a specific TCP port like this:

```
var port = 4001;
var host = '0.0.0.0';
server.listen(port, host);
```

The second argument (host) is optional. If it's omitted, the server will accept connections directed to any IP address:

```
server.listen(port);
```

Closing the Server

This method closes the server, preventing it from accepting new connections. This function is asynchronous, and the server will emit the `close` event when it closes:

```
var server = ...
server.close();
server.on('close', function() {
  console.log('server closed!');
});
```

Handling Errors

When handling a socket on the client or the server you can (and should) handle errors by listening to the `error` event like this:

```
require('net').createServer(function(socket) {
  socket.on('error', function(error) {
    // do something
  });
});
```

If you fail to catch an error, Node will handle an uncaught exception and terminate the current process.

> **NOTE** *You can choose to catch uncaught exceptions — preventing your Node process from being terminated — by doing something like this:*
>
> ```
> process.on('uncaughtException', function(err) {
>   // do something
> });
> ```
>
> *However, this practice is generally not a good idea because when an exception happens and you don't handle it properly, your application may get into an unknown state, which may later introduce more and stranger errors. Also, errors can lead to more errors, making it harder to understand the root cause. If you do this, you will also probably leak memory or resources (like file descriptors) because errors were not handled when they should have been.*
>
> *In general, you should use this event only to report everything you can about your application and then shut down your process.*

BUILDING A SIMPLE TCP CHAT SERVER

Now you should be prepared to start building a TCP-based chat server. You can start by instantiating the server, logging some important events, and then binding the server to port 4001:

LISTING 10-5: The TCP chat server — step 1.

```
var net = require('net');

var server = net.createServer();

server.on('error', function(err) {
  console.log('Server error:', err.message);
});

server.on('close', function() {
  console.log('Server closed');
});

server.listen(4001);
```

Accepting Connections

Next, you need to accept new client connections:

LISTING 10-6: The TCP chat server — step 2.

```
var net = require('net');

var server = net.createServer();

server.on('connection', function(socket) {
  console.log('got a new connection');
});

server.on('error', function(err) {
  console.log('Server error:', err.message);
});

server.on('close', function() {
  console.log('Server closed');
});

server.listen(4001);
```

Reading Data from a Connection

Every time the server gets a new connection, you need it to listen for the incoming data by binding to the `data` event.

LISTING 10-7: The TCP chat server — step 3.

```
var net = require('net');

var server = net.createServer();

server.on('connection', function(socket) {
  console.log('got a new connection');
  socket.on('data', function(data) {
    console.log('got data:', data);
  });
});

server.on('error', function(err) {
  console.log('Server error:', err.message);
});

server.on('close', function() {
  console.log('Server closed');
});

server.listen(4001);
```

Collecting All the Clients

Because you're creating a chat server in which you have to broadcast the user data to everyone, the first step is to store all the connections in a central place.

LISTING 10-8: The TCP chat server — step 4.

```
var net = require('net');

var server = net.createServer();

var sockets = [];

server.on('connection', function(socket) {
  console.log('got a new connection');

  sockets.push(socket);

  socket.on('data', function(data) {
    console.log('got data:', data);
  });

});

server.on('error', function(err) {
  console.log('Server error:', err.message);
});

server.on('close', function() {
  console.log('Server closed');
});

server.listen(4001);
```

Broadcasting Data

Every time a connected user types anything, you need to send it to every other connected user.

LISTING 10-9: The TCP chat server — step 5.

```
var net = require('net');

var server = net.createServer();

var sockets = [];

server.on('connection', function(socket) {
  console.log('got a new connection');

  sockets.push(socket);

  socket.on('data', function(data) {
    console.log('got data:', data);

    sockets.forEach(function(otherSocket) {
      if (otherSocket !== socket) {
        otherSocket.write(data);
```

continues

LISTING 10-9 *(continued)*

```
      }
    });
  });

});

server.on('error', function(err) {
  console.log('Server error:', err.message);
});

server.on('close', function() {
  console.log('Server closed');
});

server.listen(4001);
```

Removing Closed Connections

You're still missing at least one step — you also have to remove the connection when it gets closed, as shown in Listing 10-10.

LISTING 10-10: Simple TCP chat server.

```
var net = require('net');

var server = net.createServer();

var sockets = [];

server.on('connection', function(socket) {
  console.log('got a new connection');

  sockets.push(socket);

  socket.on('data', function(data) {
    console.log('got data:', data);

    sockets.forEach(function(otherSocket) {
      if (otherSocket !== socket) {
        otherSocket.write(data);
      }
    });
  });

  socket.on('close', function() {
    console.log('connection closed');
    var index = sockets.indexOf(socket);
    sockets.splice(index, 1);
  });
```

```
});

server.on('error', function(err) {
  console.log('Server error:', err.message);
});

server.on('close', function() {
  console.log('Server closed');
});

server.listen(4001);
```

Using Your TCP Chat Server

Now you should be ready to test your server. You can save the file to `chat_server.js` and launch it through the command line:

```
$ node chat_server.js
```

You can now connect to that server using `nc` or `telnet`:

```
$ nc localhost 4001
```

If you can, try launching several of these in separate terminal windows. You can then see the chat server in action.

SUMMARY

A TCP server will emit certain events during its lifecycle, namely, "listening" events when you set it to listen on a certain port, "close" events when it gets closed, and "error" events when an error occurs. You can also listen for "connection" events, which occur when a new client connects. This connection event will serve you a `socket` object that is both a readable stream and a writable stream. You can use this object to listen for data, send data, end the connection, and even pipe the connection data into another stream. You can also do the opposite, piping a readable stream into the connection.

The `socket` object allows you to control its flow by using `socket.pause()` and `socket.resume()`. It also allows you to tweak some of its parameters. For example, you can close the connection when it's been idle for some time, frequently send a keep-alive packet, or turn on or off Nagle's algorithm.

You can also create a TCP server that handles many connections and can use it for clients to communicate with each other in some form, as in the example of the chat server you created here.

11

Building HTTP Servers

WHAT'S IN THIS CHAPTER?

- Creating an HTTP server
- Making an HTTP server listen on a port
- Handling HTTP requests
- Observing request headers
- Listening for and piping request data
- Replying with a status code and headers
- Replying with a body
- Using HTTP chunked responses to stream the response body

HTTP is an application-level protocol for content and application delivery. It uses TCP as its transport protocol, and it is the foundation of data communication for the World Wide Web. One of the preferred application deployment mechanisms is to provide an HTTP service on the Internet that answers HTTP client requests.

You can easily create an HTTP server in Node. Here is the famous "Hello World!" HTTP server example, as seen in Listing 11-1.

LISTING 11-1: A "Hello World!" HTTP server.

```
var http = require('http');

var server = http.createServer();

server.on('request', function(req, res) {
  res.writeHead(200, {'Content-Type': 'text/plain'});
```

continues

LISTING 11-1 *(continued)*

```
    res.write('Hello World!');
    res.end();
  });

  server.listen(4000);
```

On line 1 you obtain the `http` module, from which you can create a `server` object by calling `http.createServer()` (line 3).

You then listen for `request` events, which happen when a new client connects. The event callback you provide gets called with two arguments: the `request` and the `response` objects. You can then use the `request` object to learn details about this request and use the `response` object to write back to the client.

On line 6 you write a header `('ContentType': 'text/plain')` and the HTTP status 200, which is a code that indicates the request succeeded.

On line 7 you reply with the string "Hello World!", and on line 8 you terminate the request.

On line 11 you bind the server to the TCP port 4000.

You can then save this script into a file named `server.js` and start it like this:

```
$ node server.js
```

Then you can point your browser to `http://localhost:4000`, and you should see the "Hello World!" string on it.

This whole example can be shortened, as seen in Listing 11-2.

LISTING 11-2: A shortened "Hello World!" HTTP server.

```
require('http').createServer(function(req, res) {
  res.writeHead(200, {'Content-Type': 'text/plain'});
  res.end('Hello World!');
}).listen(4000);
```

Here you are giving up the intermediary variables for storing the `http` module (because you need to call it only once) and the server (because you only need to make it listen on port 4000). Also, as a shortcut, the `http.createServer()` function accepts a callback function that will be invoked on every request.

Here is one last shortcut: The `response.end()` function can accept a string or buffer, which it will write to the response before ending the request.

When a client makes a request, the HTTP server emits a `request` event, passing in HTTP request and HTTP response objects. The HTTP request object allows you to query some of the request properties, and the HTTP response allows you to build an HTTP response that will be sent to the client. In the next sections, you will learn about these objects and how you can use them to accomplish these tasks.

UNDERSTANDING THE HTTP.SERVERREQUEST OBJECT

When listening for `request` events, the callback gets an `http.ServerRequest` object as the first argument. This object contains some properties you can inspect, including the `url`, `method`, and `headers` properties:

- **`req.url:`** This property contains the requested URL as a string. It does not contain the schema, hostname, or port, but it contains everything after that. Try running the following server to analyze the `request` property:

  ```
  require('http').createServer(function(req, res) {
    res.writeHead(200, {'Content-Type': 'text/plain'});
    res.end(req.url);
  }).listen(4000);
  ```

  Open `http://127.0.0.1:4000/abc` using a browser. Change the path in the URL to see how it behaves.

- **`req.method:`** This contains the `HTTP` method used on the request. It can be, for example, `GET`, `POST`, `DELETE`, or `HEAD`.

- **`req.headers:`** This contains an object with a property for every HTTP header on the request. To analyze it, you can run this server:

  ```
  var util = require('util');
  require('http').createServer(function(req, res) {
    res.writeHead(200, {'Content-Type': 'text/plain'});
    res.end(util.inspect(req.headers));
  }).listen(4000);
  ```

  Connect your browser to `http://127.0.0.1:4000` to inspect the headers of your request. Your server should output something like this:

  ```
  { host: 'localhost:4000',
    connection: 'keep-alive',
    'user-agent': 'Mozilla/5.0 (Macintosh; Intel Mac OS X 10_7_2)
  AppleWebKit/535.2
  (KHTML, like Gecko) Chrome/15.0.874.121 Safari/535.2',
    accept:
  'text/html,application/xhtml+xml,application/xml;q=0.9,*/*;q=0.8',
    'accept-encoding': 'gzip,deflate,sdch',
    'accept-language': 'en-US,en;q=0.8',
    'accept-charset': 'ISO-8859-1,utf-8;q=0.7,*;q=0.3' }
  ```

  Here you are using `util.inspect()`, a utility function that analyzes the properties of any object.

  The `header` object property keys are lowercase. For instance, if the browser sent a `"Cache-Control: max-age=0"` header, `req.headers` will have a property named `"cache-control"` with the value `"max-age=0"`. Values are untouched.

When you get the `request` event on a server, you don't immediately get the body of that request, simply because it has not arrived yet. But if you want to, you can listen for `data` events, or even pipe the request body into a WriteStream, such as a file or a TCP connection, because the `request` object is a ReadStream:

```
var writeStream = ...

require('http').createServer(function(req, res) {
  req.on('data', function(data) {
    writeStream.write(data);
  });
}).listen(4001);
```

UNDERSTANDING THE HTTP.SERVERRESPONSE OBJECT

The response object (the second argument for the `request` event callback function) is used to reply to the client. With it you can write the headers and write the body.

Writing a Header

To write a header, use `res.writeHead(status, headers)`, where `headers` is an optional argument with an object containing a property for every header you want to send. Consider this example:

```
require('http').createServer(function(req, res) {

  res.writeHead(200, {
    'Content-Type': 'text/plain',
    'Cache-Control': 'max-age=3600' });

  res.end('Hello World!');

}).listen(4000);
```

This example sets two headers, one labeled `"Content-Type: text/plain"` and another labeled `"Cache-Control: max-age=3600"`.

If you save the previous source code into `http_server.js` and run it with:

```
$ node http_server.js
```

you can query it by using your browser or using a command-line HTTP client like `curl`:

```
$ curl -i http://localhost:4000
HTTP/1.1 200 OK
Content-Type: text/plain
Cache-Control: max-age=3600
Connection: keep-alive
Transfer-Encoding: chunked
Hello World!
```

Changing or Setting a Header

You can change a header you already set or set a new one by using the following:

```
res.setHeader(name, value);
```

This works only if you haven't already sent a piece of the body by using `res.write()` or `res.end()`. This also fails to work if you have already used `res.writeHead()` on that response object, because the headers also will have already been sent.

Removing a Header

You can remove a header you have already set by calling `res.removeHeader` and providing the header name:

```
res.removeHeader('Cache-Control');
```

Again, this works only if the headers for that response haven't already been sent.

Writing a Piece of the Response Body

An HTTP server sends the response body after sending the response headers. Two ways to do this are to write a string:

```
res.write('Hello');
```

or use an existing buffer:

```
var buffer = new Buffer('Hello World');
res.write(buffer);
```

STREAMING HTTP CHUNKED RESPONSES

One of the great features of Node is the ability to consume and produce streams easily from different sources. Because HTTP is a first-class protocol in Node, the HTTP responses are no different.

HTTP *chunked encoding* allows a server to keep sending data to the client without ever sending the body size. Unless you specify a `Content-Length` header, the Node HTTP server sends the following header to the client:

```
Transfer-Encoding: chunked
```

According to the HTTP specification, this header makes the client accept several chunks of data as the response body, sending a final chunk with a length of 0 before the client can terminate the response. This can be useful for streaming text, audio, or video data into the HTTP client.

Some examples of streaming using this HTTP server feature are piping a file and piping the output of another process, both described next.

Piping a File

You can pipe any ReadStream into the response. Here is an example that pipes a file into the response. First you have to have an .mp4 file (a movie) named "test.mp4" in your current directory. Then run the server shown in Listing 11-3.

LISTING 11-3: Piping a movie to the HTTP response.

```
var fs = require('fs');

require('http').createServer(function(req, res) {
  res.writeHead(200, {'Content-Type': 'video/mp4'});
  var rs = fs.createReadStream('test.mp4');
  rs.pipe(res);
}).listen(4000);
```

With every request in Listing 11-3, you are writing the header response status and setting the content type header so that the browser correctly identifies the type of stream you are delivering to it. Then you are opening the movie file as a ReadStream and piping it to the response WriteStream.

If you open your browser to `http://127.0.0.1:4000` on any modern browser, the movie should start playing immediately, even though it's not fully loaded.

Piping the Output of Another Process

Listing 11-4 shows an example that pipes the output of a child process into the client.

LISTING 11-4: Piping the output of a process to the HTTP response.

```
var spawn = require('child_process').spawn;

require('http').createServer(function(req, res) {
  var child = spawn('tail', ['-f', '/var/log/system.log']);
  child.stdout.pipe(res);
  res.on('end', function() {
    child.kill();
  });
}).listen(4000);
```

Here, when there is a new request, you launch a new child process by executing the command `tail -f /var/log/system.log` (line 4), which produces a child process. Then you are piping the output of that child process into the response body (line 5).

When the response ends (because the browser window was closed, or the network connection was severed, for instance), you need to kill the child process so it does not hang around afterward indefinitely.

So Listing 11-4 — in nine lines of code — shows you the power of Node by building a streaming server that spawns, pipes the output of a process, and then kills the child process as needed.

SHUTTING DOWN THE SERVER

You can stop an HTTP server from accepting new connections by unbinding it from the port like this:

```
server.close();
```

If you want it to start listening again, you have to repeat the following:

```
server.listen(port[, hostname]);
```

Following are some examples of simple HTTP servers you can build without any third-party modules.

EXAMPLE 1: BUILDING A SERVER THAT SERVES STATIC FILES

In this example, you'll be building an HTTP server that serves static files (see Listing 11-5). The file path is provided in the URL like this:

```
http://localhost:4000/path/to/my/file.txt
```

LISTING 11-5: Simple HTTP static file server.

```
var path = require('path'),
    fs = require('fs');

require('http').createServer(function(req, res) {
  var file = path.normalize('.' + req.url);
  console.log('Trying to serve', file);

  function reportError(err) {
    console.log(err);
    res.writeHead(500);
    res.end('Internal Server Error');
  }

  path.exists(file, function(exists) {
    if (exists) {
      fs.stat(file, function(err, stat) {
        var rs;

        if (err) {
          return reportError(err);
        }

        if (stat.isDirectory()) {
          res.writeHead(403); res.end('Forbidden');
        } else {
          rs = fs.createReadStream(file);

          rs.on('error', reportError);

          res.writeHead(200);
```

continues

LISTING 11-5 *(continued)*

```
            rs.pipe(res);
          }
        });
      } else{
        res.writeHead(404);
        res.end('Not found');
      }
    });
  }).listen(4000);
```

EXAMPLE 2: MAKING USE OF HTTP CHUNKED RESPONSES AND TIMERS

In this example, you'll be making an HTTP server that outputs plain text with 100 newline-separated timestamps every second (see Listing 11-6).

LISTING 11-6: HTTP chunked response and timers example.

```
require('http').createServer(function(req, res) {
  res.writeHead(200, {'Content-Type': 'text/plain'});
  var left = 10;
  var interval = setInterval(function() {
    for(var i = 0; i< 100; i++) {
      res.write(Date.now() + " ");
    }
    if (-- left === 0) {
      clearInterval(interval);
      res.end();
    }
  }, 1000);
}).listen(4000);
```

SUMMARY

The Node `http` allows you to create an HTTP server and make it listen on a specific port and host. You can then listen to new `request` events where, for each request, a callback function gets the corresponding `ServerRequest` and `ServerResponse` objects.

You can observe some properties from the request object like the request URL and the headers. The `ServerRequest` object is also a ReadStream, meaning that you can, among other things, listen for `data` events containing streamed body data parts, and even pipe that data into another stream.

With the `ServerResponse` object you can reply to the client by setting the HTTP response status and sending the response headers. You can also write to the response body or even pipe any ReadStream into it. In cases where you don't know the content length or you want a continuous response stream, you can use the HTTP chunked response protocol to stream the content body, where the server sends several chunks of the response body.

12

Building a TCP Client

WHAT'S IN THIS CHAPTER?

- Connecting to a TCP server
- Sending and receiving data from a TCP server
- Reconnecting a broken connection

Sitting a level above IP, TCP is one of the most used transport protocols on the Internet, on top of which sit application protocols like HTTP. TCP is a connection-oriented protocol, which means that one endpoint requests and establishes a dedicated connection to another endpoint. This connection is a two-way dedicated stream into which both endpoints can send and receive data to/from each other at the same time. TCP guarantees that the messages you receive are in order. It has built-in mechanisms for flow control, making it a good platform for supporting machine-to-machine and human-to-machine protocols.

As you will see, Node makes it easy to build a TCP client that establishes a connection to another endpoint, usually what is called a *TCP server*. This connection then forms two streams of data that allow you to interact with the remote endpoint: One is a readable stream that receives data, and the other is a writable stream that writes data.

> **NOTE** *One point you should keep in mind is that when you write to a TCP stream, you receive no acknowledgment that the other side has received the data. Even worse, because the underlying network implementation may chop and route your packets haphazardly, the other endpoint may have received only part of the message you sent (even though TCP internally tries to resend the packets that have been lost or corrupted). Remember that TCP guarantees only that the packets are received in order by the application, not that they are received at all.*
>
> *continues*

(continued)

Furthermore, TCP is not message-oriented; it just provides a continuous stream of data. If you need to distinguish individual messages, you need to implement a framing protocol that specifies where each message starts and ends.

HTTP, for instance, solves these problems whereby an application needs a request-response workflow from a server and request and response messages are clearly delimited.

CONNECTING TO A SERVER

You can connect to a TCP server using the `net` module like this:

```
var net = require('net');
var port = 4000;
var conn = net.createConnection(port);
```

Note that the second argument for the `net.createConnection` function is omitted, which is the hostname that you want to connect to. If absent, this hostname defaults to "localhost."

```
var net = require('net');
var port = 4000;
var host = "www.acme.com";
var conn = net.createConnection(port, host);
```

You can be notified when the connection is established by passing a callback function as the last argument, like this:

```
function connectionListener(conn) {
  console.log('We have a new connection');
}


var conn = net.createConnection(port, host, connectionListener);
```

If you are connecting to the local host, you can omit the `host` argument, passing the connection listener callback function as the second argument.

```
var conn = net.createConnection(port, connectionListener);
```

You can instead listen for the `connect` event emitted by the `conn` object:

```
conn.once('connect', connectionListener);
```

SENDING AND RECEIVING DATA

The return value of the call to `net.createConnection()` is an instance of `net.Socket`, which represents the connection to the server and is both a readable and a writeable stream. It allows you to send some data:

```
conn.write('here is a string for you!');
```

You can also pass a string and specify the string encoding:

```
conn.write('SGVsbG8gV29ybGQh', 'base64');
```

You can also write a raw buffer to the server:

```
var buffer = new Buffer('Hello World!');
conn.write(buffer);
```

In any of these variants you can pass in a callback function:

```
conn.write('Hey!', function() {
  console.log('data was written out');
});
```

Note that the callback is not invoked when the server receives the data, only when the data is written to the network.

You can receive data from the server by listening to the `data` event emitted by the connection every time data is available:

```
conn.on('data', function(data) {
  console.log('some data has arrived:', data);
});
```

If you don't specify the stream encoding, the data that is passed in will be a buffer. If you want that buffer to be encoded before being emitted, you need to specify it by using `setEncoding`:

```
conn.setEncoding('base64');
```

As covered in Chapter 4, "Using Buffers to Manipulate, Encode, and Decode Binary Data," you can use `ascii`, `utf8`, or `base64` as your encoding identifiers.

ENDING THE CONNECTION

You can close the connection from your endpoint by using the connection end method:

```
conn.end();
```

This will schedule the connection to end after all the data has been written out. As you're ending the connection, you can also send some data (a buffer or a string):

```
conn.end('Bye bye!', 'utf8');
```

This is equivalent to:

```
conn.write('Bye bye!', 'utf8');
conn.end();
```

> **WARNING** *When you're ending the connection you're queuing that operation, which means that the connection does not end immediately. Also, when the connection gets "ended," a FIN packet is sent, which means that the server can still send some data through.*
>
> *For these two reasons, you can still receive "data" events after you have ended the connection.*

HANDLING ERRORS

Errors can happen when you are trying to establish a connection — the hostname is not found on DNS, the target host is not reachable, or the connection is rejected — or a network error happens when you already had an established connection. You can trap errors by listening to the `error` event like this:

```
conn.on('error', function(err) {
  console.error('this error happened:' + err.message +
    ', code: ' + err.code);
});
```

Besides the `message` property, networking-related errors also have the `code` property, which is a string that you can inspect and test against. For instance, if the requested connection is refused, you get an `ECONNREFUSED` code.

```
var net = require('net');
var conn = net.createConnection('82837');
conn.on('error', function(err) {
  console.log('I got this error code: ' + err.code);
});
```

This last piece of code should output the following:

```
I got this error code: ECONNREFUSED
```

BUILDING AN EXAMPLE COMMAND-LINE TCP CLIENT

Next you will build a simple TCP client that tries to connect to a server and then you will send and receive some data from it. You will use the TCP server you built in Chapter 10, "Building TCP Servers," and implement a client to it.

First you need to launch the TCP server in the background and leave it listening on port 4000, ready for your client-to-be to connect to.

Connecting to the Server

Here you are connecting to the server port 4000 in the local host. You are also listening for any error that may occur.

```
var net  = require('net');
var port = 4000;
var conn = net.createConnection(port);

conn.on('connect', function() {
  console.log('connected to server');
});

conn.on('error', function(err) {
  console.log('Error in connection:', err);
});
```

Sending the Command Line to the Server

When a Node process starts, `process.stdin` is a stream prepared to accept user keyboard input. This ReadStream will emit "data" events, but only after you resume it; that stream is initialized in the paused state. You can resume it by calling the `resume` method on the stream:

```
process.stdin.resume();
```

Now you have a writable stream to the server and a readable stream from the user input. You can glue them together by using the `pipe` method like this:

```
process.stdin.pipe(conn);
```

Now, every time the `process.stdin` stream is flushed — which usually happens after the user enters a new line character — the data is piped to the server through the `conn` writable stream.

Printing Server Messages

You can print every message that the server sends to the process standard output stream. The easiest way to do that is to pipe the connection output like this:

```
conn.pipe(process.stdout);
```

However, there is one problem with the last command. It happens that, by default, `sourceStream.pipe(targetStream)` ends the target stream as soon as the source stream ends, which means that the process standard output stream will close after the connection is closed, which is not the effect you are looking for. Fortunately, the `.pipe()` method accepts an `end` option that, when set to `false`, prevents that from happening.

```
conn.pipe(process.stdout, {end: false});
```

Reconnecting if the Connection Dies

A TCP connection may be closed by the remote server or in the event of a network problem or even if your connection is idling for too long. In any case, if your application so requires, it's easy to reconnect to the server, as seen in Listing 12-1.

LISTING 12-1: A TCP client that reconnects immediately.

```
var net  = require('net');
var port = 4000;
var conn;

process.stdin.resume();

(function connect() {
  conn = net.createConnection(port);

  conn.on('connect', function() {
    console.log('connected to server');
  });

  conn.on('error', function(err) {
    console.log('Error in connection:', err);
  });

  conn.on('close', function() {
    console.log('connection got closed, will try to reconnect');
    connect();
  });

  conn.pipe(process.stdout, {end: false});
  process.stdin.pipe(conn);
}());
```

Here you are connecting by immediately invoking the local function named `connect`.

When an error on the connection occurs, you will get an `error` event, then the connection will close, which will then trigger a `close` event. When the `close` event happens, this code tries to reconnect immediately (you will later see why this may be a bad idea) by invoking the local function named `connect`, which goes through all the connecting logic again.

You can test this process. While connected, terminate the server and then start it again. You should then see the client reconnecting successfully.

However, it is not recommended that you reconnect immediately after you get disconnected or that you keep retrying to connect forever. Doing so can create a kind of loop, flooding your network with connection requests. The server will probably be unreachable for a few milliseconds after the disconnection. Instead, wait a bit for the network conditions to improve or for the service to come back online. You should also quit trying to reconnect after a number of failed attempts have occurred — at this point, the problem is probably not going to be solved by reconnecting: It can be a permanent network or server problem. The user should be informed and your program should stop trying to reconnect automatically, at least for a considerable amount of time.

In Listing 12-2 you set the `retry` interval to an arbitrary value of three seconds. You also cap the number of repeated failed retries to 10. These are both arbitrary numbers that you should define based on your specific application.

LISTING 12-2: A TCP client that attempts to reconnect.

```
var net  = require('net');
var port = 4000;
var conn;

var retryInterval = 3000; // 3 seconds
var retriedTimes = 0;
var maxRetries = 10;

process.stdin.resume();

(function connect() {
  function reconnect() {
    if (retriedTimes >= maxRetries) {
      throw new Error('Max retries have been exceeded, I give up.');
    }
    retriedTimes += 1;
    setTimeout(connect, retryInterval);
  }

  conn = net.createConnection(port);

  conn.on('connect', function() {
    retriedTimes = 0;
    console.log('connected to server');
  });

  conn.on('error', function(err) {
    console.log('Error in connection:', err);
  });

  conn.on('close', function() {
    console.log('connection got closed, will try to reconnect');
    reconnect();
  });

  process.stdin.pipe(conn, {end: false});
}());
```

Here you are tracking how many times you have tried to connect after the last successful connection by storing a counter in the `retriedTimes` variable. Once you connect successfully, the `retriedTimes` variable is reset to 0.

Closing the Connection

To close the connection you just have to call `conn.end()` like this:

```
conn.end();
```

In this simple application, you know that the application user wants to disconnect when he or she types `quit` in the console. You can detect this event and act accordingly:

```
process.stdin.on('data', function(data) {
  if (data.toString().trim().toLowerCase() === 'quit') {
    conn.end();
    process.stdin.pause();
  }
});
```

Note that you are also ending the standard input stream, letting Node know you are not interested in it.

This does not work very well because you are still trying to pipe everything to the server regardless if it is the string `quit` or not, which means you might be sending data to a closed connection. Instead you need to remove the following piping command:

```
process.stdin.pipe(conn);
```

You must send that data only when the user is not quitting:

```
process.stdin.on('data', function(data) {
  if (data.toString().trim().toLowerCase() === 'quit') {
    console.log('quitting...');
    conn.end();
    process.stdin.end();
  } else {
    conn.write(data);
  }
});
```

When the connection is closed, the client will try to reconnect, overriding the user instructions. You therefore have to keep a flag indicating that the user wants to exit, which will guard against reconnecting in this case:

```
var quitting = false;
// ...

process.stdin.on('data', function(data) {
  if (data.toString().trim().toLowerCase() === 'quit') {
    quitting = true;
    console.log('quitting...');
    conn.end();
    process.stdin.pause();
  } else {
    conn.write(data);
  }
});

// ...

conn.on('close', function() {
```

```
    if (! quitting) {
      console.log('connection got closed, will try to reconnect');
      reconnect();
    }
  });
```

Putting the Client Together

Listing 12-3 shows the full source code for a TCP client that reconnects and quits.

LISTING 12-3: A new version of the command-line TCP client that reconnects when disconnected.

```
var net  = require('net');
var port = 4000;
var quitting = false;
var conn;
var retryTimeout = 3000; // 3 seconds

var retriedTimes = 0;
var maxRetries = 10;

process.stdin.resume();

process.stdin.on('data', function(data) {
  if (data.toString().trim().toLowerCase() === 'quit') {
    quitting = true;
    console.log('quitting...');
    conn.end();
    process.stdin.pause();
  } else {
    conn.write(data);
  }
});

(function connect() {
   function reconnect() {
     if (retriedTimes >= maxRetries) {
       throw new Error('Max retries have been exceeded, I give up.');
     }
     retriedTimes += 1;
     setTimeout(connect, retryTimeout);
   }

   conn = net.createConnection(port);

   conn.on('connect', function() {
     retriedTimes = 0;
     console.log('connected to server');
   });

   conn.on('error', function(err) {
     console.log('Error in connection:', err);
```

continues

LISTING 12-3 *(continued)*

```
      });

      conn.on('close', function() {
        if (! quitting) {
          console.log('connection got closed, will try to reconnect');
          reconnect();
        }
      });

      conn.pipe(process.stdout, {end: false});

   }());
```

SUMMARY

TCP is a connection-oriented protocol that handles message ordering and flow-control for you. TCP can be a good transport layer on top of which you can build client-server protocols.

Building a TCP client in Node is easy. When you try to establish a connection to a TCP server, `net.createConnection()` returns a `net.Socket` instance, which is both a readable and a writable stream that you can pipe data from and to. You can then send and receive data from that connection, either as raw buffers or as encoded strings.

You should listen to error events coming from a connection, and you can also detect when a connection is closed. You can use the `close` event to try to reestablish a connection, but you must be careful when trying to do this. Wait some time between retries and set a maximum number of failed attempts to prevent your app from looping indefinitely.

13

Making HTTP Requests

WHAT'S IN THIS CHAPTER?

- Making GET requests to an HTTP server
- Using various HTTP verbs on HTTP requests
- Inspecting request response status and headers
- Using the third-party request module

HTTP has become a central part of the infrastructure of many private and public services on the Internet. Not only used to serve static content, HTTP has become the preferred way of serving and consuming public-facing API calls.

Because it is good at handling I/O, Node is a good fit not only for providing but also for using these HTTP services. In the following sections you will learn to perform and control HTTP requests using the core `http` module and a useful third-party `request` module.

In the HTTP protocol, the request has two important properties: the URL and the method. The most common method used is the GET method, which is mainly used to request content, but other methods exist like POST (mainly used for submitting web forms), PUT, DELETE, and HEAD. Each one gets different results from the server.

MAKING GET REQUESTS

This example uses `http.get` to make an HTTP GET request to the URL `www.google.com:80/index.html`.

```
var http = require('http');

var options = {
```

```
  host: "www.google.com",
  port: 80,
  path: "/index.html"
};

http.get(options, function(res) {
  console.log('Got response:' + res.statusCode);
});
```

Here you are specifying that you want to perform a GET request to the hostname `www.google.com` and path `/index.html`, using TCP port 80. The callback is invoked when a response arrives, handing you the response object. Later in this chapter you'll learn what you can do with this response object.

USING OTHER HTTP VERBS

`http.get` is a shortcut for the generic `http.request`. The options are as follows:

- `host` — The hostname or IP address you want to make the request to.
- `port` — The TCP port of the remote server.
- `method` — A string specifying the HTTP request method. Possible values are GET (which is the default method), POST, PUT, DELETE, HEAD, or any other verb the target will understand.
- `path` — The request path, which should include a query string and fragments, if any, for example, `/index?page=2`.
- `headers` — An object containing the request headers in value-name pairs. An example of a `headers` object is as follows:

```
{
  "Accept"            : "text/json",
  "If-Modified-Since" : "Sat, 28 Jan 2012 00:00:52 GMT"
}
```

The `http.request` function returns an `http.ClientRequest` object, which is a writable stream. You can use this stream to send data as part of the request body. When you are finished writing the request body, end the stream to terminate the request.

Here is an example where you write some body content into `http://my.server.com/upload`:

```
var http = require('http');
var options = {
  host: "www.google.com",
  port: 80,
  path: "/upload",
  method: "POST"
};

var request = http.request(options, function(response) {
```

```
    console.log('STATUS:', response.statusCode);
    console.log('HEADERS:', response.headers);
    response.setEncoding('utf8');
    response.on('data', function (chunk) {
      console.log('BODY:', chunk);
    });
  });
  request.write('This is a piece of data.\n');
  request.write('This is another piece of data.\n');
  request.end();
```

The `http.request` function returns the `ClientRequest` object to which you can write the body parts by calling `request.write()`. You can pass in an encoded string — by using `request.write(str, encoding)` — a UTF-8 string, or even a raw buffer. You must end the request with `request.end()`. If you don't end the request, the server will not recognize this request as complete and will not reply.

If the server is accessible and functioning, you should get a response that triggers the `response` event. You can bind to the response event on the `request` object like so:

```
function responseHandler(res) {
  console.log('I got a response:', res);
}

request.on('response', responseHandler);
```

You can also pass a callback function as the second argument to the `http.request()` call. That callback function will also be invoked when there is a response from the server.

This callback will have the response object as the first and sole argument. By looking at this object, you can find out about the response status code the server assigned to your request and what headers it sent.

Inspecting the Response Object

When the HTTP server response comes back, the response event is fired, triggering all the registered callbacks for this event, and passing along the response object. This object is an instance of `http.ClientResponse`. You can immediately inspect some attributes of this object:

- `response.statusCode` — Contains the integer number of the HTTP response status code.
- `response.httpVersion` — The HTTP version implemented by the server on this response. Probably 1.1 or 1.0.
- `response.headers` — A plain object containing the headers' name-value pairs. The names are lowercase. Here is an example of the response `headers` object:

```
{ date: 'Wed, 01 Feb 2012 16:47:51 GMT',
  expires: '-1',
  'cache-control': 'private, max-age=0',
  'content-type': 'text/html; charset=ISO-8859-1',
  'set-cookie': [ 'NID=56=rNJVRav-ZW1Sd4f9NPsjLhaybMSzTOfbMPNHCqLeYXwKAvs4_f...],
  p3p: 'CP="This is not a P3P policy! See http://www.google.com/support/accou...',
  server: 'gws',
```

```
  'x-xss-protection': '1; mode=block',
  'x-frame-options': 'SAMEORIGIN',
  connection: 'close' }
```

Obtaining the Response Body

As stated, the response body is not present when the request `response` event is fired. If you are interested in the response body, you have to register for "data" events on the `response` like this:

```
http.request(options, function(response) {
  response.setEncoding('utf8');
  response.on('data', function(data) {
    console.log('I have a piece of the body here', data);
  });
});
```

Here you are registering for the "data" event on the response as soon as you get the `response` event. You will then get called back as the pieces of the response body arrive. The data can be a buffer or, if you specify an encoding on the response object (like you did here), it will be an encoded string.

Streaming the Response Body

The HTTP response is a readable stream that represents the response body data stream. As with any readable stream, you can pipe it into any writable stream like an HTTP request or a file. For instance, the following example shows how to pipe the response body into an open file:

```
var http = require('http');
var fs   = require('fs');
var options = {
  host: "www.google.com",
  port: 80,
  path: "/",
  method: "GET"
};

var file = fs.createWriteStream('/tmp/test.txt');

http.request(options, function(res) {
  res.pipe(file);
}).end();
```

Here you are creating a file write stream and piping the `response` body into it. As body data arrives from the server response, it's written into the file. When the body ends, the file stream is ended, which then closes the file.

POOLING SOCKETS USING HTTP.AGENT

When making HTTP requests, Node internally uses an agent. An agent is the entity in Node that makes HTTP requests for you. This agent is responsible for maintaining a pool of live TCP sockets. This pool will contain open but out-of-use network connections for a given hostname and port pair. When a new HTTP request happens, the agent will ask to keep the connection alive. When the request is completed and no additional requests are waiting on a socket to become free, the socket is closed. This means that you don't have to manually close the HTTP client and that TCP connections will tend to be reused when Node is under load.

When you make a request and an available socket gets selected or a new connection is created for that request, the `http.ClientRequest` emits a `socket` event. After the request is done, sockets are removed from the agent's pool when the socket emits a `close` event or an `agentRemove` event. If you want to keep an HTTP request open for a long time, you can remove it from the pool by doing something like this:

```
function handleResponseCallback(res) {
  console.log('got response:', res);
}

var req = http.request(options, handleResponseCallback);

req.on('socket', function(socket) {
  socket.emit('agentRemove');
});
```

Node allows a maximum of five open sockets per host-port pair on a given process. That means, under heavy load, Node will serialize the requests to the same host-port to reuse the sockets. If this process is not optimal for your usage pattern, you can disable agent socket pooling by passing in `agent: false` in the `options` object:

```
var options = {
  host: "my.server.com",
  port: 80,
  path: "/upload",
  method: "POST",
  agent: false
};

http.request(options, handleResponseCallback);
```

You can also change the maximum number of open sockets allowed in the socket pool per host-port pair by changing `http.Agent.defaultMaxSockets` like this:

```
var http = require('http');
http.Agent.defaultMaxSockets = 10;
```

The default is changed globally, which means that new HTTP agents, when created, will use this default. Note that, if you have already made requests to a given hostname and port, the respective HTTP agent instance will have already been created, so changing this default will have no effect.

When making a request you can also specify the HTTP agent like this:

```
var http = require('http');
var agentOptions = {
  maxSockets: 10
};
```

```
var agent = new Agent(options);

// Use our agent for this request:
var requestOptions = {
  host: 'www.google.com',
  port: 80,
  agent: agent
};
var req = http.request(requestOptions);
// ...
req.end();
```

This code will make an HTTP request with a given agent, which will have the socket pool stored inside it. You can share this agent you created and use it on other HTTP requests to reuse its socket pool.

USING A THIRD-PARTY REQUEST MODULE TO SIMPLIFY HTTP REQUESTS

The Node HTTP client is very powerful, but it can be somewhat cumbersome to operate. First you have to provide the object with all the options containing the URL severed into pieces and then you have to collect the response body if you want to process it. If the response is a redirect, you have to manually handle the redirect yourself.

You can avoid these issues and many others by simply using a module named *request*, authored by Mikeal Rogers, a Node core contributor.

Installing and Using Request

To install the third-party request module inside the current directory, use this command:

```
$ npm install request
```

Then you can include it in your app or module:

```
var request = require('request');
```

You can make a request by simply providing an URL and a callback function like this:

```
request('http://www.acme.com:4001/something?page=2',
  function(error, response, body) {
    // ...
  }
);
```

This performs an HTTP GET request to the specified URL and collects the response and body buffers, providing these two on one simple callback signature.

You can also use other convenience methods to change the HTTP verb as follows:

- `request.put(url)` — Issues a PUT request.
- `request.post(url)` — Issues a POST request.
- `request.head(url)` — Issues a HEAD request.
- `request.del(url)` — Issues a DELETE request.
- `request.get(url)` — Issues a GET request; exists just for uniformity, and you can instead use the default `request()`.

Instead of using a string containing a URL, you can also use an `options` object. This object can be something like the following:

```
{
  url: 'http://www.acme.com:4001/something',
  method: 'DELETE',
  headers: {Accept: 'application/json'},
  body: new Buffer('Hello world!')
}
```

Here is a list of some accepted arguments:

- **`uri`** or **`url`** — Fully qualified URI or a parsed URL object from `url.parse()`. For example, `https://my.server.com/some/path?a=1&b=2`.
- **`method`** — HTTP method; defaults to GET.
- **`headers`** — HTTP headers; defaults to `{}`.
- **`qs`** — A name-value pair to be appended as a query string into the URL; for example, `{a:1, b:2}`.
- **`body`** — A request body for POST and PUT requests. Must be a buffer or a string.
- **`form`** — Sets the body to a query-string representation of the value and adds the content-type `application/x-www-form-urlencoded; charset=utf-8` to the header.
- **`json`** — Sets the body to a JSON representation of the value and adds the content-type `application/json header`.
- **`followRedirect`** — Follows HTTP 3xx responses as redirects. Defaults to `true`.
- **`maxRedirects`** — The maximum number of redirects to follow; defaults to `10`.
- **`onResponse`** — If `onResponse` is `true`, the callback will be fired on the `response` event instead of on `end`. If `onResponse` is a function, it will be called on `response` and not affect the regular semantics of the main callback on `end`.
- **`encoding`** — Encoding to be used on `setEncoding` of the response data. If `encoding` is set to `null`, the body is returned as a buffer.
- **`pool`** — A hash object containing the agents for these requests. If this option is omitted, this request will use the global pool that's set to Node's default `maxSockets`.

- **`pool.maxSockets`** — Integer containing the maximum number of sockets in the pool.
- **`timeout`** — Integer containing the number of milliseconds to wait for a request to respond before aborting.

Creating a Testing Server

To fully understand how this third-party request module works, you'll create a simple HTTP server that prints some important information about the HTTP request, as shown in Listing 13-1.

LISTING 13-1: Request introspector HTTP server.

```
require('http').createServer(function(req, res) {

  function printBack() {
    res.writeHead(200, {'Content-Type': 'text/plain'});
    res.end(JSON.stringify({
      url: req.url,
      method: req.method,
      headers: req.headers
    }));
  }

  switch (req.url) {

    case'/redirect':
      res.writeHead(301, {"Location": '/'});
      res.end();
      break;

    case'/print/body':
      req.setEncoding('utf8');
      var body = '';
      req.on('data', function(d) {
        body += d;
      });
      req.on('end', function() {
        res.end(JSON.stringify(body));
      });
      break;

    default:
      printBack();
      break;

  }
}).listen(4001);
```

Save this server into a file named `server.js` and run it on the command line:

```
$ node server.js
```

You can then make a simple call to this server, as shown in Listing 13-2.

LISTING 13-2: Making a simple request.

```
var request = require('request');
var inspect = require('util').inspect;

request(
  'http://localhost:4001/abc/def',
  function(err, res, body) {
    if (err) { throw err; }
    console.log(inspect({
      err: err,
      res: {
        statusCode: res.statusCode
      },
      body: JSON.parse(body)
    }))
  }
);
```

Without stopping the server, you should save this into a file named `simple.js` and run it from the command line:

```
$ node simple.js
```

The result should be:

```
{ err: null,
  res: { statusCode: 200 },
  body:
   { url: '/abc/def',
     method: 'GET',
     headers:
      { host: 'localhost:4001',
        'content-length': '0',
        connection: 'keep-alive' } } }
```

You can see which headers, URLs, and methods the server derived from your request. You can see that because you are not piping anything into the request stream or writing to it, request assumes that your request body has length 0.

Following Redirects

One of the many features of the request module is that it follows redirects by default. You can observe this feature with the request introspection server that you have running, which is coded so that when the URL is `/redirect`, it will reply with a 301 redirect response status code. Using this client, you can see that request follows that URL in Listing 13-3.

LISTING 13-3: Making a request that will be redirected by the server.

```
var request = require('request');
var inspect = require('util').inspect;

request(
  'http://localhost:4001/redirect',
  function(err, res, body) {
    if (err) { throw err; }
    console.log(inspect({
      err: err,
      res: {
        statusCode: res.statusCode
      },
      body: JSON.parse(body)
    }))
  });
```

Save Listing 13-3 into a file named `redirect.js` and run it with:

```
$ node redirect.js
```

You can see that the output is the following:

```
{ err: null,
  res: { statusCode: 200 },
  body:
   { url: '/',
     method: 'GET',
     headers:
      { 'content-length': '0',
        host: 'localhost:4001',
        connection: 'keep-alive' } } }
```

You can see that the URL echoed by the server is / and not the original `/redirect`. This means that request followed the server redirect to /.

If you need to be informed about the redirects that happen, you can disable this feature by setting the request options property `followRedirect` to `false`.

Some servers can be faulty and keep redirecting in a loop. This is why request defines a maximum number of redirects by default, which is 10, but you can tweak this number as needed. For instance, you may be expecting only a maximum number of three redirects per request and want the operation to fail if that number is exceeded. However, you may be willing to endure a larger number of redirects on each request. In this case, you can set the options property `maxRedirects` to the desired number.

```
var options = {
  url: 'http://www.example.com',
  maxRedirects = 3
};
request(options, callback);
```

Setting Some Request Options

You can perform HTTP methods other than GET in request. For example, you can use the `options` method attribute and encode the HTTP method there, much like with the native Node `http.request` method. You can also use the following shortcuts:

```
request.get
request.put
request.post
request.del
```

Listing 13-4 shows an example using a POST request.

LISTING 13-4: Making a POST request.

```
var request = require('request');
var inspect = require('util').inspect;

request.post(
  'http://localhost:4001/abc/def',
  function(err, res, body) {
    if (err) { throw err; }
    console.log(inspect({
      err: err,
      res: {
        statusCode: res.statusCode
      },
      body: JSON.parse(body)
    }))
  });
```

Save this into a file named `post.js` and run it:

```
$ node post.js
```

You should get the following output:

```
{ err: null,
  res: { statusCode: 200 },
  body:
   { url: '/abc/def',
     method: 'POST',
     headers:
      { host: 'localhost:4001',
        'content-length': '0',
        connection: 'keep-alive' } } }
```

This output confirms that the server understood this was a POST request.

More generically, request accepts an `options` object instead of a string URL:

```
var request = require('request');
var inspect = require('util').inspect;

var options = {
  url: 'http://localhost:4001/abc/def',
  method: 'PUT'
};

request(options, function(err, res, body) {
  if (err) { throw err; }
console.log(inspect({
    err: err,
    res: {
      statusCode: res.statusCode
    },
    body: body
  }))
});
options.js
```

By using the `options` object, you can also send some custom headers, as shown in Listing 13-5.

LISTING 13-5: Sending some custom headers.

```
var request = require('request');
var inspect = require('util').inspect;

var options = {
  url: 'http://localhost:4001/abc/def',
  method: 'PUT',
  headers: {

    'X-My-Header': 'value'
  }
};

request(options, function(err, res, body) {
  if (err) { throw err; }
  console.log(inspect({
    err: err,
    res: {
      statusCode: res.statusCode,
      headers: res.headers
    },
    body: JSON.parse(body)
  }))
});
```

You can save Listing 13-5 into a file named `headers.js` and run it with this:

```
$ node headers.js
```

You will then get this output:

```
{ err: null,
  res:
   { statusCode: 200,
     headers:
      { 'content-type': 'text/plain',
        connection: 'keep-alive',
        'transfer-encoding': 'chunked' } },
  body:
   { url: '/abc/def',
     method: 'PUT',
     headers:
      { 'x-my-header': 'value',
        host: 'localhost:4001',
        'content-length': '0',
        connection: 'keep-alive' } } }
```

You can see that the server got the header.

Encoding the Request Body

Sometimes you have to send some data on the request body. You can use form-encoding to encode the body, which mimics how the browser encodes arguments in the body string. See Listing 13-6.

LISTING 13-6: Sending a form-encoded request body.

```
var request = require('request');
var inspect = require('util').inspect;

body = {
  a: 1,
  b: 2
};

var options = {
  url: 'http://localhost:4001/print/body',
  form: body
};

request(options, function(err, res, body) {
  if (err) { throw err; }
  console.log(inspect({
    err: err,
    res: {
      statusCode: res.statusCode,
      headers: res.headers
    },
    body: JSON.parse(body)
  }))
});
```

Save this code snippet into a file named `form.js` and run it:

```
$ node form.js
```

You will then get the following output:

```
{ err: null,
  res:
   { statusCode: 200,
     headers: { connection: 'keep-alive', 'transfer-encoding': 'chunked' } },
  body: 'a=1&b=2' }
```

You can see that request encoded the `qs` object into the body.

You can also JSON-encode some arguments into your body, as shown in Listing 13-7.

LISTING 13-7: Sending a JSON-encoded request body.

```
var request = require('request');
var inspect = require('util').inspect;

body = {
  a: 1,
  b: 2
};

var options = {
  url: 'http://localhost:4001/print/body',
  json: body
};

request(options, function(err, res, body) {
  if (err) { throw err; }
  console.log(inspect({
    err: err,
    res: {
      statusCode: res.statusCode,
      headers: res.headers
    },
    body: JSON.parse(body)
  }))
});
```

Save this code snippet into a file named `json.js` and run it:

```
$ node json.js
```

You will get the following output:

```
{ err: null,
  res:
   { statusCode: 200,
```

```
    headers: { connection: 'keep-alive', 'transfer-encoding': 'chunked' } },
  body: { a: 1, b: 2 } }
```

Streaming

A request returns a client request object, which you can pipe into a writable stream (just like I showed for Node core HTTP request function earlier in this chapter), or even into another request. For instance, if you want to pipe a request response into a file stream, you can do something like this:

```
var fs = require('fs');
var request = require('request');
var file = fs.createWriteStream('/path/to/my/file');

request.get('http://www.example.com/tmp/test.html').pipe(file);
```

You can also pipe a request into another request. For instance, you can pipe a GET request into another POST request like this:

```
var request = require('request');
var source = request.get('http://my.server.com/images/some_file.jpg');
var target = request.post('http://other.server.com/images/some_file.jpg');
source.pipe(target);
```

Using a Cookie Jar

By default, request interprets and stores all HTTP cookies in a global cookie jar. This means that, for your application, all the requests send the cookies that were received from a given hostname.

This behavior can sometimes be useful; however, you may not want to collect every single cookie because they may not be important to your application. You can choose to disable cookies globally by changing request defaults:

```
request.defaults({jar: false});
```

You can also turn this behavior off on a per-request basis by setting the options `jar` attribute to `false`:

```
var options = {
  url: 'http://www.example.com/',
  jar: false };
request(options, callback);
```

You can also define a specific cookie jar to use in each request by constructing and specifying it in the `options` object:

```
var jar = request.jar();
var options = {
  url: 'http://www.example.com/',
  jar: jar };
request(options, callback);
```

SUMMARY

Making HTTP requests in Node is easy by using the `http` module `request()` function. This method returns an `http.ClientResponse` object that emits a `response` event once the server replies. You can also stream the response body and pipe it into another writable stream if you want. You can also inspect the response headers, status code, and HTTP version.

To simplify making HTTP requests, you should probably use Mikeal Roger's *request* module, which lets you use a URL in most cases. It has some useful features like following redirects, remembering cookies, buffering the response body, setting query-string values, setting a form-encoded or a JSON-encoded request body, and streaming.

14

Using Datagrams (UDP)

WHAT'S IN THIS CHAPTER?

- When and why to use UDP
- Receiving UDP messages
- Sending UDP messages
- Multicasting UDP messages
- Understanding UDP limitations

TCP is connection-oriented protocol that provides a reliable, ordered stream of bytes from one network node to another. User Datagram Protocol (UDP), however, is a connection-less protocol that does not provide the delivery characteristics of TCP. When sending UDP packets, you are not guaranteed of the order they arrive in or even whether they arrive at all.

Despite these limitations, UDP can be quite useful; for instance, when you need to broadcast messages, you don't need hard delivery guarantees or message ordering, or when you don't know the addresses of your peers.

UNDERSTANDING UDP

UDP is a transport layer, much like TCP, that sits on top of IP. It allows you to send messages (in this case referred to as *datagrams*) to other hosts without requiring prior communications to set up the required transmission channels or data paths. Unlike TCP, UDP is not connection-oriented and does not provide any semantics for reliability, message ordering, or even data integrity. UDP provides an unreliable service, and datagrams can arrive out of order, appear duplicated, or even go missing without notice. UDP assumes that error checking either is not necessary or is performed at the application layer.

UNDERSTANDING THE USES OF UDP

Time-sensitive applications often use UDP because dropping packets is preferable to waiting for delayed ones, which may not be an option in a real-time system.

UDP's stateless nature is also useful for servers answering small queries from large numbers of clients. Unlike TCP, UDP supports packet broadcast (sending to all on local network) and multicasting (sending to all subscribers).

Common network applications that use UDP include DNS (Domain Name System), streaming media applications such as IPTV (Internet Protocol Television), VoIP (Voice over IP), IP tunneling, TFTP (Trivial File Transfer Protocol), Simple Network Management Protocol (SNMP), Dynamic Host Configuration Protocol (DHCP), and others. Other common applications include message logging when strong reliability is not a requirement and clearing a distributed cache.

BUILDING A DATAGRAM SERVER

Datagram support in Node lies inside the `dgram` module. So first you have to import it:

```
var dgram = require('dgram');
```

Then you have to create the server:

```
var server = dgram.createSocket('udp4');
```

The `dgram.createSocket` function accepts the socket type as the first argument, which can be either `udp4` (UDP over IPv4) or `udp6` (UDP over IPv6). In this example, you are sticking to Ipv4.

> **NOTE** *Also note that there is no actual server in UDP; it's just a peer listening for messages on a socket. A server generally provides some kind of feedback about receipt of a message. Later in this chapter you will see how you can reply to a UDP message.*
>
> *For simplicity and disambiguation I'll keep calling this piece of software you are building a "server."*

Listening for Messages

A UDP server will emit a `message` event when a new message is coming in, so you have to register a callback function for that event:

```
server.on('message', function(message) {
  console.log('server got message: ' + message);
});
```

Now you should bind the server to a specific UDP port like this:

```
var port = 4000;server.on('listening', function() {
  var address = peer.address();
  console.log('peer listening on ' + address.address + ':' + address.port);
});
server.bind(port);
```

You can also listen for the `listening` event, which is triggered after the server actually starts listening for messages.

Testing the Server

Listing 14-1 contains the full UDP server code.

LISTING 14-1: A simple UDP server.

```
var dgram = require('dgram');

var server = dgram.createSocket('udp4');

server.on('message', function(message) {
  console.log('server got message: ' + message);
});

var port = 4000;

server.on('listening', function() {
  var address = server.address();
  console.log('server listening on ' + address.address + ':' + address.port);
});
server.bind(port);
```

You can save the code in Listing 14-1 to a file named `udp_server_1.js` and run it:

```
$ node udp_server_1
```

This script should output the server address and the port and then just wait for messages:

```
server listening on 0.0.0.0:4000
```

You can test the script using a tool like `nc` to send:

```
$ echo hello | nc -u 0.0.0.0 4000
```

This call sends a UDP packet with `hello` to the local host port 4000. You should then get server output that's something like the following:

```
server got message: hello
```

Inspecting Additional Message Information

Because a UDP server can get messages from many senders, it may be interesting, depending on the application, that you can retrieve the message-originating address. Besides sending the message itself, the `message` event also transports some basic remote sender information, passed in as the second argument to the callback function, which you can inspect like this:

```
server.on('message', function(message, rinfo) {
  console.log('server got message: %s from %s:%d',
              message,
              rinfo.address,
              rinfo.port);
});
```

As you will see later in this chapter, you can use this origin information to reply to the remote server.

CREATING A SIMPLE DATAGRAM ECHO SERVER

Now that you have the originating address available on the `message` event, you may want to send a message back. For instance, you may want to acknowledge a command or give some kind of status back to the originating server.

As an example, you will create a simple UDP server that sends received messages back to its sender.

Waiting for Messages

You can start by creating the UDP socket and binding it to a port:

```
var dgram = require('dgram');
var server = dgram.createSocket('udp4');
var port = 4000;

server.on('message', function(message, rinfo) {
  console.log('server got message: %s from %s:%d',
              message,
              rinfo.address,
              rinfo.port);
});

server.bind(port);
```

Sending Messages Back to Senders

Then, when your server receives a message, you can return it to the sender:

```
server.on('message', function(message, rinfo) {
  server.send(message,
              0,
              message.length,
```

```
                rinfo.port,
                rinfo.address);
});
```

Here you are using the server's `send` function, which sends a message to a specific address and port.

The first three arguments specify the message — first the buffer, then the initial offset of the message inside the buffer (0 in this case because the message starts at the beginning of the buffer), and then the message length in bytes (which is the actual length of the buffer you have).

The remaining two arguments specify the destination of that message, namely, the port and address. Here you are retrieving the remote sender information contained on the `rinfo` argument — which contains the remote server address info — and using that information to address the receiver.

Putting the Echo Server Together

This is what the UDP echo server now looks like:

```
var dgram = require('dgram');
var server = dgram.createSocket('udp4');
var port = 4000;

server.on('message', function(message, rinfo) {
  server.send(message, 0, message.length, rinfo.port, rinfo.address);
});

server.bind(port);
```

You can test it by using the `nc` utility in the shell command line:

```
$ nc -u 0.0.0.0 4000
```

You can then start typing strings and pressing Enter. You should see the strings printed back.

NOTE *Be careful not to change the buffer you pass on* `client.send` *before the message has been copied into the kernel. If you need to know when your message has been flushed to the kernel and when it's safe to reuse the buffer, you have to pass a last argument to* `client.send` *with a callback function like this:*

```
var message = new Buffer('blah blah');
client.send(message,
            0,
            message.length,
            4000,
            'localhost',
            function() {
              // you can reuse the message buffer
            });
```

BUILDING A DATAGRAM CLIENT

Depending on your application, you may just want to send one or more UDP messages and not care about listening to a response or any other UDP messages. In this case you would create a send-only UDP client.

Creating the Client

To create a UDP client to send UDP packets, you can simply create a UDP socket and send messages from it like this:

```
var dgram = require('dgram');
var client = dgram.createSocket('udp4');
```

Here you are creating a client using the same `dgram.createSocket` function that was also used on the server, except that you don't bind. Because you are not binding to a specific port, the message is sent from a random UDP port. If you wanted to send from a specific port, you could have used `client.bind(port)`.

Sending Messages

Next you can create a buffer containing your message and send it to the server through the client socket.

```
var message = new Buffer('this is a message');
client.send(message, 0, message.length, 4000, 'localhost');
```

Closing the Socket

When you no longer need to send messages, you can close the datagram socket, which in this case happens when the message is flushed into the network. Fortunately the `client.send` function accepts a callback for when that happens, which you can use in this case:

```
client.send(message,
            0,
            message.length,
            4000,
            'localhost',
            function(err, bytes) {
              if (err) { throw err; }
              client.close();
            }
);
```

As you can see, the callback function you pass into `client.send` gets called with two arguments: an error if one occurs and the number of bytes that were sent.

CREATING A SIMPLE DATAGRAM COMMAND-LINE CLIENT

Now you are ready to replace the nc client with a Node-based command-line UDP client. This client program should accept the target hostname and port as command-line arguments and then read from the standard input stream, piping this stream as messages to the UDP target.

Start by creating the script file and typing the following:

```
#!/usr/bin/env node
```

Save this into a file named udp_client.js and change it to be executable:

```
$ chmod +x udp_client.js
```

Your client should be called from the shell command-line like this:

```
$ udp_client.js <host> <port>
```

Then parse the command-line arguments. Those are available inside the process.argv, which is an array containing all the command-line arguments. The first argument will always contain the path for the Node executable, and the second one will always contain the main script file path. The third will then contain the host argument, and the fourth contains the port argument.

```
var host = process.argv[2];
var port = parseInt(process.argv[3], 10);
```

Reading from the Command Line

To read from the command line after your Node process is up, you must use the process.stdin readable stream. However, the process.stdin stream starts in the paused state, which means that before you can start using it, you need to resume it like this:

```
process.stdin.resume();
```

Then you should have the standard input stream available to get lines:

```
process.stdin.on('data', function(data) {
  console.log('user typed:', data);
});
```

Sending Data to the Server

Now you can pipe the user input into the target UDP server:

```
var dgram = require('dgram');

var client = dgram.createSocket('udp4');

process.stdin.on('data', function(data) {
  client.send(data, 0, data.length, port, host);
});
```

Receiving Data from the Server

To receive messages back from the server, you need to subscribe to the `message` event:

```
client.on('message', function(message) {
  console.log('Got message back:', message.toString());
});
```

Putting the Command-Line UDP Client Together

Listing 14-2 shows what the complete UDP command-line client looks like.

LISTING 14-2: A command-line UDP client.

```
#!/usr/bin/env node
var dgram = require('dgram');

var host = process.argv[2];
var port = parseInt(process.argv[3], 10);
var client = dgram.createSocket('udp4');

process.stdin.resume();

process.stdin.on('data', function(data) {
  client.send(data, 0, data.length, port, host);
});

client.on('message', function(message) {
  console.log('Got message back:', message.toString());
});

console.log('Start typing to send messages to %s:%s', host, port)
```

You can fire it up using the shell command line:

```
$ ./udp_client.js 0.0.0.0 4000
```

You should see the following:

```
Start typing to send messages to 0.0.0.0:4000
```

If you type some characters and then press Enter, you should then see your message printed back as a response.

UNDERSTANDING AND USING DATAGRAM MULTICAST

One of the interesting uses of UDP is to distribute messages to several network nodes using only one network message. You can use this to perform logging and clean the cache and in any case where you can afford to lose some messages.

> **NOTE** *Message multicasting can be useful when you don't need to know the address of all peers. Peers just have to "tune in" and listen to that channel.*
>
> *For instance, you could have an event logging server listening on multiple "channels." When another process needs to log in to a "channel," it would multicast a message containing the event details into that "channel."*
>
> *You could also have multiple servers set up to listen to the same channel. For instance, one server could be responsible for storing the events, and another would be responsible for sending them to an analytics engine.*
>
> *Nodes can report their interest in listening to certain multicast channels by tuning in to that channel. In IP addressing, a space is reserved for multicast addresses. In IPv4 the range is between 224.0.0.0 and 239.255.255.255, but some of these are reserved.*
>
> *Addresses from 224.0.0.0 through 224.0.0.255 are reserved for local purposes (such as administrative and maintenance tasks), and addresses from 239.0.0.0 to 239.255.255.255 are also reserved for administrative scoping.*

Receiving Multicast Messages

To join a multicast address like 230.1.2.3, you can do something like this:

```
var server = require('dgram').createSocket('udp4');

server.on('message', function(message, rinfo) {
  console.log('server got message: ' + message + ' from ' + rinfo.address +
    ':' + rinfo.port);
});

server.bind(4000);
server.addMembership('230.1.2.3');
```

Line 9 tells the kernel that this UDP socket should receive multicast messages for the multicast address 230.1.2.3. When you're calling the `addMembership` method on the server, you can pass the listening interface as an optional second argument. If this argument is omitted, Node will try to listen on every network interface.

Then you can test the server using your new UDP client like this:

```
$ ./udp_client.js 230.1.2.3 4000
```

Every line of text you input here should appear on the server console log.

Sending Multicast Messages

To send a multicast message, you simply have to specify the multicast address like this:

```
var dgram = require('dgram');
var client = dgram.createSocket('udp4');

var message = new Buffer('this is a multicast message');

client.bind(4000);
client.setMulticastTTL(10);
client.send(message, 0, message.length, 4000, '230.1.2.3'); client.close();
```

Recall that you previously set the multicast time-to-live (TTL) to 10, an arbitrary value. This TTL tells the network how many hops (routers) the datagram can travel through before it is discarded. Every time a UDP packet travels through a hop, the TTL counter is decremented, and if 0 is reached, the packet is discarded.

Understanding Maximum Datagram Size

UDP is lightweight and can be a great solution if your application can tolerate some data loss and disordering, but you should be aware of some additional limitations.

The maximum datagram size depends on the network it travels through. The UDP header allows up to 65,535 bytes of data, but if your packets cross an Ethernet network, for instance, the Ethernet MTU (Maximum Transmission Unit) is 1,500 bytes, limiting the maximum datagram size to that number as well. Also, some routers will attempt to fragment large UDP packets into 512 byte chunks, so you should really limit yourself to that maximum size if you want to avoid fragmenting your datagram.

SUMMARY

UDP is a lightweight transport protocol that can serve you well if you can relax some reliability constraints. It's not connection-oriented, so it involves less overhead than TCP and can multicast and broadcast messages with just one network packet.

If you want to send or receive UDP messages, you must first create a socket into which you can send messages to other UDP peers. If you need to listen to incoming messages, you have to bind your socket to a UDP port, and then wait for `message` events.

Also, you can listen to multicast messages by attaching a multicast address membership to that socket.

15

Securing Your TCP Server with TLS/SSL

WHAT'S IN THIS CHAPTER?

- Understanding how the Public Key Infrastructure works
- Creating a TLS server
- Connecting to a TLS server
- Validating the server and client certificates
- Receiving and sending data securely

TLS (Transport Layer Security) and SSL (Secure Socket Layer) allow client/server applications to communicate across a network in a way designed to prevent eavesdropping (others looking into your messages) and tampering (others changing your message). TLS/SSL encrypts the segments of network connections above the transport layer, enabling both privacy and message authentication.

TLS is based on earlier SSL specifications developed by Netscape. In fact, TLS 1.0 is also known as SSL 3.1, and the latest version (TLS 1.2) is also known as SSL 3.3. This chapter uses TLS instead of the deprecated SSL nomenclature.

UNDERSTANDING PRIVATE AND PUBLIC KEYS

Public key cryptography refers to a cryptographic system that requires two separate keys. One key is used to encrypt the plaintext, and the other key is used to decrypt the encrypted message. One of these keys is public, and the other is private. If the plaintext is encrypted using the public key, only the private key can unlock it, enabling private communication from the public to the private key owner. If the plaintext is encrypted using the private key, the public key can decrypt it. In this case the system verifies the signatures of the documents signed by the owner of the private key.

A public key certificate (also known as a digital certificate) uses a digital signature to bind a public key to an identity — a person or an organization. The document will be signed by a Certificate Authority (CA) that went through the process of certifying that the identity information matches the public key. That Certificate Authority corresponds to another certificate that either was self-signed or was endorsed by another Certificate Authority, possibly forming a chain of delegation that forms part of the Public Key Infrastructure (PKI).

Each computer defines a root set of Certificate Authorities that are used by default when validating certificates and certificate chains. When using Node's TLS library you can use these default Certificate Authorities or define your own.

Generating a Private Key

> **NOTE** *Node TLS implementation is based on the OpenSSL library. Chances are you have the library installed. To check, open a terminal and try using the* `openssl` *command. If it's not installed, look for a package named* `openssl` *and install it.*

TLS relies on the public/private key infrastructure where each client and server must have a private key to sign messages. The `openssl` utility can create a private key on the command line like this:

```
$ openssl genrsa -out my_key.pem 1024
```

This creates a file named `my_key.pem` with your private key.

Generating a Public Key

Servers and clients involved in TLS must have a certificate if they are validating each other. Certificates are public keys signed by a Certificate Authority or are self-signed. The first step in getting a certificate is to create a Certificate Signing Request (CSR) file. This can be done by:

```
$ openssl req -new -key my_key.pem -out my_csr.pem
```

This will create a CSR file named `my_csr.pem`, but first you will need to answer some identification questions prompted by `openssl`.

To create a self-signed certificate with the CSR, you can do this:

```
$ openssl x509 -req -in my_csr.pem -signkey my_key.pem -out my_cert.pem
```

This will create a self-signed certificate file named `my_cert.pem` based on your private key and your certificate request. Alternatively you can send the CSR to a Certificate Authority for signing, but for you to work on this chapter's examples, a self-signed certificate is enough.

BUILDING A TLS SERVER

A TLS server is a subclass of `net.Server`, which I introduced in Chapter 10 — "Building TCP Servers." You can make everything with a TLS server that you can with `net.Server`. When you use a TLS server, however, you are using a secure connection.

Initializing the Server

Initializing a TLS server is a bit more complicated than initializing a plain TCP server because you have to pass in the content of the server private key and certificate files:

```
var tls = require('tls');
var fs  = require('fs');

var serverOptions = {
  key:  fs.readFileSync('./my_key.pem'),
  cert: fs.readFileSync('./my_certificate.pem')
};

var server = tls.createServer(serverOptions);
```

Here you are using the synchronous version of `fs.readFile`, which reads a whole file into memory to obtain the key and certificate that are on the filesystem.

> **NOTE** *Here you're using* `fs.readFileSync`*, a synchronous function. Won't this block the event loop? No, this will just run on the initialization phase of Node, before the event loop starts. As long as you don't use blocking functions inside an event handler, you won't block the event loop.*
>
> *But wait, what if this is a module you're writing and someone requires it inside a callback? You shouldn't require modules inside callbacks. They perform synchronous filesystem access and will block the event loop.*

Besides the `key` and `cert` options, `tls.createServer` also accepts:

- `requestCert` — If `true` the server will request a certificate from clients that connect and attempt to verify that certificate. The default value is `false`.
- `rejectUnauthorized` — If `true` the server will reject any connection that's not authorized with the list of supplied Certificate Authorities. This option has an effect only if `requestCert` is `true`. The default value is `false`.

Listening for Connections

Just like a simple TCP server, you can bind a TLS server to a TCP port like this:

```
var port = 4001;
server.listen(port);
```

When a new connection arrives, the server emits the `secureConnection` event, passing in the socket to the registered callback functions:

```
function connectionListener(stream) {
  console.log('got a new connection');
}

server.on('secureConnection', connectionListener);
```

Reading Data from the Client

When a client connects, the server emits a `secureConnection` event, passing an instance of the `tls.CleartextStream` class into the callback function. Much like the `net.Socket` object, this object implements a duplex stream interface, which means that you have all the readable stream and writeable stream methods and events available to you. You can simply bind to the `data` event to get the decrypted data sent from the client like this:

```
function secureConnectionListener(clientStream) {
  clientStream.on('data', function(data) {
    console.log('got some data from the client:', data);
  });
}
server.on('secureConnection', secureConnectionListener);
```

Sending Data to the Client

You can also use the `CleartextStream` object to send data to a connected client like this:

```
server.on('secureConnection', function(clientStream) {
  clientStream.write('Hey Hello!\n');
});
```

Ending the Connection

You may end a secure connection by simply calling `.end()` on the client stream. For instance, if the client types "quit" you can end the connection like this:

```
server.on('secureConnection', function(clientStream) {
  clientStream.on('data', function(data) {
    if (data.toString().trim().toLowerCase() === 'quit') {
      clientStream.end('Bye bye!');
    }
  });
});
```

As in the TCP case, you can pass a string or a buffer into the `clientStream.end` function, which will be the last thing that is written out to the client before the connection is closed.

BUILDING A TLS CLIENT

To make a connection to a TLS server, your key and certificate need to be issued first. If you have not done this yet, please create them as explained at the beginning of this chapter.

Initializing the Client

You must initialize the client connection with some options, which you need to gather first. Previously you should have generated the private key and digital certificate into some local files, which you must fetch using `fs.readFileSync`, the synchronous version of `fs.readFile`.

```
var fs = require('fs');
var options = {
  key: fs.readFileSync('/path/to/my/private_key.pem'),
  cert: fs.readFileSync('/path/to/my/certificate.pem')
};
```

Connecting to the Server

When you have the private key and the digital certificate, you can connect to a TLS server using the `tls.connect` function:

```
var tls = require('tls');
var host = 'localhost';
var port = 4001;

var client = tls.connect(port, host, options, function() {
  console.log('connected');
});
```

Verifying the Server Certificate

Private and public keys allow you to establish a secure channel between a client and a server. This means that the channel is secure from eavesdroppers and message changers. After a connection is established, though, you may want to ensure that the server really is the server you wanted to talk to. For this you can inspect the server certificate.

To do this, you need to learn about some TLS connection options you haven't seen yet. One of them is `ca`, which stands for Certificate Authority. If you omit this option, a default set of root certificates will be used.

> **NOTE** *Unless an internal Certificate Authority issued the certificates for your own operation, omit this option and use the default CAs.*
>
> *If you want to override these certificates with your own certificates, you must pass in an array of buffers or strings containing each CA's certificate.*

This default set of certificates will be used for authenticating the server. The server will send its identification, and the TLS client will check the signature of that identification against any of the trusted Certificate Authorities.

If the certificate is authorized, the `CleartextStream` instance (which you assigned back to a variable named `client`) will have the property named `authorized` set to `true`. If not, the stream will have that property set to `false`, and the stream `authorizationError` property will be set with the reason for the error. You can, if you want, reject the connection to the server if the server certificate is not authorized according to your root CAs, like this:

```
var client = tls.connect(port, host, options, function() {
  console.log('authorized: ' + client.authorized);
  if (! client.authorized) {
    console.log('client denied access:', client.authorizationError);
  } else {
    // ...
  }
});
```

Sending Data to the Server

Recall that the object returned from the `tls.connect` function call is a `tls.CleartextStream` instance, which is also a writable stream. That means you can use the `write()` function to send data to the server.

```
var client = tls.connect(port, host, options, function() {
  console.log('connected');
  client.write('Hey, hello!');
});
```

Reading Data from the Server

Once you are connected and the server starts sending data, you will get "data" events emitted by the `CleartextStream` object.

```
var client = tls.connect(port, host, options, function() {
  client.on('data', function(data) {
    console.log('got some data from the server:', data);
  });
});
```

Ending the Connection

Depending on your application and the agreed-upon protocol between the server and the client, the client may end the connection after it no longer needs it.

Because this only closes your end of the connection, you may still continue to receive messages from the server.

```
var client = tls.connect(port, host, options, function() {
  client.end('Bye bye!');
});
```

BUILDING SOME EXAMPLES

It's time to put everything together and create a TLS chat server and client. You need to create a separate directory for the client and the server so you can easily separate the script, key, and certificate files.

Creating a TLS Chat Server

Create a project directory named `chat_server` into which you'll place the key and certificate files.

First create the server key:

```
$ openssl genrsa -out server_key.pem 1024
```

Then create the certificate request:

```
$ openssl req -new -key server_key.pem -out server_csr.pem
```

To create a self-signed certificate with the CSR, you can do this:

```
$ openssl x509 -req -in server_csr.pem -signkey server_key.pem \
-out server_cert.pem
```

Now that you have the file `server_cert.pem` file sitting in the `chat_server` directory, you can put the server script together inside a file named `server.js`. See Listing 15-1.

LISTING 15-1: A TLS chat server.

```
var tls = require('tls');
var fs  = require('fs');
var port = 4001;

var clients = [];

var options = {
  key:  fs.readFileSync('server_key.pem'),
  cert: fs.readFileSync('server_cert.pem')
};

function distribute(from, data) {
  var socket = from.socket;
  clients.forEach(function(client) {
    if (client !== from) {
      client.write(socket.remoteAddress + ':' + socket.remotePort +
        ' said: ' + data);
    }
```

continues

LISTING 15-1 *(continued)*

```
  });
}

var server = tls.createServer(options, function(client) {

  clients.push(client);

  client.on('data', function(data) {
    distribute(client, data);
  });

  client.on('close', function() {
    console.log('closed connection');
    clients.splice(clients.indexOf(client), 1);
  });

});

server.listen(port, function() {
  console.log('listening on port', server.address().port);
});
```

This server keeps a list of all connected clients in a module-global array stored on a variable named `clients`. Each time a client connects it is added to that array. Each time a client sends any data, that data is distributed to all the other clients, prefixed with the source IP address and TCP port. Also, when the client is disconnected, that client is removed from the list.

Now you simply have to start up your script:

```
$ node server.js
```

Creating a TLS Command-Line Chat Client

After you have created the `chat_client` directory, you can start creating the client key and certificates:

```
$ openssl genrsa -out client_key.pem 1024
$ openssl req -new -key client_key.pem -out client_csr.pem
$ openssl x509 -req -in client_csr.pem -signkey client_key.pem -out client_cert.pem
```

With your client key and certificate files you can create the client code inside a file named `client.js`. See Listing 15-2.

LISTING 15-2: A TLS chat client.

```
var tls = require('tls');
var fs  = require('fs');

var port = 4001;
var host = '0.0.0.0';
```

```
var options = {
  key:  fs.readFileSync('client_key.pem'),
  cert: fs.readFileSync('client_cert.pem')
};

process.stdin.resume();

var client = tls.connect(port, host, options, function() {
  console.log('connected');
  process.stdin.pipe(client, {end: false});
  client.pipe(process.stdout);
});
```

The client is simple — it connects to the TLS server in a local host and then pipes the process standard input into the server, which writes every line you type to the server. It also pipes the server stream into the standard output, which makes it output every character the server sends.

You can test the client on multiple windows by launching

```
$ node client.js
```

You will then see what you type in the client window appear on all the other clients.

Verifying the Client Certificate

One thing that your server does not do yet is verify client credentials. If you turn on the `requestCert` option, you will see that the `authorized` property on the client stream is set to `false`:

```
var options = {
  key:  fs.readFileSync('server_key.pem'),
  cert: fs.readFileSync('server_cert.pem'),
  requestCert: true
};

var server = tls.createServer(options, function(client) {
  console.log('client.authorized:', client.authorized);
  // ...
});
```

If you make these changes to the server and then execute the client, you will see that the server outputs the following:

```
client.authorized: false
```

You can also resolve not to accept any unauthorized client by setting the `rejectUnauthorized` option to `true`:

```
var options = {
  key:  fs.readFileSync('server_key.pem'),
  cert: fs.readFileSync('server_cert.pem'),
  requestCert: true,
  rejectUnauthorized: true
};
```

This ensures that the clients that fail to pass the certification chain are not served. If you try this option, you will see that the client does not enter the server callback.

This happens because the client certificate is self-signed, and the server is using the default Certificate Authorities. These default CAs don't validate the self-signed certificate of the client.

You can do a small trick to test this feature on the server — copy the client certificate and say that it is a Certificate Authority:

```
$ cd chat_server
$ cp ../chat_client/client_cert.pem fake_ca.pem
```

Then override the Certificate Authority option on the server:

```
var options = {
  key: fs.readFileSync('server_key.pem'),
  cert: fs.readFileSync('server_cert.pem'),
  ca: [fs.readFileSync('fake_ca.pem')],
  requestCert: true
};
```

Then, if you start the server and connect with a client, you will see that the client is authorized:

```
client.authorized: true
```

SUMMARY

TLS provides an encrypted stream of communication on top of TCP and uses a public/private key infrastructure to authenticate clients and servers. To communicate you need to have a private key and a signed certificate. This certificate can be self-signed or, if the server or client demands it, can be signed by a Certificate Authority.

A TLS server and client follow the existing pattern in the `net` module but have some extensions to allow the specification of the principal private key and the certificate. They also allow you to set whether to perform authentication.

16

Securing Your HTTP Server with HTTPS

WHAT'S IN THIS CHAPTER?

- Setting up an HTTPS server
- Making requests to an HTTPS server
- Validating client and server certificates

HTTPS adds the security capabilities of TLS to the standard HTTP protocol. In Node HTTPS is implemented as a separate module from HTTP. The HTTPS API is very similar to the HTTP one, with some small differences.

The `https` Node core module extends the core `http` module and uses the `tls` module as a transport mechanism. For instance, the `https.Server` pseudo-class simply inherits from the `http.Server` pseudo-class, overriding the way that connections are constructed inside the corresponding `Agent` class, which instantiates a TLS connection instead of a plain TCP one.

BUILDING A SECURE HTTP SERVER

In this section you will set up an HTTP server that talks to clients through a secured encrypted channel. This HTTP server can provide self-authentication to clients and authenticate client identification.

First you have to create the server private key and self-signed certificate like you did in the previous chapter:

```
$ openssl genrsa -out server_key.pem 1024
$ openssl req -new -key server_key.pem -out server_csr.pem
$ openssl x509 -req -in server_csr.pem -signkey server_key.pem
        -out server_cert.pem
```

The second step prompts you with some questions — you can answer them as you like.

Setting Up the Server Options

To create a server, you can do something like this:

```
var fs = require('fs');
var https = require('https');

var options = {
  key: fs.readFileSync('server_key.pem'),
  cert: fs.readFileSync('server_cert.pem')
};

var server = https.createServer(options, function(req, res) {
  res.writeHead(200, {'Content-Type': 'text/plain'});
  res.end('Hello World!');
});
```

The first argument of `https.createServer` is an `options` object that, much like with the TLS module, provides the private key and the certificate strings. Just as you did in Chapter 15, "Securing Your TCP Server with TLS/SSL," you are loading the private key and certificate from the filesystem using the `fs.readFileSync` function, which, as the name indicates, loads the file content synchronously.

> **NOTE** *As mentioned in Chapter 15, the fact that you do this synchronously does not create any danger of blocking the event loop because it is done during the module loading phase, which happens before the Node event loop starts.*

Listening for Connections

You can then — as with the bare HTTP server model — register your server to listen to a specific TCP port:

```
var port = 4001;
server.listen(port);
```

You can also specify which interface you want to listen on:

```
port = 4001;
var address = '192.168.1.100';
server.listen(port, address);
```

If you don't specify an address, the server will listen on all network interfaces.

This `listen` command is asynchronous, which means that the server will not listen for connections immediately after you command it to. You can, however, provide a callback function that will be invoked once the server does start listening, which you pass in as the second or third argument of the `server.listen` function (whether you are specifying a network interface to bind to or not):

```
server.listen(port, address, function() {
  console.log('Server is listening on port', server.address().port);
});
```

Validating the HTTPS Client Certificate

If you are building an HTTPS server, your main concern may be that the communication channel between the server and each client be encrypted. You might also need each client to be able to identify the server in a certified way. You might require the server to verify the authenticity of the clients. This last example is not a very common use case, but it can be helpful when you want to build a highly secured machine-to-machine communication scheme or even if you want to issue identification certificates to clients like some home-banking services do.

You can require that the server verify the clients' authenticity by simply specifying some option arguments on the server startup:

```
var options = {
  key: fs.readFileSync('server_key.pem'),
  cert: fs.readFileSync('server_cert.pem'),
  requestCert: true,
  rejectUnauthorized: true
};
```

You are now using two new options — `requestCert` and `rejectUnauthorized` — and setting them both to `true`. The first one asks the client to send over the certificate. The second one tells the server to reject certificates that are not validated by the Certificate Authority chain.

> **NOTE** *For more information about Certificate Authorities, consult Chapter 15, "Securing Your TCP Server with TLS/SSL."*

Also, if you omit the `rejectUnauthorized` attribute, you can still determine whether the client was authenticated by inspecting the `authorized` attribute on the client stream:

```
var server = https.createServer(options, function(req, res) {
  console.log('authorized:', req.socket.authorized);
});
```

You can also access the client certificate, but note that you will only be able to trust the authenticity of that information if `socket.authorized` is `true`. Here is how you can do that:

```
var server = https.createServer(options, function(req, res) {
  console.log('authorized:', req.socket.authorized);
  console.log('client certificate:', req.socket.getPeerCertificate());
});
```

By inquiring if the stream is authenticated (`req.socket.authorized`) and by obtaining the peer certificate (`req.socket.getPeerCertificate()`), you can identify and authenticate the client connection.

CREATING AN HTTPS CLIENT

In Node, making an HTTPS request is very similar to making an HTTP one. In fact, it can be exactly the same because you don't really need to pass in the client private key or client certificate unless the server requires it.

Initializing the Client

You can make an HTTPS request to an HTTPS server like this:

```
var fs = require('fs');
var https = require('https');

var options = {
  host: '0.0.0.0',
  port: 4001,
  method: 'GET',
  path: '/'
};
```

Much like the HTTP counterpart, you need to construct an object containing the options for your request. This should include values for host, port, and path. You can also specify the method if you want to make a request using a method other than GET.

Making the Request

You have to pass these last options that specify host, port, method, and path to the `request` function in the `https` module, which accepts the `options` object and a function callback and returns an `http.ClientRequest` instance.

```
var request = https.request(options, function(response) {
   console.log('response.statusCode:', response.statusCode);

   response.on('data', function(data) {
     console.log('got some data back from the server:', data);
   });
});

request.write('Hey!\n');
request.end();
```

This client request is a writable stream to which you can write, or into which you can pipe a readable stream. You should then end the request so that the server can respond.

Once a response from the server is received — triggering the `response` event on the `request` object — the callback gets the `response` object. If you are interested in the body content, this `response` object is a readable stream, which means that you can pipe it into a writable stream or simply register a callback function for any `data` events.

Validating the HTTPS Server Certificate

Besides the secure communication channel, client-side validation of the server certificate is the most common reason for using HTTPS on the web. Most web browsers want to be sure that the server they are talking to is the same one that shows up in the URL bar. You can perform this kind of validation using the built-in Node HTTPS client.

While performing a request, when you get a `response` event and the `response` object, you can inspect that object. The `response` object has the `stream` object embedded inside its `socket` attribute. Because this is a TLS stream, you can invoke the `getPeerCertificate` function on it to obtain the server certificate like this:

```
var fs = require('fs');
var https = require('https');

var options = {
  host: 'google.com',
  method: 'GET',
  path: '/'
};

var req = https.request(options, function(res) {
  console.log('res.socket.authorized:', res.socket.authorized);
  console.log('peer certificate:');
  console.log(res.socket.getPeerCertificate());
});

req.end();
```

If you run this small HTTPS client, you will get output similar to this:

```
res.socket.authorized: true
peer certificate:
{ subject:
   { C: 'US',
     ST: 'California',
     L: 'Mountain View',
     O: 'Google Inc',
     CN: '*.google.com' },
  issuer: { C: 'US', O: 'Google Inc', CN: 'Google Internet Authority' },
  subjectaltname: 'DNS:*.google.com, DNS:google.com, DNS:*.youtube.com, ...',
  modulus: 'CAB66CCEFADF0EF63AC7B5DC1647EB9F31E196929391D28DAB0747C42276...',
  exponent: '10001',
  valid_from: 'Jul 26 00:34:27 2012 GMT',
  valid_to: 'Jun  7 19:43:27 2013 GMT',
  fingerprint: '56:7E:72:30:90:DB:16:E1:A9:65:8F:5A:7B:18:59:52:01:F7:64:D7',
  ext_key_usage: [ '1.3.6.1.5.5.7.3.1', '1.3.6.1.5.5.7.3.2' ] }
```

This identification data, together with the fact that `res.socket.authorized` is `true`, enables you to securely assert that the subject's common name matches the hostname or the domain to which you made the request.

SUMMARY

HTTPS is a way to secure the communication channel and to provide an authentication framework between communicating peers. With HTTPS you can authenticate the client or the server. The Node `https` module extends the functionality of the HTTP module and uses the TLS module to provide the underlying transport on top of HTTP.

You can identify servers and clients by tapping into the underlying TLS socket and extracting the peer certificate identification data.

PART IV
Building and Debugging Modules and Applications

17

Testing Modules and Applications

WHAT'S IN THIS CHAPTER?

- Running tests using node-tap
- Using the Node assert module
- Testing a sample module

To minimize the number of errors that users encounter while using your software, you must test the code you produce. You can do some of this testing manually, but optimally, you need a program that automates this process.

Automated testing is one of the most important practices that improve code quality. The goal is to have a series of tests that cover your entire code base, including the main and edge cases of your software. Some disciplines like TDD (test-driven development) even advocate that you write your tests, make them fail, and then implement the code that makes them work.

Whatever your approach, writing automated tests is a good investment. This chapter shows you how to do that in your Node modules and programs.

USING A TEST RUNNER

To create an automated test, you first need a way to define your tests. Then you need a tool that compiles and runs these tests, outputting the results.

Many such tools for Node.js and JavaScript exist. This chapter features one called node-tap. I picked it for several reasons: It's simple, it easily supports asynchronous testing, and the output format is based on a standard.

You can install node-tap by including it inside the `dev-dependencies` section of your `package.json` file:

```
{
  "name": "MyApp",
  "version": "0.1.0",
  "devDependencies": {
    "tap": "*"
  }
}
```

You then issue this command:

```
$ npm install
```

When NPM downloads and installs node-tap and its dependencies, you can start using it.

> **NOTE** *If you declare a dependency in the* `devDependencies` *property of your* `package.json` *file, you are telling your program that it does not need that dependency once it's running in production.*
>
> *This is a good place to store all dependencies that will be used solely for developing and testing your application.*
>
> *When you install your application in a production environment, you can use the* `-production` *option to skip the installation of the modules listed in the* `devDependencies` *section:*
>
> ```
> $ npm install -production
> ```

Writing Tests

To create tests, you need first to set up a directory where you place the test scripts. As a general rule, this directory is usually called `tests` and contains one file per module you want to test.

You create your first test script inside this directory. To do so, require the `tap` module and obtain the `test` constructor as follows:

```
var test = require('tap').test;
```

Then you can define your first test. For that you need to provide a test name and a function that contains the test code:

```
test("addition of 2 and 2 works", function(t) {
  t.equal(2+2, 4, "2+2 should be 4");
  t.end();
});
```

In this code, you are declaring a test named `addition of 2 and 2 works` and then passing a function that contains the test code. The function receives an argument named `t`, which contains the control object for this test. With this object you can test your expectations and end the current test. It's important that you end the test explicitly. Node-tap supports asynchronous tests, which means that if you're performing any IO, the test will still run after your test function returns. Node-tap ends a test only when you call the `end` method on it.

Running Tests

Save the file you created in the previous section and name it `my_test.js`. You can run this test by invoking the test script directly:

```
$ node my_test
```

You should then get output that is similar to this:

```
# addition of 2 and 2 works
ok 1 2+2 should be 4

1..1
# tests 1
# pass  1

# ok
```

USING AN ASSERTION TESTING MODULE

To build a valid test, you need a way to verify that the results you are getting match your expectations. For this, the previous example used node-tap's built-in assertion functions — which you'll learn about later — but for now you can use Node's built-in `assert` module.

Using the assert Module

Node uses the built-in `assert` module in its tests. Node also exposes the `assert` module, which means you can use it to verify assumptions inside your own tests.

To use the `assert` module, import the module into your test script:

```
var assert = require('assert');
```

Now you can use the assertion functions. Each of these functions sets an expectation, and an exception will be thrown if the expectation is not met.

First, you can test if a value is *truthy*:

```
var a = true;
assert(a);
```

> **NOTE** *In JavaScript, a value that can be used successfully inside an* `if` *statement is said to be* truthy. *Truthy values are usually defined by all possible values, minus the* falsy *values, which are:*
>
> - *false*
> - *null*
> - *undefined*
> - *The empty string " "*
> - *The number 0*
> - *The number NaN*

In this and other assertion functions, you can also provide a message as the last argument, providing more information that is shown when the test fails:

```
assert(a, 'a should be truthy');
```

You can also use this alias to determine whether a value is truthy:

```
assert.ok(a, 'a should be truthy');
```

`assert` also tests for equality in two ways: shallow or deep. Shallow equality just tests the two objects you provide and doesn't test the equality of objects embedded inside the objects you provided. In contrast, deep equality recursively tests all the nested objects. Shallow equality is normally used to compare scalar objects like strings and numbers, while deep equality is normally used to compare two objects.

You test shallow equality like this:

```
assert.equal(a, 10, 'a should be 10');
```

This operator is equivalent to the JavaScript equality operator (==), which means that the following assertion is valid:

```
assert.equal('10', 10);
```

You can also use the reverse — the inequality assertion — which is the equivalent of the JavaScript coercive inequality operator (`!=`). It makes the following assertion fail:

```
assert.notEqual('10', 10);
```

The `assert` module also supports the strict equality semantics, similar to the JavaScript strict equality operator (===). The following assertion fails:

```
assert.strictEqual('10', 10, 'string 10 should  equal to number 10');
```

and the following assertion is valid:

```
assert.notStrictEqual('10', 10, 'string 10 should not be equal to number 10');
```

So far you have tested for shallow equality. In shallow equality, if you are testing two objects, these two object references have to point to the same object for the equality assertion to be valid:

```
assert.equal({a:1}, {a:1});
```

The previous assertion fails with this:

```
AssertionError: {"a":1} == {"a":1}
```

Shallow comparison fails here because, even though these two objects appear identical, they are in fact two different objects.

If you wish to compare object *properties*, you need to use deep comparison.

For deep comparison, you can use the `assert.deepEqual` function. The following assertion is valid:

```
var obj = {b:1, a:[1,2,3,4]};
assert.deepEqual(obj, {a:[1,2,3,4], b:1});
```

You can also use it to compare dates:

```
var a = new Date(),
    b = new Date();
assert.deepEqual(a, b);
```

Since version 0.7 you can also use it to compare regular expressions. If you are using Node 0.7 or greater, the following assertion is valid:

```
assert.deepEqual(/a/ig, /a/gi);
```

The `deepEqual` function verifies only the object's enumerable properties, which means that if two objects have different prototypes but all the enumerable properties are the same, they won't register as different. For instance, the following assertion is valid:

```
var EventEmitter = require('events').EventEmitter;
var ee = new EventEmitter();
assert.deepEqual(ee, {});
```

This happens because the following assertion is valid:

```
assert.strictEqual(Object.keys(ee).length, 0);
```

Using the Built-in Assertion Functions in Node-Tap

The node-tap module also provides a set of assertion-testing functions. By using them instead of the ones defined in the Node core module, you can take advantage of the built-in test count metrics, error reporting, and aggregated reports of node-tap. The testing functions are somewhat similar to the native assert module, but they are different enough that it's worth taking a look at them separately.

By using t.ok() and t.notOk, you can test for truthyness:

```
test("truthyness of numbers", function(t) {
  t.ok(1, '1 should be truthy');
  t.notOk(0, '0 should not be truthy');
  t.end();
});
```

You can also test for strict equality by using the t.equal function:

```
test("sum works", function(t) {
  var a = 2 + 2;
  t.equal(a, 4, '2 + 2 should be equal to 4');
  t.notEqual(a, '4', '2 + 2 should not be equal to the string "4"');
  t.end();
});
```

You can also use t.equal to test for shallow equality. The following test fails:

```
test("object equality", function(t) {
  var a = {a:1};
  t.equal(a, {a:1});
  t.end();
});
```

In this case you should use the equivalency test. This test succeeds:

```
test("object equivalency", function(t) {
  var a = {a:1, b:2};
  t.equivalent(a, {b:2, a:1});
  t.end();
});
```

You can also test for object similarity. For instance, you may want to determine if an object contains a series of attributes and then assert their values. For that you can use t.similar like this:

```
test("object similarity", function(t) {
  a = {a:1, b:2};
  t.similar(a, {a:1});
  t.similar('abc', 'abc');
  t.similar(10, 10);
  t.end();
});
```

Object similarity also works for number and string objects:

```
test("object similarity", function(t) {
  t.similar('abc', 'abc');
  t.similar(10, 10);
  t.end();
});
```

You can also test for object types using `t.type()` like this:

```
test("object type", function(t) {

  t.type(1, "number");

  t.type('abc', 'string');

  t.type({}, Object);

  var EventEmitter = require('events').EventEmitter;
  var ee = new EventEmitter();
  t.type(ee, EventEmitter);
  t.type(ee, Object);

  t.end();
});
```

You can see in the previous example that you can determine whether an object inherits from a certain constructor by passing the constructor into the `t.type()` assertion function.

TESTING YOUR ASYNCHRONOUS MODULE

Now that you know how to use node-tap, you can build an example of an interesting module to test. To make it even more interesting, this module can perform some I/O so you can do some asynchronous tests.

This module adds two integers by invoking a remote HTTP service. First, create an HTTP server that takes two integers and adds them, as in Listing 17-1:

LISTING 17-1: An HTTP server that sums two integers.

```
var parse = require('url').parse;

require('http').createServer(function(req, res) {
  params = parse(req.url, true).query;
  var a = parseInt(params.a, 10);
  var b = parseInt(params.b, 10);
  var result = a + b;
  res.end(JSON.stringify(result));
}).listen(8080);
```

Create two directories: one named "client" and another named "server." You can then save Listing 17-1 into a file named `server/sum_server.js`, which the following will launch:

```
$ node server/sum_server.js
```

This starts the integer-adding HTTP service.

Then you need to create a client module that uses this service and exposes a client API. First you will declare the dependencies in the `package.json` manifest inside the "client" directory, as in Listing 17-2:

LISTING 17-2: Client package.json manifest.

```
{
  "name": "sum-client",
  "version": "1.0.0",
  "dependencies": {
    "request": "*"
  }
}
```

Now you need to install the dependencies, which in this case are only for the "request" module:

```
$ npm install
request@2.10.0 ./node_modules/request
```

Now you can plant the client module in a file named `index.js` inside the client directory by copying Listing 17-3 into a file named `sum_client.js` inside the client directory.

LISTING 17-3: The sum client module.

```
var request = require('request');

function sum(a, b, callback) {
  var options = {
    uri: 'http://localhost:8080/',
    qs: {
      a: a,
      b: b
    }
  };

  request(options, function(err, res, body) {
    var result;
    if (err) {
      return callback(err);
    }
    try {
      result = JSON.parse(body);
    } catch(err) {
      return callback(err);
    }
    return callback(null, result);
  });
}

module.exports = sum;
```

This module simply exports a function that provides the sum service.

Now you're ready to test this module. Create a "tests" directory at the same level as the "client" and "server" directories.

Then you have to create a `package.json` manifest inside that directory where you list "tap" as a development dependency:

```
{
  "name": "sum-tests",
  "version": "1.0.0",
  "devDependencies": {
    "tap": "*"
  }
}
```

Step into the "tests" directory and install the development dependencies:

```
$ cd tests
$ npm install
tap@0.3.0 node_modules/tap
├── buffer-equal@0.0.0
├── deep-equal@0.0.0
├── mkdirp@0.3.3
├── slide@1.1.3
├── nopt@2.0.0 (abbrev@1.0.3)
├── difflet@0.2.1 (charm@0.0.8, traverse@0.6.3)
└── runforcover@0.0.2 (bunker@0.1.2)
$ cd ..
```

Then save the contents of Listing 17-4 inside the file `tests/sum.js`.

LISTING 17-4: The sum client tests.

```
var sum = require('../client/sum_client');
var test = require('tap').test;

test('sums 1 and 2', function(t) {
  sum(1, 2, function(err, result) {
    t.notOk(err, 'no error');
    t.equal(result, 3, '1 + 2 should be equal to 3');
    t.end();
  });
});

test('sums 5 and 0', function(t) {
  sum(5, 0, function(err, result) {
    t.notOk(err, 'no error');
    t.equal(result, 5, '5 + 0 should be equal to 3');
    t.end();
  });
});
```

continues

LISTING 17-4 *(continued)*

```
test('sums 5 and -2', function(t) {
  sum(5, -2, function(err, result) {
    t.notOk(err, 'no error');
    t.equal(result, 3, '5 + -2 should be equal to 3');
    t.end();
  });
});
```

In this test file, you first import your sum client module, which you use further down in the test definitions.

Then you perform a series of tests, invoking the sum client module function with varying arguments for each one, always checking to see that there is no error and that the result matches the expected value, and finally ending the test.

Making sure that your sum server is still running, run these tests:

```
$ node tests/sum.js
```

You will then get the output of a successful test run:

```
...
1..6
# tests 6
# pass  6

# ok
```

SUMMARY

Testing your application and modules not only is considered a best practice but is imperative to minimize the defects in the code you produce. In Node you can use, among others, the node-tap module for running your tests.

To test your expectations in your tests, you can use Node's native `assert` module, or you can use the functions provided with the node-tap module.

18

Debugging Modules and Applications

WHAT'S IN THIS CHAPTER?

- Formatting and outputting variables
- Using variable interpolation
- Using the Node debugger
- Using a visual Node debugger

Building functional software is not a trivial task. Dividing your application code into small modules and testing each one thoroughly can help, but you're still bound to find problems. If you find yourself in a situation where you need to inspect the inner workings of your Node application or module code, several tools can help. This chapter covers several of those debugging tools — `console.log`, Node's built-in debugger, and Node Inspector.

USING CONSOLE.LOG

Node has some global objects that you can use without requiring them explicitly. One of them is the console object, which enables you to output formatted strings.

The simplest debugging tool at your disposal is `console.log`. This function call does two things — it serializes and concatenates your objects into a string and outputs the result to the standard output stream. You can use it to inspect objects like this:

```
var obj = {a: 1, b: 2};
console.log(obj);
```

This last snippet prints the following:

```
{ a: 1, b: 2 }
```

This simple example passes in an object that is translated into a literal string representation. You can pass in any type of object, and `console.log` will inspect its properties and values.

> **NOTE** *Actually,* `console.log` *does not do any formatting. All the formatting is done by the* `util.format` *function. Whatever arguments you pass in to* `console.log` *are handed over to* `util.format`, *and the result is flushed to the standard output stream. This means that any of these example calls to* `console.log` *can be directly applied to* `util.format`.

The `console.log` function inspects only the object's own enumerable properties, which means that properties on the prototype chain and properties that are not enumerable are not shown. As an example, this code instantiates an `EventEmitter` object on the Node console:

```
> var EventEmitter = require('events').EventEmitter;
undefined
> var emitter = new EventEmitter();
undefined
> console.log(emitter);
{}
undefined
> emitter.on('data', function() { });
{ _events: { data: [Function] } }
> console.log(emitter);
{ _events: { data: [Function] } }
undefined
```

In the previous interactive example, you can see that the first time you call `console.log` on the `emitter` variable value, it prints an empty object. That is because the `emitter` object has no properties set at the time of construction. Then, after you attach an event listener, it gains a property named `_events`, which is printed on the following `console.log` call.

The `console.log` function can also comprehensibly log arrays:

```
> var arr = [1, 2, 3];
undefined
> console.log(arr);
[ 1, 2, 3 ]
undefined
```

The `console.log` function also provides — via the `util.format` function — the ability to interpolate values into strings, where you can specify placeholders that are prefixed by `%` inside a string like this:

```
> console.log('an object: %j and a number: %d', {a:1, b:2}, 0xfa);
an object: {"a":1,"b":2} and a number: 250
undefined
```

You can use `%j` to JSON-encode an object, `%d` to output a number (integer or float), and `%s` to output another string.

If you supply `console.log` with extra arguments that don't have placeholders in the template string or if you just supply a list of arguments with no template string, `console.log` will simply format and concatenate them, separated by space characters.

```
> console.log({a:1, b:2}, 0xfa);
{ a: 1, b: 2 } 250
undefined
> console.log('an object: %j and a number:', {a:1, b:2}, 0xfa);
an object: {"a":1,"b":2} and a number: 250
undefined
```

> **NOTE** *The* `console.log` *function simply outputs the resulting string from* `util.format`*, appends a newline character, and pushes it into the standard output stream. However, writing to process output streams in Node is a blocking operation, which means that you are blocking your event loop while you are logging. Depending on your application and on how frequently you use this function, you may reduce responsiveness, which means that you should avoid using* `console.log` *in production code.*

USING NODE'S BUILT-IN DEBUGGER

Using `console.log` to inspect variables can quickly become unmanageable, especially when the problem you are trying to fix is nontrivial. When addressing a problem that is hard to find, you would probably have to add many log instructions and your program output would become too verbose. Worst of all, you would have to run your program and try to reproduce the problem every time you introduce new logging instructions.

Fortunately, the JavaScript V8 Virtual Machine exports a debugging interface, which Node also supports. If you need to halt execution to carefully inspect your app, you can use Node's built-in debugger. Even though it's simple and basic, it can be just enough to help you debug your app without having to install another tool.

First, create a simple example application with an error so you can experiment with the debugger (see Listing 18-1).

LISTING 18-1: An application with a bug.

```
var a = 0;

function init() {
  a = 1;
}

function incr() {
```

continues

LISTING 18-1 *(continued)*

```
  var a = a + 1;
}

init();
console.log('a before: %d', a);

incr();
console.log('a after: %d', a);
```

If you run this application, you can see that the output is this:

```
a before: 1
a after: 1
```

You can see that the a variable was not incremented as you intended it to be. Your next step is to start Node in debug mode so you can observe what is happening.

```
$ node debug my_app.js
```

This code snippet launches Node in debug mode and starts the debugger. This will start the app but will break at the first line of your main module. You should now get the debugger prompt and the current instruction position:

```
< debugger listening on port 5858
connecting... ok
break in my_app.js:1
  1 var a = 0;
  2
  3 function init() {
```

You can use the prompt to list all the commands:

```
debug> help
Commands: run (r), cont (c), next (n), step (s), out (o), backtrace (bt),
setBreakpoint (sb), clearBreakpoint (cb), watch, unwatch, watchers,
repl, restart, kill, list, scripts, breakpoints, version
```

Now you can continue to the next instruction:

```
debug> next
```

This will continue and break the execution in the next instruction on the same scope:

```
break in my_app.js:11
  9 }
 10
 11 init();
 12 console.log('a before: %d', a);
 13
```

Now, instead of using the `next` command to continue to the next instruction on the same scope, you enter the `init()` function call:

```
debug> step
break in my_app.js:4
  2
  3 function init() {
  4   a = 1;
  5 }
  6
```

You can now see the state of the call stack like this:

```
debug> backtrace
#0 my_app.js:4:3
#1 my_app.js:11:1
```

You can also watch over a variable by adding a `watch` like this:

```
debug> watch('a')
```

This command adds a `watch` to the watch list, which you can inspect like this:

```
debug> watchers
  0: a = 0
```

Here you can see that the variable named `a` has a value of `0` in the local scope.

Now you can step into the next command like this:

```
debug> next
break in my_app.js:5
Watchers:
  0: a = 1

  3 function init() {
  4   a = 1;
  5 }
  6
  7 function incr() {
```

This debugger instruction runs the next command and shows the watch list and the next line of execution. You can see that the `a` variable now has a value of `1`.

You are now at the end of the `init` function, ready to return. You can use the `out` command to skip to the next instruction on the parent scope, or — because you've reached the end of the current scope — you can also use the `next` command:

```
debug> next
break in my_app.js:12
Watchers:
  0: a = 1
```

```
10
11 init();
12 console.log('a before: %d', a);
13
14 incr();
```

What if you wanted to skip line 12 and jump right into the execution of the `incr` function call? To do so, you set a breakpoint on line 8 of the `my_app.js` file:

```
debug> sb ('my_app.js', 8)
  7 function incr() {
* 8   var a = a + 1;
  9 }
 10
 11 init();
 12 console.log('a before: %d', a);
 13
 14 incr();
 15 console.log('a after: %d', a);
 16 });
```

You can see that you have a breakpoint on line 8, and that the current instruction is on line 12. Now you are ready to fast-forward to the breakpoint:

```
debug> cont
< a before: 1
break in my_app.js:8
Watchers:
  0: a = undefined

  6
  7 function incr() {
* 8   var a = a + 1;
  9 }
 10
```

By examining the output of the debugger, you can detect the problem in the application. The debugger is saying that the previous value of the `a` variable was `1` and that the new value is undefined. That is because you use the `var` keyword on line 8, which creates a local variable instead of using the global one. Now that you know what you did wrong, you can exit the debugger by hitting Ctrl-D and fix the problem by removing the `var` keyword from line 8:

```
var a = 0;

function init() {
  a = 1;
}

function incr() {
  a = a + 1;
}
```

```
init();
console.log('a before: %d', a);

incr();
console.log('a after: %d', a);
```

Run the application again:

```
$ node my_app.js
a before: 1
a after: 2
```

Now the output is what you expected; the bug is fixed.

USING NODE INSPECTOR

Another debugging tool you might find helpful is Node Inspector. Instead of using a text-only debugger, this one provides a graphical interface by bringing the full-fledged Google Chrome inspector to your Node app using a web browser.

You can install Node Inspector globally like this:

```
$ npm install -g node-inspector
```

Node Inspector runs as a daemon by default on port 8080. You can launch it like this:

```
$ node-inspector &
```

This sends the `node-inspector` process to the background.

Next you need to fire up your app, by using the `--debug` or `--debug-brk` option on the Node executable like this:

```
$ node --debug-brk my_app.js
```

The `--debug-brk` option makes your app break on the first line, whereas the `--debug` option simply enables debugging.

> **NOTE** *When debugging servers you should use* `--debug`, *and when debugging other scripts you might want to break on the first line by using* `--debug-brk`.

Now you can open your browser and point it to `http://localhost:8080`, and you should get something like the screen shown in Figure 18-1.

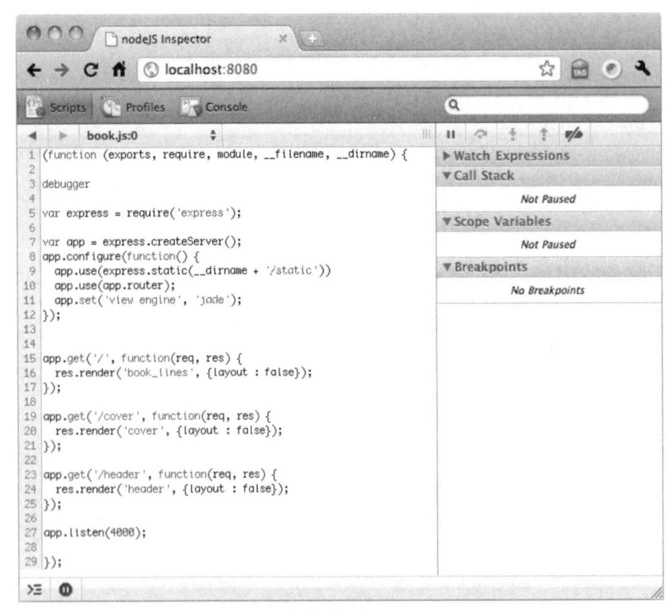

FIGURE 18-1: Start screen of Node Inspector.

You can set and unset breakpoints by clicking on the line numbers.

When a breakpoint is reached, your app freezes and Node Inspector shows the context, as shown in Figure 18-2.

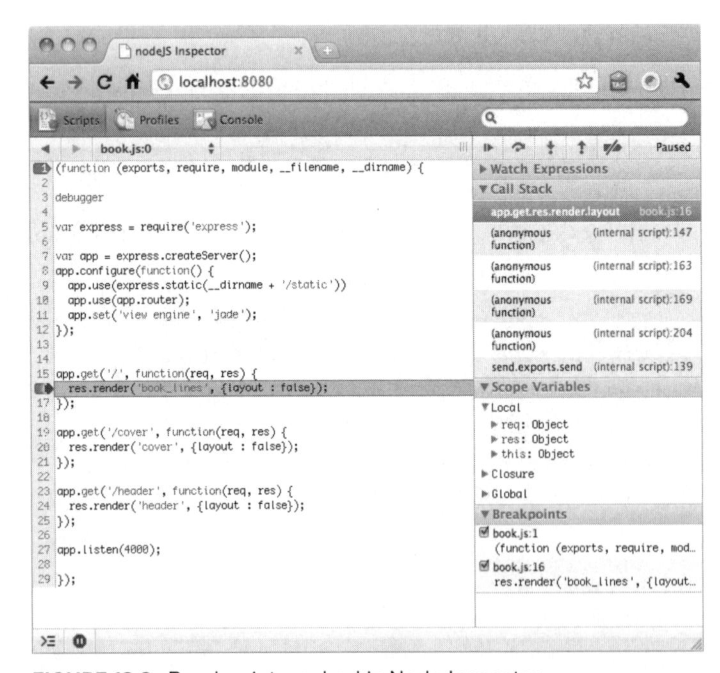

FIGURE 18-2: Breakpoint reached in Node Inspector.

You can see the two most interesting context panes on the right:

- The call stack, where you can see which functions were invoked to get to this point.
- The scope variables, where you can inspect the local variables, the global variables, and the closure variables, which are variables that are defined on a higher function scope.

Above those panes are some buttons that you can use to manipulate the executed instructions, as shown in Figures 18-3 through 18-6.

FIGURE 18-3: Fast-forward execution until a breakpoint is reached.

FIGURE 18-4: Execute this function and stop on the next line.

FIGURE 18-5: Step into this function.

FIGURE 18-6: Continue, and when this function ends return to the caller.

> **NOTE** *Live Edit describes the process whereby you change code while you are debugging. You simply double-click on a line of code and edit it. Change the code and press the Tab key or click outside the edit area. You just changed the running code!*
>
> *However, note that changing the code using Live Edit will not save the changes — use it only to test quick fixes.*

SUMMARY

You can use `console.log()` to output some state of your application to help you debug it. Using this function you can format and output variables to expose the state of your application.

If you have a more complex problem, you can use Node's built-in console debugger. If you prefer, you can use Node Inspector, which is a graphical alternative that uses a browser and provides some more complex options. Node Inspector also allows you to edit your code as you are debugging.

19

Controlling the Callback Flow

WHAT'S IN THIS CHAPTER?

- Understanding the boomerang effect
- Avoiding deeply nested callbacks
- Building an asynchronous flow control routine
- Using `async` to control callback flow
- Using `async` to iterate asynchronously

When Node is performing an asynchronous operation, the result of that operation is not communicated back using the function return value. Instead, asynchronous programming relies on callback functions that are usually passed in as arguments.

When you need to leave your process and do some I/O, most of the time you need to specify a callback function that gets invoked when that operation is finished.

If your task involves a lot of I/O operations, organizing the flow of callback functions can become difficult and may lead to a pattern that is sometimes called "callback soup" or the "boomerang effect."

UNDERSTANDING THE BOOMERANG EFFECT

The "boomerang effect" happens when a group of callbacks is executed in chain — when one I/O operation completes, the next operation starts. The name "boomerang" derives from the shape of your code when there are many nested callback functions. The increasing left indentation and the return of that indentation makes a boomerang-like shape.

To illustrate the boomerang effect, you'll build a script that appends bytes 0 to 10 from a file named `a.txt` into a file named `b.txt`. Both files exist in the current directory. Listing 19-1 shows an example of the boomerang effect.

LISTING 19-1: A demonstration of the boomerang effect.

```
var fs = require('fs');

function append_some_a_to_b(callback) {
  fs.open(__dirname + '/a.txt', 'r', function(err, aFd) {

    if (err) {
      return callback(err);
    }

    var buffer = new Buffer(10);

    fs.read(aFd, buffer, 0, buffer.length, 0, function(err) {

      if (err) {
        return callback(err);
      }

      fs.close(aFd, function(err) {

        if (err) {
          return callback(err);
        }

        fs.open(__dirname + '/b.txt', 'a', function(err, bFd) {

          if (err) {
            return callback(err);
          }

          fs.fstat(bFd, function(err, bStats) {

            if (err) {
              return callback(err);
            }

            fs.write(bFd, buffer, 0, buffer.length, bStats.size,
                     function(err) {
              if (err) {
                return callback(err);
              }

              fs.close(bFd, callback);

            });
          });

        });
      });
```

```
      });

    });
  }

  console.log('starting...');

  append_some_a_to_b(function(err) {

    if (err) {
      throw err;
    }

    console.log('done');
  });
```

Note that the function named `append_some_a_to_b`, which implements the callback flow for the task, places the declaration of the callback functions inline, which leads to this deeply nested code. To the untrained eye, code structured this way can be hard to read.

Worse yet, if you needed to conditionally perform some I/O before the final operation, structuring the code this way could lead to a lot of duplication.

> **NOTE** *Declaring the callback functions inline has at least one advantage, though. By visually placing the callback function code after you have started the I/O call, you get a better sense of the actual sequence of operations.*
>
> *As with most things in programming, this is not an all-or-nothing proposition — nested callbacks can sometimes make sense, as long as you don't abuse them.*

AVOIDING THE BOOMERANG EFFECT BY DECLARING FUNCTIONS

You can avoid the boomerang effect altogether by naming the functions and declaring them in the same scope. Listing 19-2 shows the previous example, but this time, the functions are named and declared in the same scope.

LISTING 19-2: Declaring named functions.

```
var fs = require('fs');

function append_some_a_to_b(callback) {

  var aFd, bFd,
      buffer = new Buffer(10);

  function open_a() {
    fs.open(__dirname + '/a.txt', 'r', read_from_a);
```

continues

LISTING 19-2 *(continued)*

```
}

function read_from_a(err, fd) {

  if (err) {
    return callback(err);
  }

  aFd = fd;
  fs.read(aFd, buffer, 0, buffer.length, 0, close_a);
}

function close_a(err) {

  if (err) {
    return callback(err);
  }

  fs.close(aFd, open_b);
}

function open_b(err) {

  if (err) {
    return callback(err);
  }

  fs.open(__dirname + '/b.txt', 'a', stat_b);
}

function stat_b(err, fd) {

  if (err) {
    return callback(err);
  }

  bFd = fd;
  fs.fstat(bFd, write_b);
}

function write_b(err, bStats) {

  if (err) {
    return callback(err);
  }

  fs.write(bFd, buffer, 0, buffer.length, bStats.size, close_b);
}

function close_b(err) {

  if (err) {
```

```
        return callback(err);
      }

      fs.close(bFd, callback);
    }

    open_a();

  }

  console.log('starting...');

  append_some_a_to_b(function(err) {

    if (err) {
      throw err;
    }

    console.log('done');
  });
```

Listing 19-2 declares all the functions inside the same scope. Using this technique you lose the closure nesting effect and now have to store the necessary values inside a scope that is above each function.

You may have noticed, though, that this code has at least two problems:

- Each function must know the name of the next function in the flow.
- You always have to deal with the errors, which means there is a lot of repetitive code.

Because you are chaining all the callbacks, you can make this code more generic and flexible, as shown in Listing 19-3.

LISTING 19-3: Using a generic flow control mechanism.

```
var fs = require('fs');

function cascade(callbacks, callback) {

  // clone the array
  var functions = callbacks.slice(0);

  function processNext(err) {

    if (err) {
      return callback(err);
    }

    var args = Array.prototype.slice.call(arguments);

    var func = functions.shift();
    if (func) {
```

continues

LISTING 19-3 *(continued)*

```
        // remove first argument containing the error
        args.shift();
      } else {
        func = callback;
      }

      args.push(processNext);

      func.apply(this, args);
    }

    processNext.call(this);

  }


  function append_some_a_to_b(callback) {

    var aFd, bFd,
        buffer = new Buffer(10);

    cascade([
      function open_a(next) {
        fs.open(__dirname + '/a.txt', 'r', next);
      },

      function read_from_a(fd, next) {
        aFd = fd;
        fs.read(aFd, buffer, 0, buffer.length, 0, next);
      },

      function close_a(bytesRead, buf, next) {
        fs.close(aFd, next);
      },

      function open_b(next) {
        fs.open(__dirname + '/b.txt', 'a', next);
      },

      function stat_b(fd, next) {
        bFd = fd;
        fs.fstat(bFd, next);
      },

      function write_b(bStats, next) {
        fs.write(bFd, buffer, 0, buffer.length, bStats.size, next);
      },

      function close_b(bytesWritten, buf, next) {
        fs.close(bFd, next);
      }
    ], callback);
```

```
};

console.log('starting...');

append_some_a_to_b(function done(err) {

  if (err) {
    throw err;
  }

  console.log('done');
});
```

Listing 19-3 declares a function named `cascade` that takes two arguments. The first argument contains all the callback functions that should be invoked. The second argument contains a final callback function to be called when all the callbacks are done or in case of an error.

This `cascade` function will invoke the callbacks, one by one, passing in the `processNext` function as the last argument for each callback. This way, each callback function does not have to know which function to call next.

Then, the `append_some_a_to_b` function calls the cascade function with the list of callback functions, plus a final callback function.

USING THE ASYNC FLOW CONTROL LIBRARY

Sometimes, as in the previous example, you can roll your own generic flow control routines. However, many third-party modules can simplify this and other asynchronous patterns. One of these is a module called `async`.

To install `async` you include it in your `package.json` manifest or simply install it on your application root directory like this:

```
$ npm install async
```

The `async` module comes with a series of helper functions that allow you to perform asynchronous iteration and flow control.

For example, Listing 19-4 implements an HTTP server that returns the square of the number you give it.

LISTING 19-4: A simple squaring server.

```
var port = process.argv[2] && parseInt(process.argv[2], 10) || 8080;

require('http').createServer(function(req, res) {

  var body = '';

  req.setEncoding('utf8');

  req.on('data', function(data) {
```

continues

LISTING 19-4 *(continued)*

```
      body += data;
    });

    req.once('end', function() {
      var number = JSON.parse(body);
      var squared = Math.pow(number, 2);
      res.end(JSON.stringify(squared));
    });

}).listen(port, function() {
  console.log('Squaring Server listening on port %d', port);
});
```

You can save this script into a file named `server.js` and start it by using the following:

```
$ node server.js
Squaring Server listening on port 8080
```

The next sections will cover several useful helper functions in the `async` library.

Executing in Series

You can execute a series of functions that return their results asynchronously. Use the squaring server code from Listing 19-4 to learn how to use `async` to execute asynchronous functions in series.

First, for these examples, you need to install the `request` third-party module, as follows:

```
$ npm install request
```

Listing 19-5 shows an example of how you can chain the execution of two I/O operations using the `async.series` helper function.

LISTING 19-5: Async.series example.

```
var async   = require('async'),
    request = require('request');

function done(err, results) {
  if (err) {
    throw err;
  }
  console.log('results: %j', results);
}

async.series([

  function(next) {
    request.post({uri: 'http://localhost:8080', body: '4'},
      function(err, res, body) {
```

```
          next(err, body && JSON.parse(body));
        }
      );
    },

    function(next) {
      request.post({uri: 'http://localhost:8080', body: '5'},
        function(err, res, body) {
          next(err, body && JSON.parse(body));
        }
      );

    }

  ], done);
```

This listing performs two calls. The calls are similar, but one passes the `body` value of `4` and the other one the `body` value of `5`.

You can save the script into a file named `series.js` and run it:

```
$ node series.js
results: [16,25]
```

The `done` callback is invoked after all the functions are terminated with the asynchronous result of each function. In this case, the results contain the output of each call to the squaring server, which contains the square value of 4 and 5.

Executing in Parallel

In the previous example, the calls were performed one after another. However, these calls can also be done in parallel. For that, you simply need to change the `async.series` call to a `async.parallel` call, as shown in Listing 19-6.

LISTING 19-6: Async.parallel example.

```
var async   = require('async'),
    request = require('request');

function done(err, results) {
  if (err) {
    throw err;
  }
  console.log('results: %j', results);
}

async.parallel([

  function(next) {
    request.post({uri: 'http://localhost:8080', body: '4'},
      function(err, res, body) {
```

continues

LISTING 19-6 *(continued)*

```
        next(err, body && JSON.parse(body));
      }
    );
  },

  function(next) {
    request.post({uri: 'http://localhost:8080', body: '5'},
      function(err, res, body) {
        next(err, body && JSON.parse(body));
      }
    );

  }

], done);
```

If you save this into a file named `parallel.js` and run it, you will get the same results:

```
$ node parallel.js
results: [16,25]
```

Cascading

You can also execute a series of functions where the execution of the next callback depends on the result of the previous one. For instance, say that you want to calculate 3^4 using the squaring HTTP server. You can easily do this using the `async.waterfall` function, as shown in Listing 19-7.

LISTING 19-7: Cascading using async.waterfall.

```
var async   = require('async'),
    request = require('request');

function done(err, res, body) {
  if (err) {
    throw err;
  }

  console.log("3^4 = %d", body);
}

async.waterfall([

  function(next) {
    request.post({uri: 'http://localhost:8080', body: "3"}, next)
  },

  function(res, body, next) {
    request.post({uri: 'http://localhost:8080', body: body}, next);
  }

], done);
```

You can see that each callback gets all the callback arguments of the last operation, minus the first error argument. If an error occurs, the final callback (which is named `done` in this case) gets called with an error in the same argument.

Queuing

If you need to perform some repetitive asynchronous jobs and you want to control the *concurrency* — the maximum number of pending jobs that exist at any given time — you can use the `async.queue` function.

This function lets you create a queue that will process elements based on a function. The clients of the queue can push work into it, and a maximum number of concurrent workers perform each of them in order.

Listing 19-8 creates a queue to calculate the square value of a number using the squaring server.

LISTING 19-8: Using async.queue.

```
var async   = require('async'),
    request = require('request');

function done(err, results) {
  if (err) {
    throw err;
  }
  console.log('results: %j', results);
}

var maximumConcurrency = 5;

function worker(task, callback) {
  request.post({uri: 'http://localhost:8080',
                body: JSON.stringify(task)},
    function(err, res, body) {
      callback(err, body && JSON.parse(body));
    }
  );
}

var queue = async.queue(worker, maximumConcurreny);

[1, 2, 3, 4, 5, 6, 7, 8, 9, 10].forEach(function(i) {

  queue.push(i, function(err, result) {

    if (err) {
      throw err;
    }

    console.log(i + '^2 = %d', result);

  });
});
```

This listing declares a function named `worker` that receives a task and processes it. In this case, the task is a number and the worker is calling the squaring server to obtain the square value of this number.

The code then creates a queue based on the `worker` function and defines a maximum concurrency. The maximum concurrency is set to 5 in this example, but it's an arbitrary value and you should define it for your own cases.

Then the example pushes 10 jobs as numbers 1 through 10 into the queue by using `queue.push`. This function accepts a callback to receive the result of this job once the job is done.

You can run this script by saving it into a file named `queue.js` and running it:

```
$ node queue.js
5^2 = 25
1^2 = 1
2^2 = 4
3^2 = 9
4^2 = 16
6^2 = 36
10^2 = 100
8^2 = 64
9^2 = 81
7^2 = 49
```

> **NOTE** *You can see here that the results are not in the order you placed them. That's the nature of asynchronicity: The results are shown in the order in which they finish. If you want to order the results, you should use* `async.forEach` *or a similar function — which is covered later in this chapter.*

One of the nice things about using a queue is that it limits the number of concurrent requests. You can use it to limit concurrent access to some resources like a database, preventing flooding, and so on. But how can you determine and adapt the optimal maximum concurrency? Determining it depends on your application. The maximum concurrency can be, for instance, a function of the observed latency, or it can be provided by an external setting. Any way you do this, it's good to know that you can change the maximum concurrency after the queue is created by changing the `concurrency` property on the queue:

```
queue.concurrency = 10;
```

A queue also emits some events regarding its state. You can know when a queue has reached the maximum concurrency limit — and further tasks have to wait to start — by plugging a function into the queue's `saturated` property, like this:

```
queue.saturated = function() {
  console.log('queue is saturated');
};
```

Likewise, you can know when the last item in the queue is given to a worker by listening to the `empty` event like this:

```
queue.empty = function() {
  console.log('queue is empty');
};
```

When the worker returns the last work in the queue, the queue emits the `drain` event:

```
queue.drain = function() {
  console.log('queue is drained, no more work!');
};
```

This event and others can be emitted many times throughout the lifetime of a queue, because you can add jobs to a queue at any point in the future.

Iterating

JavaScript has some nice functions for synchronously iterating over collections. `async` provides some of these functions but with asynchronous semantics. For example, in JavaScript, if you have an array, you can use `array.forEach` to iterate over it:

```
[1, 2, 3, 4].forEach(function(i) {
  var squared = Math.pow(i, 2);
  console.log('%d ^ 2 is %d', i, squared);
});
```

If, instead of using a synchronous function, you need to perform some I/O based on the value of each element, this approach doesn't work.

You can use `async.forEach` to iterate asynchronously over a collection of objects, as shown in Listing 19-9.

LISTING 19-9: Iterating over a collection using async.forEach.

```
var async   = require('async'),
    request = require('request');

var results = {};

function done(err) {
  if (err) {
    throw err;
  }
  console.log('done! results: %j', results);
}

var collection = [1, 2, 3, 4];

function iterator(value, callback) {
  request.post({
      uri: 'http://localhost:8080',
      body: JSON.stringify(value)
    },
```

continues

LISTING 19-9 *(continued)*

```
      function(err, res, body) {
        if (err) {
          return callback(err);
        }
        results[value] = JSON.parse(body);
        callback();
      });
  }

  async.forEach(collection, iterator, done);
```

This example defines an `iterator` function that you use in `async.forEach`. This function will take an element, perform the required I/O, and call the callback when it's done. When asynchronous iteration over all of the elements is complete, the final callback (called `done` in this example) is called.

If you use this `async.forEach` function, you are invoking an iterator for each element in parallel. If you want `async` to wait for the completion of one iteration before starting the next, you can use `async.forEachSeries`. In this case you can simply replace the last line in the previous listing with the following:

```
async.forEachSeries(collection, iterator, done);
```

You can also do the calls in parallel, but control the maximum concurrency. By using `async.forEachLimit`, you can set the maximum number of pending iterators at any given time. In this case, you replace the last line in the previous listing with the following:

```
var maximumConcurrency = 5;
async.forEachLimit(collection, maximumConcurrency, iterator, done);
```

Mapping

JavaScript also provides an `array.map()` function for synchronously iterating over all elements, gathering the results.

You can use `async.map` to make the same thing, but asynchronously, as shown in Listing 19-10.

LISTING 19-10: Mapping a collection using async.map.

```
var async   = require('async'),
    request = require('request');

var collection = [1, 2, 3, 4];

function done(err, results) {
  if (err) {
    throw err;
  }
  console.log('done! results: %j', results);
}
```

```
function iterator(value, callback) {
  request.post({
      uri: 'http://localhost:8080',
      body: JSON.stringify(value)
    },

    function(err, res, body) {
      callback(err, body && JSON.parse(body));
    });
}

async.map(collection, iterator, done);
```

This example is similar to the previous one, except that you don't have to manually gather the results — you just have to pass each result to the callback inside the iterator function. Each iteration can take an arbitrary amount of time to complete, but `async.map` provides the results to the `done` callback function in the correct order when all of them are finished.

Reducing

JavaScript also has an `array.reduce` function that takes an initial value and an iterator function and returns a new value that is fed into the next iteration alongside the new element.

For instance, a typical use of the `reduce` function is to sum elements:

```
var collection = [1, 2, 3, 4];
function iterator(sum, elem) {
  return sum + elem;
}
var sum = collection.reduce(iterator, 0);
console.log('sum is %d', sum);
```

The `async.reduce` function offers these same semantics, but for asynchronous iterators. For instance, if you wanted to sum the square value of all elements in a collection using the squaring server, you can use the code in Listing 19-11 to do so.

LISTING 19-11: Reducing a collection asynchronously using async.reduce.

```
var async   = require('async'),
    request = require('request');

var collection = [1, 2, 3, 4];

function done(err, result) {
  if (err) {
    throw err;
  }
  console.log('The sum of the squares of %j is %d', collection, result);
}

function iterator(memo, item, callback) {
  request.post({
```

continues

LISTING 19-11 *(continued)*

```
        uri: 'http://localhost:8080',
        body: JSON.stringify(item)
      },

      function(err, res, body) {
        callback(err, body && (memo + JSON.parse(body)));
      });
  }

  async.reduce(collection, 0, iterator, done);
```

Like the synchronous `array.reduce` version, `async.reduce` takes the initial value as the second argument, which in this case is 0. Then it goes on to call the iterator on each element of the collection, one at a time, passing the new `memo` value into a callback when the operation is finished. In this case the new `memo` value is the squared value of the element, plus whatever the `memo` value was.

Filtering

In JavaScript you can also filter a collection based on a filtering function like this:

```
var collection = [1, 2, 3, 4];
function isEven(value) {
  return value % 2 === 0;
}
var evenElements = collection.filter(isEven);
console.log('even elements of %j are: %j', collection, evenElements);
```

This last example filters a collection of numbers and returns the even ones.

The `async.filter` function behaves similarly for asynchronous operations. You can, for instance, use the squaring server to filter all the elements whose square value is greater than 10, as shown in Listing 19-12.

LISTING 19-12: Using async.filter.

```
var async   = require('async'),
    request = require('request');

var collection = [1, 2, 3, 4, 5];

function done(results) {
  console.log('These are the elements of %j whose ' +
              'square value is greater than 10: %j', collection, results);
}

function test(value) {
  return value > 10;
}

function filter(item, callback) {
```

```
    request.post({
        uri: 'http://localhost:8080',
        body: JSON.stringify(item)
      },

      function(err, res, body) {
        if (err) {
          throw err;
        }
        callback(body && test(JSON.parse(body)));
      });
}

async.filter(collection, filter, done);
```

The `filter` function has to call the callback with a boolean stating whether that value should remain or not. You can see that the `filter` function has to call the callback with the boolean value as the first argument. If there is an error in the filtering function, you have to handle it yourself.

`async` also provides the inverse function, which is named `reject`. By changing `async.filter` to `async.reject` on the last line of the previous listing, you can filter all numbers whose square value is less than or equal to 10.

The `async.filter` and `async.reject` functions invoke the `filter` function for each element in parallel. Async provides a serialized version of these functions:

```
async.filterSeries(collection, filter, done);
```

and

```
async.rejectSeries(collection, filter, done);
```

Using any of these functions, you will have at most one `filter` function pending at any given time.

Detecting

You might want to stop iterating when you have reached a certain point. For example, you might want to detect the first value in a collection whose squared value is greater than 10. Listing 19-13 shows how to do this.

LISTING 19-13: Using async.detect.

```
var async   = require('async'),
    request = require('request');

var collection = [1, 2, 3, 4, 5];

function done(result) {
  console.log('The first element on %j whose square value '+
              'is greater than 10: %j', collection, result);
}
```

continues

LISTING 19-13 *(continued)*

```
function test(value) {
  return value > 10;
}

function detect(item, callback) {
  request.post({
      uri: 'http://localhost:8080',
      body: JSON.stringify(item)
    },

    function(err, res, body) {
      if (err) {
        throw err;
      }
      callback(body && test(JSON.parse(body)));
    });
}

async.detect(collection, detect, done);
```

Here, `async.detect` invokes the `detect` function in parallel for each element, which means that you might not get the first item in the list that meets the criteria — it depends on the order in which the asynchronous operations finish.

If order is important to you or you just want to have one pending active operation at any given time, you can use the serialized version of this function: `async.detectSeries`. You can replace the last line of the listing with the following:

```
async.detectSeries(collection, detect, done);
```

Here, `async.detectSeries` invokes the `detect` function and waits for it to finish. Then, if the element fails the detection test, `async.detectSeries` goes on to the next element until one is detected or until there are no more elements.

SUMMARY

It can be difficult to control asynchronous flow, and it can easily lead to poorly structured code. One way to avoid these issues is to declare callbacks as named functions beforehand and avoid nesting them.

You can also create a generic flow-control routine or use one of the many provided by the `async` third-party module. Using them, you can perform function calls in series or in parallel, or you can iterate over a collection in an asynchronous fashion. This chapter covered some of the most commonly used functions, but `async` provides more than these. If you're interested, check out the official `async` documentation at

```
https://github.com/caolan/async#readme
```

PART V
Building Web Applications

20

Building and Using HTTP Middleware

WHAT'S IN THIS CHAPTER?

- Understanding how Connect works
- Making Connect-compatible middleware
- Making a middleware component that handles errors
- Using some of the built-in middleware components bundled in Connect
- Serving static files using Connect middleware
- Parsing query string, request body, and cookies
- Maintaining a session

Node is particularly fit to be an HTTP server. It has a great HTTP parser and can efficiently handle many concurrent connections in one single process.

When you are building an HTTP application server, you usually need it to perform some routine tasks like parsing the cookie headers, parsing the query string on the request URL, maintaining and associating a session, persisting session data, serving static files, parsing the request body, logging the request and response, and others. When coding the core logic of your application, you shouldn't have to explicitly perform these tasks; these should be handled by the HTTP server application logic.

Some of these tasks involve inspecting the request — headers or body — others involve inspecting and changing the response, and some involve both. An example of where you may want to do both is when you want to log the details of each incoming request together with the respective response HTTP status code. In this case you need to inspect both the request and the response objects. You may also want to set or change the response headers, as is the case of when you are maintaining a session ID using browser cookies.

In typical HTTP application frameworks like Django, Cake, Rails, or Sinatra, components generally called *middleware* perform these tasks. These middleware components wrap the request-response cycle, extending the request object before your application code is reached or changing the response before or after it.

UNDERSTANDING THE CONNECT HTTP MIDDLEWARE FRAMEWORK

Node also includes some frameworks that ease the development of an HTTP-based application. One of the most popular is called *Connect*. Connect defines a model for middleware components and an engine to run them.

In general, middleware components are pieces that the programmer can stack together. When Connect receives an HTTP request, the middleware engine calls each of these components in order. Any of these components has access to the request object, which means that they can parse some headers and buffer and parse the request body. They can also change the response headers, write a part of the body, or end the response.

Connect comes bundled with a series of middleware components, but you can easily build your own.

BUILDING YOUR OWN HTTP MIDDLEWARE

As you will see, a middleware component is not much more than a function that receives the request and response objects, much like the standard Node HTTP server `request` listener. To run an example of a simple middleware component, you need to first install the `connect` module inside a working directory you choose:

```
$ npm install connect
```

Listing 20-1 shows a simple middleware component that responds with the string `"Hello World!"` and ends the response.

LISTING 20-1: A simple HelloWorld middleware.

```
function helloWorld(req, res) {
  res.end('Hello World!');
}

module.exports = helloWorld;
```

You can save this code listing as a local file named `hello_world.js` to be used later.

This middleware component simply exports a function that will be called by Connect to handle new requests. This function writes the string `"Hello World"` into the body and then ends the request.

You can test this middleware component by creating a Connect server, as shown in Listing 20-2.

LISTING 20-2: A Connect server that uses the HelloWorld middleware.

```
var connect = require('connect');

// import middlewares
var helloWorld = require('./hello_world');

var app = connect.createServer(helloWorld);
app.listen(8080);
```

Here you are creating a Connect HTTP server and initializing it with the `HelloWorld` middleware component. Save this listing as a file named `hello_world_app.js` and run it:

```
$ node hello_world_app
```

Point your browser to `http://localhost:8080`, and you will see the `"Hello World!"` response rendered.

You can also create a more generic component that responds with any optional text, as shown in Listing 20-3.

LISTING 20-3: A more generic ReplyText middleware.

```
function replyText(text) {
  return function(req, res) {
    res.end(text);
  };
}

module.exports = replyText;
```

Instead of directly exporting a function that handles the request, this middleware component exports a function that, when invoked, returns a function that replies with a custom text string.

You can change the server code to use this more generic component to behave the same way, as shown in Listing 20-4.

LISTING 20-4: A Connect server that uses the ReplyText middleware.

```
var connect = require('connect');

// import middlewares
var replyText = require('./reply_text');

var app = connect.createServer(replyText('Hello World!'));
app.listen(8080);
```

Save this listing as a file named `hello_world_app_v2.js` and run it:

```
$ node hello_world_app_v2
```

By pointing your browser to `http://localhost:8080`, you should see the `"Hello World!"` response rendered again.

Creating Asynchronous Middleware

A middleware function can be asynchronous: When the work is done, it needs to call a callback for the middleware engine to continue to do its work. The previous example didn't use this feature because it just ended the response without handing over control to the next middleware in line.

To practice, you can create a middleware component that introduces a header into the response header section, as shown in Listing 20-5.

LISTING 20-5: A Connect middleware that writes a header.

```
function writeHeader(name, value) {
  return function(req, res, next) {
    res.setHeader(name, value);
    next();
  };
}

module.exports = writeHeader;
```

This middleware component uses a third argument that contains the callback to be invoked when this component is done.

Save this listing as a file named `write_header.js`.

You can now incorporate this middleware component into your HelloWorld app by including it in the middleware stack you pass into the server constructor, right before the ReplyText middleware, as shown in Listing 20-6.

LISTING 20-6: Including the WriteHeader middleware in the HelloWorld app.

```
var connect = require('connect');

// import middlewares
var writeHeader = require('./write_header');
var replyText = require('./reply_text');

var app = connect.createServer(
  writeHeader('X-Powered-By', 'Node'),
  replyText('Hello World!')
);

app.listen(8080);
```

You can save this listing as a file named `hello_world_app_v3.js` and run it.

```
$ node  hello_world_app_v3
```

You can then run a command-line utility to make an HTTP request where you can inspect the headers like *curl*:

```
$ curl -i http://localhost:8080HTTP/1.1 200 OK
X-Powered-By: Node
Connection: keep-alive
Transfer-Encoding: chunked

Hello World!
```

Here you can see that the header is written out into the response as expected.

Here it's important that the middleware that writes the header is inserted before the middleware that writes and ends the response. If you placed the `ReplyText` middleware first, the second middleware would never be called because `ReplyText` does not invoke the "next" callback.

Registering Callbacks Inside Middleware

Besides inspecting the request and changing the response, middleware components can register some callbacks to be executed later. As an example, you can create one that saves all the data of each request into a file (see Listing 20-7).

LISTING 20-7: A middleware that saves every request into a file.

```
var fs = require('fs'),
  path = require('path'),
  util = require('util');

function saveRequest(dir) {

  return function(req, res, next) {

    var fileName = path.join(dir, Date.now().toString() + '_' +
      Math.floor(Math.random() * 100000) + '.txt');
    var file = fs.createWriteStream(fileName);
    file.write(req.method + ' ' + req.url + '\n');
    file.write(util.inspect(req.headers) + '\n');
    req.pipe(file);
    next();
  }
}

module.exports = saveRequest;
```

For every request this middleware component gets, it creates a new file inside a specified directory and saves all the headers into it. Then, it pipes the request into that file. No part of the request body is written out at this time. The data and other event listeners are set up so that when future data arrives, that data is sent into the file writable stream.

Now you can modify the server to include this middleware component, as shown in Listing 20-8.

LISTING 20-8: This HelloWorld server includes the SaveRequest middleware.

```
var connect = require('connect');

// import middlewares
var saveRequest = require('./save_request');
var writeHeader = require('./write_header');
var replyText = require('./reply_text');

var app = connect.createServer(
  saveRequest(__dirname + '/requests'),
  writeHeader('X-Powered-By', 'Node'),
  replyText('Hello World!')
);

app.listen(8080);
```

Here you are commanding the `SaveRequest` middleware to save all the requests into a directory named `requests`, under the local directory. You can save this code listing into a file named `hello_world_app_v4.js` and create the directory for storing the requests:

```
$ mkdir requests
```

Now you can start the server:

```
$ node hello_world_app_v4
```

You can then feed the server with a local file using *`curl`*:

```
$ curl -T hello_world_app_v4.js http://localhost:8080
```

This command is telling `curl` to upload the file into this URL. After this command is done, you can look in the `requests` directory. There should be a file similar to "1340373961878_15062.txt" that contains something like the following:

```
PUT /hello_world_app_v4.js
{ 'user-agent': 'curl/7.21.4 (universal-apple-darwin11.0) libcurl/7.21.4
OpenSSL/0.9.8r zlib/1.2.5',
  host: 'localhost:8080',
  accept: '*/*',
  'content-length': '349',
  expect: '100-continue' }

var connect = require('connect');

// import middlewares
var saveRequest = require('./save_request');
var writeHeader = require('./write_header');
var replyText = require('./reply_text');
```

```
var app = connect.createServer(
  saveRequest(__dirname + '/requests'),
  writeHeader('X-Powered-By', 'Node'),
  replyText('Hello World!')
);
```

As expected, this file contains the HTTP method, the URL, the headers, and the request body.

Handling Errors Inside Middleware

A middleware component can also handle errors. To test one of these, first you must create a "faulty" middleware component that throws an error, as shown in Listing 20-9.

LISTING 20-9: A middleware component that throws an error.

```
function errorCreator() {
  return function(req, res, next) {
    throw new Error('This is an error');
  }
}

module.exports = errorCreator;
```

This component just throws an exception back into the stack. You can do this because Connect catches the exceptions and hands it to the next middleware error handler. But if you are inside a callback and you catch an error, you should call the "next" callback with the error as the first argument, as shown in Listing 20-10.

LISTING 20-10: Another middleware component that throws an error.

```
function errorCreator() {
  return function(req, res, next) {
    next(new Error('This is an error'));
  }
}

module.exports = errorCreator;
```

By default, if no middleware is set up to handle errors, Connect will present the error trace in plaintext. You can try this by including the error creator middleware, as shown in Listing 20-11.

LISTING 20-11: A server with a middleware that throws an error.

```
var connect = require('connect');

// import middlewares
var errorCreator = require('./error_creator');
var saveRequest  = require('./save_request');
```

continues

LISTING 20-11 *(continued)*

```
var writeHeader  = require('./write_header');
var replyText    = require('./reply_text');

var app = connect.createServer(
  errorCreator(),
  saveRequest(__dirname + '/requests'),
  writeHeader('X-Powered-By', 'Node'),
  replyText('Hello World!')
);

app.listen(8080);
```

Save this listing as a file named `hello_world_app_v5.js` and run it:

```
$ node  hello_world_app_v5
```

Refresh the browser. You should get an error similar to this one:

```
Error: This is an error
    at Object.handle (/Users/pedroteixeira/projects/wiley-node/code/20/error_creato
r.js:3:10)
    at next (/Users/pedroteixeira/projects/wiley-node/code/20/node_modules/connect/
lib/proto.js:190:15)
    at Function.handle (/Users/pedroteixeira/projects/wiley-node/code/20/node_modul
es/connect/lib/proto.js:198:3)
    at Server.app (/Users/pedroteixeira/projects/wiley-node/code/20/node_modules/co
nnect/lib/connect.js:66:31)
    at Server.emit (events.js:70:17)
    at HTTPParser.onIncoming (http.js:1514:12)
    at HTTPParser.onHeadersComplete (http.js:102:31)
    at Socket.ondata (http.js:1410:22)
    at TCP.onread (net.js:374:27)
```

Now you can build your custom error handler. Error handlers in Connect must take four arguments — the error, the request, the response, and the "next" callback (see Listing 20-12).

LISTING 20-12: An error handling middleware.

```
function errorHandler() {
  return function(err, req, res, next) {
    if (err) {
      res.writeHead(500, {'Content-Type': 'text/html'});
      res.end('<h1>Oh no! We have an error!</h1>\n<pre>' + err.stack + '</pre>');
    } else {
      next();
    }
  }
}

module.exports = errorHandler;
```

You can save this listing as a file named error_handler.js.

This error handler formats the error and outputs it as HTML. Now you can integrate this middleware into the server by placing it in the last position, as shown in Listing 20-13.

LISTING 20-13: An application with a custom error handler.

```
var connect = require('connect');

// import middlewares
var errorCreator = require('./error_creator');
var saveRequest  = require('./save_request');
var writeHeader  = require('./write_header');
var replyText    = require('./reply_text');
var errorHandler = require('./error_handler');

var app = connect.createServer(
  errorCreator(),
  saveRequest(__dirname + '/requests'),
  writeHeader('X-Powered-By', 'Node'),
  replyText('Hello World!'),
  errorHandler()
);

app.listen(8080);
```

You can save this listing as a file named hello_world_app_v6.js and run it:

```
$ node  hello_world_app_v6
```

If you refresh the browser, you will get an HTML output of the error. You can also use the *curl* command-line utility to inspect the response:

```
$ curl http://localhost:8080
HTTP/1.1 500 Internal Server Error
Content-Type: text/html
Connection: keep-alive
Transfer-Encoding: chunked

<h1>Oh no! We have an error!</h1>
<pre>Error: This is an error
    at Object.handle (/Users/pedroteixeira/projects/wiley-node/code/20/error_creato
r.js:3:10)
    at next (/Users/pedroteixeira/projects/wiley-node/code/20/node_modules/connect/
lib/proto.js:190:15)
    at Function.handle (/Users/pedroteixeira/projects/wiley-node/code/20/node_modul
es/connect/lib/proto.js:198:3)
    at Server.app (/Users/pedroteixeira/projects/wiley-node/code/20/node_modules/co
nnect/lib/connect.js:66:31)
    at Server.emit (events.js:70:17)
    at HTTPParser.onIncoming (http.js:1514:12)
    at HTTPParser.onHeadersComplete (http.js:102:31)
    at Socket.ondata (http.js:1410:22)
    at TCP.onread (net.js:374:27)</pre>
```

Here you can see that the header does not contain the custom "X-Powered-By" entry. This is because when an error happens, Connect executes the first error-handling middleware in the next middleware components, skipping all the other "normal" middleware components.

In fact, Connect only executes error-handling middleware components when there is an error, which means that you can reduce the error-handling middleware, as shown in Listing 20-14.

LISTING 20-14: A simplified error-handling middleware component.

```
function errorHandler() {
  return function(err, req, res, next) {
    res.writeHead(500, {'Content-Type': 'text/html'});
    res.end('<h1>Oh no! We have an error!</h1>\n<pre>' + err.stack + '</pre>');
  }
}

module.exports = errorHandler;
```

USING THE HTTP MIDDLEWARE BUNDLED IN CONNECT

Connect not only lets you fabricate and use HTTP middleware components but also comes with a set of some commonly used ones. You can pick and choose which ones fit the requirements of your application, customizing your stack, and perhaps mixing in some of your own with these generic middleware components.

Logging Requests

Connect has a middleware component for logging some request and response data. You can simply use it, as shown in Listing 20-15.

LISTING 20-15: Using a logger middleware.

```
var connect = require('connect');

var app = connect();

// setup logger middleware
app.use(connect.logger());

// actually respond
app.use(function(req, res) {
  res.end('Hello World!');
});

app.listen(8080);
```

> **NOTE** *You see here that you are using an alternative syntax for creating the server and attaching the middleware. Here you're creating the server by invoking the module function directly and then adding middleware to it by using the* `.use()` *method. This is an alternative to the previous syntax you saw, which can be more convenient because it doesn't require you to pass all the middleware components at the time of creation.*

You can save this code listing as a file named `logger.js` and run it like this:

```
$ node logger
```

Now, if you point your browser to `http://localhost:8080`, you will observe something like this in your server output:

```
127.0.0.1 - - [Sat, 23 Jun 2012 15:23:07 GMT] "GET / HTTP/1.1" 200 - "-" "Mozilla/5
.0 (Macintosh; Intel Mac OS X 10_7_4) AppleWebKit/536.5
(KHTML, like Gecko) Chrome/19.
0.1084.56 Safari/536.5"
127.0.0.1 - - [Sat, 23 Jun 2012 15:23:08 GMT] "GET /favicon.ico HTTP/1.1" 200 - "-"
"Mozilla/5.0 (Macintosh; Intel Mac OS X 10_7_4) AppleWebKit/536.5
(KHTML, like Gecko
) Chrome/19.0.1084.56 Safari/536.5"
```

You can see that your server is outputting some request and response details. You will probably see that the server is outputting two requests. This is because the browser also requests the `/favicon.ico` URL, looking for a favorite icon to show in the URL bar.

Here you can also see that the logger is outputting the remote client address, followed by the current date, the HTTP method, the HTTP version, the response status code, the response content length, the referrer, and the user agent string. This is the default format of the logging statement, and you can change it at will. You can choose to log almost every element available on the request (and you'll soon see how), but there are some predefined shortcuts for the short and tiny formats. You need to specify the format when creating the middleware component:

```
app.use(connect.logger('tiny'));
```

If you change the format to tiny and restart the server, it will output something like:

```
GET / 200 - - - ms
GET /favicon.ico 200 - - 2 ms
```

This format will output the HTTP method, URL, HTTP status code, content length header (not present in this case), and response time.

You can choose a more verbose output than the "short" one, which will output something like the following:

```
127.0.0.1 - GET / HTTP/1.1 200 - - - ms
127.0.0.1 - GET /favicon.ico HTTP/1.1 200 - - 1 ms
```

It adds the remote address and the HTTP version.

You can also define your own custom format by specifying a string containing any of the following tokens:

- `:req[header]` — You can specify any request header, such as `:req[Accept]`. You can also output as many headers as you want throughout the format string.
- `:http-version` — The HTTP version.
- `:response-time` — The difference between the time the request reaches the logger and the time when the request is ended, in milliseconds.
- `:remote-addr` — The remote IP address of the client making the request.
- `:date` — The formatted date of when the log was created.
- `:method` — The HTTP method (`GET`, `PUT`, `DELETE`, `HEAD`, and so on).
- `:url` — The requested URL.
- `:referrer` — The content of the referrer header.
- `:user-agent` — The user agent string.
- `:status` — The numeric HTTP response status code.

For instance, if you want to output only the method, URL, status code, and response time, you can use the following format:

```
var format = ':method :url - :status - :response-time ms';
app.use(connect.logger(format));
```

Handling Errors

Connect comes with a more elaborate error handler. One of its capabilities is using content negotiation to understand what output is best. For instance, if the client accepts the text/html content type, it outputs the content as HTML. If the client accepts `application/json`, it will output the error as a JSON-encoded object containing the `error` and `stack` properties. If any of these content types is not supported by the client, the error handler outputs the error as plaintext.

You can use this error handler middleware by adding it to the server, as shown in Listing 20-16.

LISTING 20-16: Using the Connect error handler.

```
var connect = require('connect');

var app = connect();

app.use(function(req, res, next) {
  next(new Error('Hey!'));
});

// actually respond
```

```
app.use(function(req, res) {
  res.end('Hello World!');
});

app.use(connect.errorHandler());

app.listen(8080);
```

Here you are provoking an error and setting up the error handler middleware at the end of the middleware stack. If you save this listing as a file named `errorHandler.js`, you can run it like this:

```
$ node errorHandler
```

If you refresh your browser, you will see a formatted HTML page containing the title `Connect`, the error message, and the error trace. You can change the title by setting the `errorHandler` title property and introducing a line of code like this:

```
connect.errorHandler.title = 'My Application';
```

Serving Static Files

An HTTP application usually needs to serve some static assets like CSS, JavaScript, images, and HTML files. Connect already has a middleware component that provides this function (see Listing 20-17).

LISTING 20-17: Using the Connect static server middleware.

```
var connect = require('connect');

var app = connect();

// setup the static file server
app.use(connect.static(__dirname + '/public'));

// actually respond
app.use(function(req, res) {
  res.end('Hello World!');
});

app.listen(8080);
```

Here you are saying that the static file server should look for files under the `public` directory. If a file is found, that file is served, and the middleware chain is interrupted.

Now you can create a directory named `public` inside the current folder and put a static file there that you can rename `pic.jpg`. Just pick any JPEG picture you have. Then, save this previous listing into a file named `static.js` on the parent folder and run it like this:

```
$ node static
```

Then point your browser to the URL `http://localhost:8080/pic.jpg`. You should see the picture rendered in your browser.

Now point the browser to any other URL, such as `http://localhost:8080/abc`. You should see the `"Hello World"` string rendered. This means that the static component passes control to the next one, which in this case is the `"Hello World!"` renderer.

> **NOTE** *Just as an interesting experiment, if you remove the* `"Hello World!"` *renderer and then try a URL that the static server can't reply to, you will find that Connect replies with the following:*
>
> ```
> Cannot GET <URL>
> ```
>
> *This happens when Connect can't find any middleware that responds to the request.*

Parsing the Query String

A typical convention for passing arguments into a server-side page generator is using a query string. A query string is where you encode a string containing name and value pairs. It comes at the end of a URL, after the `?` character. Here is an example of a URL with a query string:

```
/search?q=node.js&where=mailinglist
```

Connect has a middleware component that parses this string if available and then populates the `query` property on the request, making it available for subsequent middleware components.

Listing 20-18 shows an example.

LISTING 20-18: Using the Connect query string parser middleware.

```
var connect = require('connect');

var app = connect();

// setup the query middleware
app.use(connect.query());

// actually respond
app.use(function(req, res) {
  res.end(JSON.stringify(req.query));
});

app.listen(8080);
```

Here you are setting up the query string parser middleware and then replying with the content of `req.query`. You can save this listing as a file named `query.js` and then run it:

```
$ node query
```

If you point your browser to the URL `http://localhost:8080/?a=b&c=d`, you should see the following response rendered:

```
{"a":"b","c":"d"}
```

You can now change the query string part of the URL and see how it reflects the `req.query` object.

Parsing the Request Body

In HTTP, the request body is the part of the request that comes right after the header. It can contain any content the application chooses and is typically used to upload files, post forms, and pass remote API arguments.

When posting forms, there are two types of request body encoding: URL-encoded and multipart. The URL-encoded format is similar to the query string format, and the multipart encoding is a more complex format that is mainly used to upload files and pass more complex data types.

When passing arguments to an API call that is hosted by your server, the remote client can encode the call arguments as a JSON-encoded body.

All of these main types of encoding are specified by the request content type string, and you would have to switch between these body decoders depending on it. Fortunately, Connect comes with a generic body parser middleware component that makes this for you, providing a final `body` property on the request object that can be consumed later in the request.

You can use it as shown in Listing 20-19.

LISTING 20-19: Using the Connect body parser middleware.

```
var connect = require('connect');

var app = connect();

// setup the middlewares
app.use(connect.logger(':method :req[content-type]'));
app.use(connect.bodyParser());

// actually respond
app.use(function(req, res) {
  res.end(JSON.stringify(req.body));
});

app.listen(8080);
```

Here you also added the logger middleware so you can inspect the HTTP method and the request content type header.

You can save this listing as a file named `body.js` and run it like this:

```
$ node body
```

Now you can make some requests to your server using the *curl* utility. First, post using the simple URL encoding:

```
$ curl -X POST --data-urlencode a=b --data-urlencode c=d http://localhost:8080
```

Here you are saying that the argument named `a` will have the value `b` and that the argument named `c` will have the value `d`. You can see that the response is what is expected:

```
{"a":"b","c":"d"}
```

You should also see that the server logs the following:

```
POST application/x-www-form-urlencoded
```

Now you can test the multipart encoding:

```
$ curl -X POST -F a=b -F c=d http://localhost:8080
```

The response should also be the following:

```
{"a":"b","c":"d"}
```

And the server should contain a new log message similar to:

```
POST multipart/form-data; boundary=----------------------------cfb73467cea3
```

Now you can test the JSON encoding. `curl` doesn't natively support this encoding; you have to do it yourself:

```
$ curl -d '{"a":"b","c":"d"}' http://localhost:8080
{"{\"a\":\"b\",\"c\":\"d\"}":""}
```

Here you can see that `req.body` contains a string; Connect failed to parse the request body and handed you a string instead. That's because you didn't indicate that the content type would be `application/json`. You should set this request header when using *curl* like this:

```
$ curl -d '{"a":"b","c":"d"}' -H 'Content-Type: application/json' \
http://localhost:8080
{"a":"b","c":"d"}
```

Now you can see that the `bodyParse` middleware was able to recognize the content type and decode it properly.

Parsing Cookies

Cookies are a standard used to store data as short strings on the web browser. A server can send one or many cookies, and each cookie has a name. The server can send one or more of these in the response of any request by using `Set-Cookie` response headers. The web browser has to store each of them and send them along as a single `Cookie` header on the following requests until the cookie expires. The `Cookie` header has its own encoding mechanism because many name-value pairs can be encoded there. Setting a cookie with a name of a cookie that is already stored on the browser overrides the original cookie.

Connect comes with a cookie middleware that takes care of parsing the request cookies, setting the `cookies` property on the request object. You can use it as shown in Listing 20-20.

LISTING 20-20: Using the Connect body parser middleware.

```
var connect = require('connect');

var app = connect();

// setup middleware
app.use(connect.cookieParser());

// actually respond
app.use(function(req, res) {
  res.end(JSON.stringify(req.cookies));
});

app.listen(8080);
```

Here you are replying with the content of `req.cookies`, which should contain an object with a property for each cookie that the client sends. To test this save the previous listing into a file named `cookie.js` and start it:

```
$ node cookie
```

You can test this server with the *`curl`* command-line utility, using the `-b` option, which sets the content on a cookie header:

```
$ curl -b 'a=b; c=d' http://localhost:8080
{"a":"b","c":"d"}
```

Here you can see that the cookies were correctly parsed into the `req.cookie` object.

Using a Session

Connect has a middleware component that allows you to keep a session on the server side, allowing you to save session values that can be used on future requests. When the client first connects, a session identifier is created, and Connect sends a browser cookie containing it to associate that browser with the created session. In future requests, the browser sends that cookie, which allows the server to identify the session and retrieve the stored session objects to be further used and modified.

On the server side, a session is an object that allows you to store name-value pairs. By default, Connect stores the session in memory but has a pluggable interface that allows you to define a different store. Several third-party session stores allow you to use Memcache, Redis, and other database servers as a session store for Connect.

> **NOTE** *If you use a memory store, the sessions won't survive a process restart. If you use a persistent session store, you will have an external service where the sessions will be kept and survive a Node process restart. Also, using an external session store allows you to force two or more Node processes to share the session state, which means that if you use a load balancer, any request can hit any Node process running your app at any given time and always have the session data available.*
>
> *For this example, though, you will use the built-in and default memory store, but you should use an external persistent store if your production setup involves more than one Node process.*

Listing 20-21 shows how you can set up the session middleware.

LISTING 20-21: Using the Connect session middleware.

```
var connect = require('connect');
var format = require('util').format;

var app = connect();

// setup middleware
app.use(connect.query());

app.use(connect.cookieParser('this is my secret string'));

app.use(connect.session({
  cookie: { maxAge: 24 * 60 * 60 * 1000 }
}));

// actually respond
app.use(function(req, res) {
  for (var name in req.query) {
    req.session[name] = req.query[name];
  }
  res.end(format(req.session) + '\n');
});

app.listen(8080);
```

In this listing, you are setting up some middleware components.

First, you are using the query string parser. This is only because the example requires it, as you will see later.

Then you set up the cookie parser, but you pass a string into the middleware constructor. This string contains a secret that will be used for the server to sign the data in the cookies, ensuring that the data cannot be modified by the client.

After this you set up the session middleware, where you define the `cookie.maxAge` option, which defines how long the session cookie can live in the browser before expiring.

Then, when a request arrives, you cycle through every attribute on the `req.query` object and copy it into the session. This is an easy (and not very secure) way for you to easily test the session object later by changing the query string portion of the request URL.

Finally, you reply to the request by serializing the contents of the `req.session` property.

You can save this code listing into a file named `session.js` and run it:

```
$ node session
```

Then point your browser to `http://localhost:8080`. You should see something similar to this rendered:

```
{ cookie:
   { path: '/',
     _expires: Sun, 24 Jun 2012 10:58:24 GMT,
     originalMaxAge: 60000,
     httpOnly: true } }
```

This shows that the session has a `cookie` property that stores some cookie information. This internal data is used by the session middleware.

Now you can set the session by using the query string. Try loading the following URL in the browser:

```
http://localhost:8080/?a=b
```

You will then see something like this rendered:

```
{ cookie:
   { path: '/',
     _expires: Sun, 24 Jun 2012 11:02:22 GMT,
     originalMaxAge: 60 * 60 * 1000,
     httpOnly: true },
  a: 'b' }
```

Here you can see that the session is getting the names and values that were present on the query string.

Now you can try passing a URL with no query string (like `http://localhost:8080`), just to observe the session data. You should see something like this rendered:

```
{ cookie:
   { path: '/',
     _expires: Sun, 24 Jun 2012 11:04:17 GMT,
     originalMaxAge: 60000,
     httpOnly: true },
  a: 'b' }
```

You can now see that the session is being successfully recorded and restored on subsequent requests.

You can try now to perform another request, setting a different variable name, like `http://localhost:8080/?c=d`. You should now see the previous session data plus the new name-value pair you just provided:

```
{ cookie:

   { path: '/',
     _expires: Sun, 24 Jun 2012 12:06:44 GMT,
     originalMaxAge: 3599999,
     httpOnly: true },
  a: 'b',
  c: 'd' }
```

Other Available Middleware

This chapter describes some of the most popular and useful middleware components available in Connect, but others provide things like CSRF (cross-site request forgery) protection, Gzip compression, static file memory cache, virtual-host support, a request body size limiter, and others.

You already read about a session store using Redis or Memcache, but others are also available for various databases like MongoDB, CouchDB, and MySQL.

Also, many third-party middleware components are compatible with Connect that allow you to do things like provide JSONP support, render templates, support request timeout, integrate with various methods of authentication, support LESS (the CSS DSL), and others. A list of these is maintained by the Connect project patron at the following URL:

```
https://github.com/senchalabs/connect/wiki
```

SUMMARY

Connect has become a bit of a standard for defining and running middleware components in an HTTP server on Node. You can easily create components that respond, log data, pipe the request body, handle errors, and do other things in a reusable way.

You can also use the middleware components provided by Connect. These include modules for parsing the query string, parsing the request body, parsing cookies, serving static files, handling errors, and maintaining sessions.

Also, many third-party modules allow you to easily extend the functions provided by your Node HTTP server.

21

Making a Web Application Using Express.js

WHAT'S IN THIS CHAPTER?

- Installing Express
- Starting a web application using Express
- Defining Express middleware
- Rendering Jade templates
- Defining URL route listeners
- Creating route middleware

For some languages and platforms there are frameworks that simplify the job of crafting an HTTP-based application. Perhaps the best known is Rails (for the Ruby language), but countless others include Django, Sinatra, and Cake. Most have the goal of simplifying and structuring the development of HTML applications and solving some common problems like routing the HTTP request to the correct controller code, serving static assets, and rendering HTML templates.

In the Node world several modules and frameworks also solve some of these and other problems. Some are separate modules that you can glue together, and some, like Express.js, offer an integrated solution that you can rapidly implement.

Express.js is based on the Connect middleware engine: Any Connect-specific middleware will also work with Express. Besides allowing you to set up middleware to respond to HTTP requests, Express.js allows you perform different actions based on the HTTP method and URL — by letting you define a routing table. It also allows you to dynamically render HTML documents based on supplying arguments to templates.

INITIALIZING YOUR EXPRESS.JS APPLICATION

This section shows you how to create an Express application from scratch, but first you must install Express globally using `npm`:

```
$ npm install -g express@2.5.x
```

> **NOTE** *If this command fails because it doesn't have enough permissions, depending on your system, you may be able to run it using sudo like this:*
>
> ```
> $ sudo npm install -g express@2.5.x
> ```
>
> *If you can't do it, try fixing the permissions in your file system.*

Now you can use the `express` binary module to locally initialize your application:

```
$ express my_app
   create : my_app
   create : my_app/package.json
   create : my_app/app.js
   create : my_app/public
   create : my_app/public/javascripts
   create : my_app/public/images
   create : my_app/public/stylesheets
   create : my_app/public/stylesheets/style.css
   create : my_app/routes
   create : my_app/routes/index.js
   create : my_app/views
   create : my_app/views/layout.jade
   create : my_app/views/index.jade
```

Express creates a directory named `my_app`, followed by a set of files on which you can base your new application. Step into that directory and open your code editor to analyze what Express created.

First there is the `package.json` manifest file, which contains something like this:

```
{
    "name": "application-name"
  , "version": "0.0.1"
  , "private": true
  , "dependencies": {
      "express": "2.5.11"
    , "jade": ">= 0.0.1"
  }
}
```

This manifest file's main purpose is to contain the module dependency list that NPM can use to install dependencies. Let's install those dependencies now:

```
$ npm install
...
jade@0.26.2 ./node_modules/jade
├── commander@0.5.2
└── mkdirp@0.3.0

express@2.5.11 ./node_modules/express
├── qs@0.4.2
├── mime@1.2.4
├── mkdirp@0.3.0
└── connect@1.9.0 (formidable@1.0.11)
```

This code will download and install the Express module and the Jade templating language modules and their dependencies into the local `node_modules` directory. You can see that Express depends on, among others, the Connect module.

Next, by exploring the `public` directory Express created for you, you can see that it contains directories for the static files you may need in your app. These are somewhat standard directories for separating the location of style sheets, images, and client-side JS files, but you can change them at will.

```
$ ls public
images     javascripts     stylesheets
```

You will also find that Express created a file named `app.js` containing some initialization code for your server, as seen in Listing 21-1.

LISTING 21-1: The app.js file Express creates for you.

```
/**
 * Module dependencies.
 */

var express = require('express')
  , routes = require('./routes');

var app = module.exports = express.createServer();

// Configuration

app.configure(function(){
  app.set('views', __dirname + '/views');
  app.set('view engine', 'jade');
  app.use(express.bodyParser());
  app.use(express.methodOverride());
  app.use(app.router);
  app.use(express.static(__dirname + '/public'));
});
```

continues

LISTING 21-1 *(continued)*

```
app.configure('development', function(){
  app.use(express.errorHandler({ dumpExceptions: true, showStack: true }));
});

app.configure('production', function(){
  app.use(express.errorHandler());
});

// Routes

app.get('/', routes.index);

app.listen(3000, function(){
  console.log("Express server listening on port %d in %s mode", app.address().port,
     app.settings.env);
});
```

After the initial dependency has loaded, you will find that you are instantiating an Express server using `express.createServer()`. This server inherits from the Connect HTTP server, which in turn inherits from the Node HTTP server.

After this the code goes into configuring some application settings. First it sets the `views` setting to the root of the template files used for composing HTML pages. Then it sets the `view engine` setting to `jade`. Jade is a templating language for HTML that does what you would expect from a templating language — it allows you to render HTML blocks, render dynamic values, perform loops, and include other templates. You can take a look at some simple Jade templates that are inside the `views` directory that Express just created.

In the next section, you learn how to define the middleware for your application.

SETTING UP MIDDLEWARE IN YOUR APPLICATION

Continuing with the code in the `app.js` file, you can see that some middleware components are added to the app:

```
app.configure(function(){
  app.use(express.bodyParser());
  app.use(express.methodOverride());
  app.use(app.router);
  app.use(express.static(__dirname + '/public'));
});
```

This code is wrapped inside a callback function passed to the `app.configure` call. This callback is invoked synchronously and is shown here to make the code more consistent with the environment-specific configuration part that follows.

Inside this callback you are setting up the body parser middleware component — covered in the previous chapter — which is used to parse the request body according to the content type defined in the request.

> **NOTE** *The Connect framework is bundled with a set of useful middleware components that Express simply exposes. For instance,* `express.bodyParser` *exposes the Connect body parser middleware. This prevents you from needing to install the Connect module dependency to use the middleware.*

The method override middleware is then added to the app. This middleware component enables browsers to simulate using HTTP methods other than `GET` and `POST`. The HTTP standard defines many methods like `GET`, `POST`, `DELETE`, `PUT`, and others, but web browsers are not capable of using them. When posting a form or making an AJAX request, most browsers are capable of using only `GET` or `POST` requests. But placing the pretend HTTP method inside a hidden argument named `_method`, they can, with the help of the server and the method override middleware, pretend to be using any other method.

> **NOTE** *There are several advantages of using the method overriding middleware. First, you can make your routing decisions richer based on a standard HTTP method. Second, you can treat HTTP clients that can request this method the same way you treat browsers, which may lead to simplified server-side code.*

Next in the list is the router middleware. This middleware component dispatches each request to the proper listener as defined in a routing table, depending on HTTP method and URL. You will return to this subject later.

The code then sets up a static file server middleware, which will serve static files inside your `public` directory.

After this block of code in `app.js`, you proceed to some parts that are environment-specific:

```
app.configure('development', function(){
  app.use(express.errorHandler({ dumpExceptions: true, showStack: true }));
});

app.configure('production', function(){
  app.use(express.errorHandler());
});
```

In Express, you can have independent initialization code blocks for each environment your app runs on. For instance, you may want to use the in-memory session store in the development environment, but you may want to use an external service like Memcache or Redis as the session store in a production environment.

In this case you want the error handler to dump exceptions and show the stack trace in a development environment, but you want to keep those private when you are running in production.

> **NOTE** *You can change the environment by setting the* `NODE_ENV` *environment variable. For instance, set the environment to* `production` *when you start your Node process in this way:*
>
> ```
> $ NODE_ENV=production node my_app
> ```
>
> *In Express, the environment defaults to* `development`.

You can also specify many environments where you want that block of code to run by listing them before the last argument:

```
app.configure('production', 'staging', function(){
  app.use(express.errorHandler());
});
```

ROUTING REQUESTS

When you define an HTTP server request listener or a middleware component, that piece of code is invoked for every request. But obviously, different parts of your application need to trigger different server behaviors. For instance, `GET` requests should probably be treated differently than `POST` requests, and a different URL should also trigger different responses. For instance, if you want some part of the application you're building to show user profiles, you would want the following combinations of method and URLs to behave differently:

- `GET /users` — To show a list of users or to search for users.
- `GET /users/:username` — Generally, show the profile of the user with the given username, like in the next line.
- `GET /users/joe` — To show the profile of the user who has the name "joe."
- `POST /users` — To create a user profile.
- `PUT /users/:username` — Generally, to update a profile of a user with the specified username, like in the next line.
- `PUT /users/joe` — Update profile of user with name "joe."

The list above defines what is called a routing table. This table maps HTTP methods and URL patterns into actions. The next section shows how to define these methods and patterns in Express.

Handling Routes

In line 32 of the `app.js` file that Express created (Listing 21-1), the code reads as follows:

```
app.get('/', routes.index);
```

This code indicates to the app that, if a `GET` request is sent to the `/` URL, the `routes.index` handler should be called. This `routes` object is imported in line 7 and defined in the file `routes/index.js`. You need to change this model a bit to accommodate the new set of routes.

Change the `routes/index.js` file to the one shown in Listing 21-2.

LISTING 21-2: The new version of routes/index.js.

```
/*
 * GET home page.
 */

module.exports = function(app) {
  app.get('/', function(req, res){
    res.render('index', { title: 'Express' })
  });
};
```

Then you should change line 32 of `app.js` to the following:

```
require('./routes/index')(app);
```

Then you can define the new routes in the file `routes/users.js`, as shown in Listing 21-3.

LISTING 21-3: The users routes.

```
/*
 * User Routes
 */

module.exports = function(app) {

    app.get('/users/:name', function(req, res){
    res.render('users/profile', {title: 'User profile'});
  });

};
```

Then you need to add the following line to `app.js`, right after line 32:

```
require('./routes/users')(app);
```

> **NOTE** *This model of setting up the routes delegates the route setup to each route group. This keeps the* `app.js` *file from being cluttered with all the routes.*

Here you are defining two new route handlers for your application. The first is activated when a request has the `GET` method and the URL `/users`. In this case you render the template `users/index`, passing the title as an available argument.

The next one is a dynamic route. It matches any route that begins with `/users/` followed by a non-empty string. This final string will be available to the route handler in `req.params.name`.

In Express routing, strings prefixed by `:` are handled as placeholders, and the captured value will match any string except for the / character.

Now you can start the server:

```
$ node app
```

Then you can point a web browser to `http://localhost:3000`. You should then see the default index view rendered. If you go to the URL `http://localhost:3000/users`, you will see an error message rendered, and the server output should contain something like this:

```
failed to locate view "users/index", tried:
  - /Users/myusername/projects/my_app/views/users/index.jade
  - /Users/myusername/projects/my_app/views/users/index/index.jade
  - /Users/myusername/projects/my_app/views/users/../index/index.jade
```

Express helps you with the location of the missing template file. Now you must create the file shown in Listing 21-4 within `views/users/index.jade`.

LISTING 21-4: The users list view.

```
h1 Users

p User list should be here
```

After you have saved this file and refreshed the page, you will see a simple HTML page containing a placeholder for the user list. Just to simplify rendering, you will now create a list of fake user data under `data/users.json`. Create a project root directory named `data` and then a file named `users.json` with some content, as shown in Listing 21-5.

LISTING 21-5: Fake users.

```
{

  "frank": {
    "username": "frank",
    "name": "Frank Sinatra",
    "bio": "Singer"
  },

  "jobim": {
    "username": "jobim",
    "name": "Antonio Carlos Jobim",
    "bio": "Composer"
  },

  "fred": {
    "username": "fred",
    "name": "Fred Astaire",
    "bio": "Dancer and Actor"
  }

}
```

Now you can complete the user route listeners, as shown in Listing 21-6.

LISTING 21-6: Completed user route listeners.

```
/*
 * User Routes
 */

var users = require('../data/users');

module.exports = function(app) {

  app.get('/users', function(req, res){
    res.render('users/index', {title: 'Users', users: users});
  });

  app.get('/users/new', function(req, res) {
    res.render('users/new', {title: "New User"});
  });

  app.get('/users/:name', function(req, res, next){
    var user = users[req.params.name];
    if (user) {
      res.render('users/profile', {title: 'User profile', user: user});
    } else {
      next();
    }

  });

  app.post('/users', function(req, res) {
    if (users[req.body.username]) {
      res.send('Conflict', 409);
    } else {
      users[req.body.username] = req.body;
      res.redirect('/users');
    }
  });

  app.del('/users/:name', function(req, res, next) {
    if (users[req.params.name]) {
      delete users[req.params.name];
      res.redirect('/users');
    } else {
      next();
    }
  });

};
```

This code implements all the basic functions of listing, showing, creating, and removing users. Let's go through each block of code, one at a time.

In the beginning, the listing imports the user's fake database, which is just a JSON structure you parse and load into memory.

```
app.get('/users', function(req, res){
  res.render('users/index', {title: 'Users', users: users});
});
```

The listener for the `GET /users` route simply passes the users "database" into the `views/users/index.jade` template. Now you need to change that template to render the users, as shown in Listing 21-7.

LISTING 21-7: User list template.

```
h1 Users

p
  a(href="/users/new") Create new profile

ul
  - for(var username in users) {
    li
      a(href="/users/" + encodeURIComponent(username))= users[username].name
  - };
```

This listing iterates over the users object, rendering for each user a list item that contains a link to the detail URL. Here you can see an example of a Jade template and how you can intersperse code with markup.

You can now restart the server to test this new code.

When you point your browser to `http://localhost:3000/users` you should see the user list rendered. If you click on one of those user links, you activate the following route listener:

```
app.get('/users/:name', function(req, res, next){
  var user = users[req.params.name];
  if (user) {
    res.render('users/profile', {title: 'User profile', user: user});
  } else {
    next();
  }
});
```

This route listener uses the request `param` containing the username and uses it to look up the user object. If a user is found, it is applied to the `users/profile.jade` template. If not, the control is passed back to the middleware engine, which in this case will render a `"Not found"` message.

If you click on one of the users in the list, you will get an error screen stating that Express failed to locate the `users/profile` template. You need to create this under `views/users/profile.jade`, as shown in Listing 21-8.

LISTING 21-8: User profile template.

```
h1= user.name

h2 Bio
p= user.bio

form(action="/users/" + encodeURIComponent(user.username), method="POST")
  input(name="_method", type="hidden", value="DELETE")
  input(type="submit", value="Delete")
```

In the first section, you are showing the username and bio. Then you are providing a simple form with a button to delete the user from the database. You are also taking advantage of the method override middleware component to pass in a body parameter named `_method` containing the string `"DELETE"`. When this middleware sees this parameter, it will change the request method from `POST` to `DELETE`, thereby activating this route listener:

```
app.del('/users/:name', function(req, res, next) {
  if (users[req.params.name]) {
    delete users[req.params.name];
    res.redirect('/users');
  } else {
    next();
  }
});
```

This listener will look up the user in the database, and if the user exists, the listener will delete it from the database and redirect the request to the users list.

From the users list you can also create a new user by clicking on the `Create new profile` link, which directs you to the `GET /users/new` route listener:

```
app.get('/users/new', function(req, res) {
  res.render('users/new', {title: "New User"});
});
```

This listener simply renders the `views/users/new.jade` template, which you need to create, as shown in Listing 21-9

LISTING 21-9: New user form template.

```
h1 New User

form(method="POST", action="/users")
  p
    label(for="username") Username<br />
    input#username(name="username")
  p
    label(for="name") Name<br />
    input#name(name="name")
  p
    label(for="bio") Bio<br />
```

continues

LISTING 21-9 *(continued)*

```
    textarea#bio(name="bio")
  p
    input(type="submit", value="Create")
```

This template contains a simple form for creating a user. When pressing the Create button, a `POST` request is made to the `/users` URL, activating this route listener:

```
app.post('/users', function(req, res) {
  if (users[req.body.username]) {
    res.send('Conflict', 409);
  } else {
    users[req.body.username] = req.body;
    res.redirect('/users');
  }
});
```

In the first line of this listener function you are checking whether this username is already in the "database." If it is, you respond with a `409 status` code, which indicates to the client that there was a conflict. The code also renders a `"Conflict"` string as the body response by using `res.send`, a utility provided by Express that allows you to respond with a string and set the response status code.

If there was no conflict, you save the user object in the database and then redirect the user to the `/users` URL by using the `res.redirect` utility function.

NOTE *Here you are storing the user database in memory. In a real application you would obviously want to keep this data, which would imply doing I/O and going asynchronous. If you have a generic and simple key-value store module to access the database, your code for this last route listener would look something like this:*

```
app.post('/users', function(req, res, next) {
  db.get(req.body.username, function(err, user) {
    if (err) {
      return next(err);
    }
    if (user) {
      res.send('Conflict', 409);
    } else {
      db.set(req.body.username, req.body, function(err) {
        if (err) {
          return next(err);
        }
        res.redirect('/users');
      });
    }
  }
```

In Chapters 23, 24, and 25, you will learn how to connect to some popular databases using Node.

Using Sessions

Now you have a very basic HTTP-based user management application (or part of an application) that can be improved in many ways. One way is to provide some sort of authentication mechanism and session management, allowing the users to log in with a username and password. First you need to set up the session middleware in the `app.js` file:

```
app.configure(function(){
  app.set('views', __dirname + '/views');
  app.set('view engine', 'jade');
  app.use(express.bodyParser());
  app.use(express.methodOverride());
  app.use(express.cookieParser('my secret string'));

  app.use(express.session({
    secret: 'my secret string',
    maxAge: 3600000
  }));
  app.use(app.router);
  app.use(express.static(__dirname + '/public'));
});
```

Here you are setting up the cookie parser middleware with a secret string (which you should change) because, as covered before, the session middleware requires the cookie parser middleware to be set up because it maintains the session using cookies.

You are also setting up the session middleware and defining the shared secret and the maximum session age. The maximum session defines the maximum amount of time a session will be kept alive on the server without any user HTTP activity.

Then you need to create a session routing listener, which you can put in a file with the path `routes/session.js` (see Listing 21-10).

LISTING 21-10: Session routes.

```
/*
 * Session Routes
 */

var users = require('../data/users');

module.exports = function(app) {

  app.dynamicHelpers({
    session: function(req, res) {
      return req.session;
    }
  });

  app.get('/session/new', function(req, res) {
    res.render('session/new', {title: "Log in"});
```

continues

LISTING 21-10 *(continued)*

```
    });

    app.post('/session', function(req, res) {
      if (users[req.body.username] &&
        users[req.body.username].password === req.body.password) {
          req.session.user = users[req.body.username];
          res.redirect('/users');
        } else {
          res.redirect('/session/new')
        }
    });

    app.del('/session', function(req, res, next) {
      req.session.destroy();
      res.redirect('/users');
    });

  };
```

Going through each block of code in this last listing, you have the following:

```
app.dynamicHelpers({
  session: function(req, res) {
    return req.session;
  }
});
```

This is an alternative way of passing local variables into views. Instead of explicitly inserting an argument on every `res.render` call, you can define a dynamic helper that will be evaluated for each request whose result will be available as a local variable. Here you are exposing the session, which can be later used inside any view template.

Now you can change the layout and create a header that will, for every page, show the user's login status. For this you will create a new file under `views/session/user.jade` with the code shown in Listing 21-11.

LISTING 21-11: The app.js file Express creates for you.

```
- if (session.user) {

  p
    span Hello 
    span= session.user.name
    span !
  p
    form(method="POST", action="/session")
      input(type="hidden", name="_method", value="DELETE")
      input(type="submit", value="Log out")
```

```
- } else {

  p
    a(href="/session/new") Login
    span  or 
    a(href="/users/new") Register

- }
```

This partial renders in two modes: when a user is present in the session and when no one is in the session. In the first case, you present some user data and a button to end the session. In the last case you present a link for the user to log in.

Now you need to include this partial in the `views/layout.jade` file, as shown in Listing 21-12.

LISTING 21-12: Changed layout file to include user info on header.

```
!!!
html
  head
    title= title
    link(rel='stylesheet', href='/stylesheets/style.css')
  body
    header!= partial('session/user')
    section#main!= body
```

Here you're assigning the content of the partial in `views/session/user.jade` into the header tag.

> **NOTE** *In Jade, content that is assigned in a tag can be HTML-encoded or not. If you want to assign a string that should appear exactly as that string in the browser (even HTML-specific characters like < and >), use the = operator. It will encode these special characters for you:*
>
> ```
> span= session.user.name
> ```
>
> *If your content has HTML you want to see rendered as tags (as is the case of the result of a partial), you should use !=:*
>
> ```
> header!= partial('session/user')
> ```

If you click on the `login` link, you will activate the following route:

```
app.get('/session/new', function(req, res) {
  res.render('session/new', {title: "Log in"});
});
```

This will simply render the `views/session/new.jade` template file, which is a login form, as shown in Listing 21-13.

LISTING 21-13: The login form.

```
h1 Log in

form(method="POST", action="/session")
  p
    label(for="username") User name:<br />
    input#username(name="username")
  p
    label(for="password") Password:<br />
    input#password(type="password", name="password")
  p
    input(type="submit", value="Log in");
```

This form will post this data into the `/session` URL, activating the following route:

```
app.post('/session', function(req, res) {
  if (users[req.body.username] &&
    users[req.body.username].password === req.body.password) {
      req.session.user = users[req.body.username];
      res.redirect('/users');
    } else {
      res.redirect('/session/new')
    }
});
```

This route listener checks the username and password against the fake user database and, if there is a match, saves the user object in the session and then redirects the user to the `/users` URL.

When the user is logged in, the header part of the page shows the username and a button to log out. This button makes a `DELETE` request (again, using the method override middleware trick) to the `/session` URL, activating this route:

```
app.del('/session', function(req, res, next) {
  req.session.destroy();
  res.redirect('/users');
});
```

This route listener simply destroys the session and redirects to the `/users` URL.

Next, add these new session routes' initialization to `app.js` by adding the following line on the routes section:

```
require('./routes/session')(app);
```

Now you should be able to log in, except that none of the existing users in the fake database have a password. You can insert a password for them and try restarting the app.

To insert a password you need to change each user record in the `data/users.json` file to something like this:

```
{

  "frank": {
    "username": "frank",
    "name": "Frank Sinatra",
    "bio": "Singer",
    "password": "theladyisatramp"
  },

  "jobim": {
    "username": "jobim",
    "name": "Antonio Carlos Jobim",
    "bio": "Composer",
    "password": "garotadeipanema"
  },

  "fred": {
    "username": "fred",
    "name": "Fred Astaire",
    "bio": "Dancer and Actor",
    "password": "tophat"
  }

}
```

Also, you'll need to add a password field to the signup form (`views/users/new.jade`), seen in Listing 21-14:

LISTING 21-14: The new version of the user signup form.

```
h1 New User

form(method="POST", action="/users")
  p
    label(for="username") Username<br />
    input#username(name="username")
  p
    label(for="name") Name<br />
    input#name(name="name")
  p
    label(for="password") Password<br />
    input#password(type="password", name="password")
  p
    label(for="bio") Bio<br />
    textarea#bio(name="bio")
  p
    input(type="submit", value="Create")
```

Now you can create users with passwords and log in and out.

Now you should restrict user access to some of the routes. For instance, users should be able to create a profile only if they aren't logged in and should only be able to remove only their own profiles. For these tasks, you need to use a new feature called *route middleware*.

Using Route Middleware

You might want to restrict certain actions based on session info. You might, for instance, restrict the execution of some routes to users who are logged in or even users who have certain internal profile characteristics (like being the administrator).

You can make each of the relevant route listeners perform this task, but this would lead to repetitive or inelegant code. Instead, you can define route middleware that can be executed on chosen routes.

For instance, if you want to restrict access to the `GET /users/new`, `POST /users`, `GET /sessions/new`, and `POST /session` to users who are not logged in, you can create the following generic route middleware that you can save into `routes/middleware/not_logged_in.js` (see Listing 21-15).

LISTING 21-15: The not_logged_in middleware.

```
function notLoggedIn(req, res, next) {
  if (req.session.user) {
    res.send('Unauthorized', 401);
  } else {
    next();
  }
}

module.exports = notLoggedIn;
```

This middleware piece simply checks if a user is in the session. If there is one, it sends a `401 Unauthorized` status. If there is no user, it proceeds to the next middleware in place.

You can then import this middleware piece at the top of the `routes/session.js` file and proceed to include the middleware piece in every route needed (see Listing 21-16).

LISTING 21-16: New version of the session routes.

```
/*
 * Session Routes
 */

var users = require('../data/users');
var notLoggedIn = require('./middleware/not_logged_in');

module.exports = function(app) {

  app.dynamicHelpers({
    session: function(req, res) {
      return req.session;
    }
  });

  app.get('/session/new', notLoggedIn, function(req, res) {
```

```
    res.render('session/new', {title: "Log in"});
  });

  app.post('/session', notLoggedIn, function(req, res) {
    if (users[req.body.username] &&
      users[req.body.username].password === req.body.password) {
        req.session.user = users[req.body.username];
        res.redirect('/users');
      } else {
        res.redirect('/session/new')
      }
    });

  app.del('/session', function(req, res, next) {
    req.session.destroy();
    res.redirect('/users');
  });

};
```

Here you are placing the new route middleware callback function right before the final listener one. Express will take care of chaining the route middleware calls for you.

You also need to use this function inside the user routes, as shown in Listing 21-17.

LISTING 21-17: New version of the user routes.

```
/*
 * User Routes
 */

var users = require('../data/users');
var notLoggedIn = require('./middleware/not_logged_in');

module.exports = function(app) {

  app.get('/users', function(req, res){
    res.render('users/index', {title: 'Users', users: users});
  });

  app.get('/users/new', notLoggedIn, function(req, res) {
    res.render('users/new', {title: "New User"});
  });

  app.get('/users/:name', function(req, res, next){
    var user = users[req.params.name];
    if (user) {
      res.render('users/profile', {title: 'User profile', user: user});
    } else {
      next();
    }
```

continues

LISTING 21-17 *(continued)*

```
    });

    app.post('/users', notLoggedIn, function(req, res) {
      if (users[req.body.username]) {
        res.send('Conflict', 409);
      } else {
        users[req.body.username] = req.body;
        res.redirect('/users');
      }
    });

    app.del('/users/:name', function(req, res, next) {
      if (users[req.params.name]) {
        delete users[req.params.name];
        res.redirect('/users');
      } else {
        next();
      }
    });

};
```

You can use this strategy and take this opportunity to remove some redundant code where you load the user. To do so, create a new route middleware component in file `routes/middleware/load_user.js` that loads the user based on the username parameter, as shown in Listing 21-18.

LISTING 21-18: Load user route middleware.

```
var users = require('../../data/users');

function loadUser(req, res, next) {
  var user = req.user = users[req.params.name];
  if (! user) {
    res.send('Not found', 404);
  } else {
    next();
  }
}

module.exports = loadUser;
```

This piece of middleware loads the user into the `req.user` attribute, making it available to the middleware that will execute next.

Now you can include this middleware and reuse some redundant code in the `routes/users.js` file, as shown in Listing 21-19.

LISTING 21-19: New version of the user routes.

```
/*
 * User Routes
 */

var users = require('../data/users');
var notLoggedIn = require('./middleware/not_logged_in');
var loadUser = require('./middleware/load_user');

module.exports = function(app) {

  app.get('/users', function(req, res){
    res.render('users/index', {title: 'Users', users: users});
  });

  app.get('/users/new', notLoggedIn, function(req, res) {
    res.
/*
 * User Routes
 */

var users = require('../data/users');
var notLoggedIn = require('./middleware/not_logged_in');
var loadUser = require('./middleware/load_user');

module.exports = function(app) {

  app.get('/users', function(req, res){
    res.render('users/index', {title: 'Users', users: users});
  });

  app.get('/users/new', notLoggedIn, function(req, res) {
    res.render('users/new', {title: "New User"});
  });

  app.get('/users/:name', loadUser, function(req, res, next){
    res.render('users/profile', {title: 'User profile', user: req.user});
  });

  app.post('/users', notLoggedIn, function(req, res) {
    if (users[req.body.username]) {
      res.send('Conflict', 409);
    } else {
      users[req.body.username] = req.body;
      res.redirect('/users');
    }
  });

  app.del('/users/:name', loadUser, function(req, res, next) {
    delete users[req.user.username];
    res.redirect('/users');
  });

};
```

You now need to protect some of the user profile actions from other users. For this you can create a new piece of middleware that checks whether the loaded user is the same as the one logged in, as shown in Listing 21-20 in `routes/middleware/restrict_user_to_self.js`.

LISTING 21-20: New middleware to restrict user to the session user.

```
function restrictUserToSelf(req, res, next) {
  if (! req.session.user || req.session.user.username !== req.user.username) {
    res.send('Unauthorized', 401);
  } else {
    next();
  }
}

module.exports = restrictUserToSelf;
```

Now you can import this new piece of routing middleware at the top of the user routes:

```
var restrictUserToSelf = require('./middleware/restrict_user_to_self');
```

And use this middleware in the last listener in the user routes:

```
  app.del('/users/:name', loadUser, restrictUserToSelf, function(req, res, next) {
    delete users[req.user.username];
    res.redirect('/users');
  });
```

You can then restart the server and ensure that, when you're logged in, you cannot delete any profile other than your own.

> **NOTE** *This application needs many improvements before it is safe. Improvements include sanitizing and validating the user input, providing feedback messages when actions are performed, and rendering more friendly messages when an error happens.*
>
> *You should also use a persistent database for storing user data, which is covered later in the book.*

SUMMARY

Express is one of the most popular web frameworks used to build HTML-based websites. It builds up on the middleware functionality provided by Connect and allows you to view rendering and routing on top of that.

You can start your project by using the Connect command-line and evolve from there, adding or removing middleware components and defining the routing table.

Routing uses a simple form of pattern-matching against the method and request URL. You should not stick all the routes in your main module. Instead, use separate modules for different sets of functionality.

In Express, routing works much like global middleware, where you can define a stack of listener functions listening on a certain route. Using this feature you can make your final route listeners more secure and less redundant.

22

Making Universal Real-Time Web Applications Using Socket.IO

WHAT'S IN THIS CHAPTER?

- Understanding the history of HTTP in relation to real-time applications
- Understanding how WebSockets enable real-time applications on the web
- Using Socket.IO to write real-time applications for Node.js
- Writing a web-based real-time chat with Socket.IO for Node.js
- Using namespaces to separate Socket.IO apps
- Scaling to several Node processes with Redis

For many years, HTTP and real-time applications didn't really go together very well. The reason lies in the very nature of the HTTP protocol, which is stateless and based on a request-response cycle — an HTTP server only reacts upon requests from the client but doesn't have a stateful continuous connection to the client.

An HTML and JavaScript-based application is capable of reacting to client events and sending them to the server, but the reverse is not easy. If an event on the server occurs, the server has no way of actively informing its clients about this event in real time. Only when clients ask the server for its current state can the information be delivered from the server to its clients.

A browser-based chat is a good example of a web-based real-time application that shows the limitations of HTTP. Multiple users share a chatroom, which technically means that a message sent by any of the participating users needs to be delivered to all other users in the same room.

To achieve real-time, or at least near real-time, behavior in traditional web chats, certain workarounds were common. In its simplest form, the traditional request-response flow was used: The browser of every chat user polled the HTTP server at regular intervals for new messages. Polling fast enough, such as every second or less, gave the impression of interacting in real time.

However, this technique was highly inefficient; the client had to poll every second, even if no new messages were available, and the server had to handle a request from all connected chat users every second, even if no new messages were available. In a chatroom where new messages where posted only every 10 seconds, the clients and the server had to do a lot of computation, which in 90 percent of the cases wasn't necessary.

More clever workarounds were developed, but they were all still based on the request-response cycle, only using it in slightly more efficient ways. *Long polling* is a technique whereby the client sends a request to the server only once, and then the server keeps this connection open, sending new data whenever it's available. But because HTTP was never designed for this kind of use, implementations remained hacky — browsers showed different behaviors when faced with long-running request responses, and keeping the connection open usually resulted in inefficient load behavior on the server.

Today, the situation is much better. The WebSocket protocol was developed (and recently standardized) to overcome the shortcomings of HTTP in relation to real-time applications, which now enables HTTP clients and browsers to talk to each other in an efficient and full-duplex way, without the need for workarounds.

For the first time, real-time web applications can use only web technologies, without the need to for external technologies like Java Applets, Flash, or ActiveX.

UNDERSTANDING HOW WEBSOCKETS WORK

At its core, a WebSocket connection is just a conventional TCP connection between an HTTP server and an HTTP client. It's established using a handshake protocol, which is very similar to an HTTP handshake.

The client initializes the connection. To do this, the browser sends a special HTTP/1.1 request to the server, asking it to turn the connection of this request into a WebSockets connection:

```
GET /chat HTTP/1.1
Host: server.example.com
Upgrade: websocket
Connection: Upgrade
Sec-WebSocket-Key: dGhlIHNhbXBsZSBub25jZQ==
Origin: http://example.com
Sec-WebSocket-Protocol: chat, superchat
Sec-WebSocket-Version: 13
```

Although this starts out as a regular HTTP connection, the client asks to "upgrade" this connection to a WebSocket connection. If the server supports the WebSocket protocol, it answers like this:

```
HTTP/1.1 101 Switching Protocols
Upgrade: websocket
Connection: Upgrade
Sec-WebSocket-Accept: s3pPLMBiTxaQ9kYGzzhZRbK+xOo=
Sec-WebSocket-Protocol: chat
```

This marks the end of the handshake, and the connection switches to data transfer mode. Both sides can now send messages back and forth without any HTTP overhead or additional handshakes, making it a bi-directional full-duplex communication connection in which both client and server can send messages to one another at any time without having to wait for one another.

USING SOCKET.IO TO BUILD WEBSOCKET APPLICATIONS

Although implementing your own WebSocket server for Node.js is possible, it's not necessary. Many low-level details need to be taken care of before you can implement an actual application on top of it, which makes using a library a lot more practical.

The de facto standard library for building WebSocket Node.js applications is Socket.IO. Not only is it a wrapper library that makes building WebSocket servers very convenient, it also provides transparent fallback mechanisms like long polling for clients that don't support the WebSocket protocol. Furthermore, it ships with a client-side library that provides a convenient API for developing the browser part of the application.

Using Socket.IO, you never need to grapple with the low-level implementation details of a WebSocket server or client. You get a clean and expressive API on both sides, which allows writing real-time applications with ease.

Installing and Running Socket.IO on the Server

Like many other Node.js libraries, Socket.IO ships as an NPM module and can therefore be installed with the following:

```
$ npm install socket.io
```

After you've installed it, you can implement a very basic WebSocket server, as shown in Listing 22-1.

LISTING 22-1: Setting up a Socket.IO server.

```
var io = require('socket.io').listen(4000);

io.sockets.on('connection', function (socket) {
  socket.on('my event', function(content) {
    console.log(content);
  });
});
```

Save this code to `server.js`.

The corresponding client part looks like Listing 22-2.

LISTING 22-2: A basic Socket.IO client.

```
<html>
  <head>
    <title>Socket.IO example application</title>
    <script src="http://localhost:4000/socket.io/socket.io.js"></script>
    <script>
      var socket = io.connect('http://localhost:4000');
      socket.emit('my event', 'Hello world.');
    </script>
  </head>
  <body>
  </body>
</html>
```

Save this in the same directory as `index.html`.

As you can see, both sides use a similar vocabulary. On the server, the first step is to bind to a TCP port, 4000 in this case. As soon as the server is running, it listens to incoming WebSocket connections. The `connection` event is triggered as soon as a new client connects. The server then listens for incoming messages on this connection, logging the content of any message it receives.

> **NOTE** *As you can see, Socket.IO provides a message-oriented communication mechanism. This is an improvement over the underlying WebSockets protocol, which doesn't provide message framing.*
>
> *You can also see that Socket.IO does not distinguish between a client that is connected using WebSockets or any other type of mechanism: It provides a unified API that abstracts away those implementation details.*

The event name `my event` is arbitrary — it's just a label the client gives the messages it sends, and it is used to distinguish among different types of messages within an application.

On the client, a WebSocket connection is created by connecting to the server. This socket is then used to emit (or send) a message with the label `my event` to the server. This triggers the listener in the server code and results in the message content being logged to the console.

Now, it would be great if you could just open the HTML file locally via `file:///path/to/index.html`, but that doesn't work reliably in all browsers because of security constraints that apply when opening local files.

Therefore, you need to serve the HTML through the Node.js server, which allows you to request `http://localhost:4000/`, which doesn't impose any security restrictions because it's a "real" HTTP request.

You can achieve this by piggybacking the Socket.IO server on a regular Node.js HTTP server and serving the HTML through this HTTP server. Sounds complicated? It's not, as Listing 22-3 shows.

LISTING 22-3: Serving the HTML file with Node.js HTTP server.

```
var httpd = require('http').createServer(handler);
var io = require('socket.io').listen(httpd);
var fs = require('fs');

httpd.listen(4000);

function handler(req, res) {
  fs.readFile(__dirname + '/index.html',
    function(err, data) {
      if (err) {
       res.writeHead(500);
       return res.end('Error loading index.html');
      }

      res.writeHead(200);
      res.end(data);
    }
  );
}

io.sockets.on('connection', function (socket) {
  socket.on('my event', function(content) {
    console.log(content);
  });
});
```

What happens here is that the WebSocket server links into the HTTP server and listens to certain requests. Whenever a client requests anything below `/socket.io`, Socket.IO handles these requests, returning the `socket.io.js` script or setting up a WebSocket connection. Any other request receives the `index.html` file as a response.

Now you can point your browser to `http://localhost:4000/` — the string `"Hello World."` will be logged to the console of your server.

Next, you will see how to rewrite this example code as a full application.

Building a Real-Time Web Chat with Socket.IO

Node.js provides the building blocks for any real-time application on the web: It's based on the web standard JavaScript and is non-blocking at heart, which is crucial for enabling real-time behavior.

Therefore it's no surprise that the poster child of real-time web applications, that is, browser-based chatrooms, have become the most popular example application for demonstrating Node.js capabilities.

The example application is a good starting point for a basic chat application. It needs to be extended on the server and the client side, which is explained step by step in the following sections.

Application Structure and Use Case

The application is very simple. The user interacts with the chat system through a very frugal interface that provides only two elements — the text input field and an area that displays all received chat messages.

When the user types text into the input field and presses Enter, the entered text is sent to the server via Socket.IO. Whenever a message is received on the Socket.IO connection, the client will add it to the message area.

Every client will receive all messages sent by any other client, and these messages are echoed back as well.

The Chat Server

You'll first rewrite the server application created in Listing 22-3. You need to listen for new connections and new messages. Whenever a new message from a client arrives, you need to echo it back to the client, and then broadcast it to all other connected clients. You could implement the broadcasting part by keeping an array of all currently connected clients, but this is not necessary — Socket.IO already provides a convenient broadcast mechanism that sends messages to all connected sockets, except the one that sent the message.

Because the file serving part of the chat server doesn't need to be changed, you just need to rewrite the part that handles socket connections:

```
io.sockets.on('connection', function (socket) {
  socket.on('clientMessage', function(content) {
    socket.emit('serverMessage', 'You said: ' + content);
    socket.broadcast.emit('serverMessage', socket.id + ' said: ' +
      content);
  });
});
```

You now need to listen to `clientMessage` events on each connection socket, handle these events by echoing the content back to the sender, and emit them to all other clients. To make chat messages distinguishable on the client, you prefix messages with either `You said:` or `<client id> said:`, whereby `client id` is the internal socket ID number for now.

Again, the name of the incoming event is not a special keyword that bears any meaning in regard to Socket.IO — it's a label that can be chosen at will. Of course, you need to make sure that the client uses the same label when emitting messages on the socket.

Listing 22-4 shows how the full server code looks at this point.

LISTING 22-4: A simple Socket.IO chat server.

```
var httpd = require('http').createServer(handler);
var io = require('socket.io').listen(httpd);
var fs = require('fs');

httpd.listen(4000);

function handler(req, res) {
  fs.readFile(__dirname + '/index.html',
    function(err, data) {
      if (err) {
       res.writeHead(500);
       return res.end('Error loading index.html');
      }

      res.writeHead(200);
      res.end(data);
    }
  );
}

io.sockets.on('connection', function (socket) {
  socket.on('clientMessage', function(content) {
    socket.emit('serverMessage', 'You said: ' + content);
    socket.broadcast.emit('serverMessage', socket.id + ' said: ' +
      content);
  });
});
```

The Chat Client

Because message handling on the server side of the application is still basic, most of the heavy lifting actually happens on the client side.

Therefore, you need to rewrite large parts of the previous example code. The client needs an element that allows the user to enter chat messages and an area that displays all incoming chat messages. First, you should style and position these on the page with some CSS in the `<head>` section of the page:

```
<style type="text/css">
  #input {
    width: 200px;
  }
  #messages {
    position: fixed;
    top: 40px;
    bottom: 8px;
    left: 8px;
    right: 8px;
    border: 1px solid #EEEEEE;
    padding: 8px;
  }
</style>
```

The `input` element, which is a simple text input field, will sit at the top of the page, followed by a `div` for the messages that fills the rest of the page:

```
Your message:
<input type="text" id="input">

<div id="messages"></div>
```

Before the closing `body` tag, you need to load the Socket.IO client library and add the client-side application logic. It's crucial to have the JavaScript at the end of the document to make sure that all DOM elements are available to the JavaScript code.

First, you need to load the Socket.IO client library:

```
<script src="http://localhost:4000/socket.io/socket.io.js"></script>
```

Then, after opening another script block with `<script type="text/javascript">` for your code, you need to handle two use cases — a message from the server arrives and a message has to be sent to the server. Let's start with a function that knows how to append new messages to the message area:

```
var messagesElement = document.getElementById('messages');
var lastMessageElement = null;

function addMessage(message) {
  var newMessageElement = document.createElement('div');
  var newMessageText = document.createTextNode(message);

  newMessageElement.appendChild(newMessageText);
  messagesElement.insertBefore(newMessageElement, lastMessageElement);
  lastMessageElement = newMessageElement;
}
```

New messages arrive on the Socket.IO wire, so you need to connect to the backend and add a handler for the `serverMessage` events that the server code emits:

```
var socket = io.connect('http://localhost:4000');
socket.on('serverMessage', function(content) {
  addMessage(content);
});
```

The last step is to emit `clientMessage` events with the message of the users as their content. This can be achieved by binding to the `onkeydown` event of the input text field and writing to the socket whenever the user presses Enter:

```
var inputElement = document.getElementById('input');

inputElement.onkeydown = function(keyboardEvent) {
  if (keyboardEvent.keyCode === 13) {
    socket.emit('clientMessage', inputElement.value);
    inputElement.value = '';
```

```
      return false;
    } else {
      return true;
    }
  };
```

When everything is put together, `index.html` looks Listing 22-5.

LISTING 22-5: A simple Socket.IO chat client.

```
<html>
  <head>
    <title>Node.js WebSocket chat</title>
    <style type="text/css">
      #input {
        width: 200px;
      }
      #messages {
        position: fixed;
        top: 40px;
        bottom: 8px;
        left: 8px;
        right: 8px;
        border: 1px solid #EEEEEE;
        padding: 8px;
      }
    </style>
  </head>

  <body>

    Your message:
    <input type="text" id="input">

    <div id="messages"></div>

    <script src="http://localhost:4000/socket.io/socket.io.js"></script>
    <script type="text/javascript">
      var messagesElement = document.getElementById('messages');
      var lastMessageElement = null;

      function addMessage(message) {
        var newMessageElement = document.createElement('div');
        var newMessageText = document.createTextNode(message);

        newMessageElement.appendChild(newMessageText);
        messagesElement.insertBefore(newMessageElement,
          lastMessageElement);
        lastMessageElement = newMessageElement;
      }

     var socket = io.connect('http://localhost:4000');
      socket.on('serverMessage', function(content) {
```

continues

LISTING 22-5 *(continued)*

```
          addMessage(content);
        });

        var inputElement = document.getElementById('input');

        inputElement.onkeydown = function(keyboardEvent) {
          if (keyboardEvent.keyCode === 13) {
            socket.emit('clientMessage', inputElement.value);
            inputElement.value = '';
            return false;
          } else {
            return true;
          }
        };
      </script>

    </body>
  </html>
```

This implements the simplest chat use case. When you start the chat server with `node server.js` and open `http://localhost:4000/`, you will be presented with a very Spartan interface that allows sending and receiving messages from other users. It makes sense to open another browser window or tab to simulate real multi-user interaction.

Extending the Chat Application

At this point, the chat exchange protocol between client and server isn't exactly vast — each side emits one type of message and reacts to one type of message. This will change when the use cases within the application become more complex.

For example, it's not convenient that chat users are identified by their internal socket connection ID. It would be nice if before entering the chat, users could identify themselves by name.

This can be implemented by adding another type of client-to-server Socket.IO message type, which could be called `login`.

The server needs to handle this message by associating the name of the user — which is the content part of the `login` message — with the socket connection.

```
socket.on('login', function(username) {
  socket.set('username', username, function(err) {
    if (err) { throw err; }
    socket.emit('serverMessage', 'Currently logged in as ' + username);
    socket.broadcast.emit('serverMessage', 'User ' + username +
      ' logged in');
  });
});
```

This code on the server is setting the `username` on the socket. Using `socket.set` you can set any key-value pair on the socket, keeping any information around you may find useful for the current socket connection.

Then you need to send a `login` message from the client. For that, the browser asks the user for the username. Now you need something to trigger this question, which can be a `login` server event.

```
socket.on('login', function() {
  var username = prompt('What username would you like to use?');
  socket.emit('login', username);
});
```

The server then needs to send a `login` event when the user connects:

```
socket.on('login', function(username) {
  socket.set('username', username, function(err) {
    if (err) { throw err; }
    socket.emit('serverMessage', 'Currently logged in as ' + username);
    socket.broadcast.emit('serverMessage', 'User ' + username +
      ' logged in');
  });
});
```

And the server emits a `login` event when the user connects:

```
socket.emit('login');
```

The login flow works like this now: The user connects and the server sends a `login` event. The browser, upon receiving this event, prompts the user about the username and then sends it to the server with a `login` event. The server processes this event, associating the username with that socket, to be used in the future.

Listing 22-6 contains the full server code, and Listing 22-7 contains the complete client code.

LISTING 22-6: A Socket.IO chat server that supports user login.

```
var httpd = require('http').createServer(handler);
var io = require('socket.io').listen(httpd);
var fs = require('fs');

httpd.listen(4000);

function handler(req, res) {
  fs.readFile(__dirname + '/index.html',
    function(err, data) {
      if (err) {
       res.writeHead(500);
       return res.end('Error loading index.html');
      }

      res.writeHead(200);
      res.end(data);
    }
  );
}
```

continues

LISTING 22-6 *(continued)*

```
io.sockets.on('connection', function (socket) {
  socket.on('clientMessage', function(content) {
    socket.emit('serverMessage', 'You said: ' + content);

    socket.get('username', function(err, username) {
      if (! username) {
        username = socket.id;
      }
      socket.broadcast.emit('serverMessage', username + ' said: ' +
        content);
    });
  });

  socket.on('login', function(username) {
    socket.set('username', username, function(err) {
      if (err) { throw err; }
      socket.emit('serverMessage', 'Currently logged in as ' + username);
      socket.broadcast.emit('serverMessage', 'User ' + username +
        ' logged in');
    });
  });

  socket.emit('login');

});
```

LISTING 22-7: A Socket.IO chat client that supports user login.

```
<html>
  <head>
    <title>Node.js WebSocket chat</title>
    <style type="text/css">
      #input {
        width: 200px;
      }
      #messages {
        position: fixed;
        top: 40px;
        bottom: 8px;
        left: 8px;
        right: 8px;
        border: 1px solid #EEEEEE;
        padding: 8px;
      }
    </style>
  </head>

  <body>
```

```
    Your message:
    <input type="text" id="input">

    <div id="messages"></div>

    <script src="http://localhost:4000/socket.io/socket.io.js"></script>
    <script type="text/javascript">
      var messagesElement = document.getElementById('messages');
      var lastMessageElement = null;

      function addMessage(message) {
        var newMessageElement = document.createElement('div');
        var newMessageText = document.createTextNode(message);

        newMessageElement.appendChild(newMessageText);
        messagesElement.insertBefore(newMessageElement,
          lastMessageElement);
        lastMessageElement = newMessageElement;
      }

      var socket = io.connect('http://localhost:4000');
      socket.on('serverMessage', function(content) {
        addMessage(content);
      });

      socket.on('login', function() {
        var username = prompt('What username would you like to use?');
        socket.emit('login', username);
      });

      var inputElement = document.getElementById('input');

      inputElement.onkeydown = function(keyboardEvent) {
        if (keyboardEvent.keyCode === 13) {
          socket.emit('clientMessage', inputElement.value);
          inputElement.value = '';
          return false;
        } else {
          return true;
        }
      };
    </script>

  </body>
</html>
```

Now you can save the client as a file named `index.html` and the server code as a file named `app.js`, running it like this:

```
$ node app.js
```

Then, open several browser windows pointing to `http://localhost:4000`. You should be able to run different chat sessions, all communicating with each other.

Detecting Disconnections

The only way users can now leave the chat is by closing the browser window. That will trigger a `disconnect` event on the server-side socket. It would be interesting for other connected users to be informed that a certain user has left the chat.

```
socket.on('disconnect', function() {
  socket.get('username', function(err, username) {
    if (! username) {
      username = socket.id;
    }
    socket.broadcast.emit('serverMessage', 'User ' + username + ' disconnected');
  });
});
```

Now, when a given socket is disconnected, the server broadcasts that information to all other connected clients. Listing 22-8 contains the full server code.

LISTING 22-8: A Socket.IO chat server that detects disconnections.

```
var httpd = require('http').createServer(handler);
var io = require('socket.io').listen(httpd);
var fs = require('fs');

httpd.listen(4000);

function handler(req, res) {
  fs.readFile(__dirname + '/index.html',
    function(err, data) {
      if (err) {
       res.writeHead(500);
       return res.end('Error loading index.html');
      }

      res.writeHead(200);
      res.end(data);
    }
  );
}

io.sockets.on('connection', function (socket) {
  socket.on('clientMessage', function(content) {
    socket.emit('serverMessage', 'You said: ' + content);

    socket.get('username', function(err, username) {
      if (! username) {
        username = socket.id;
      }
      socket.broadcast.emit('serverMessage', username + ' said:' +
        content);
    });
  });
```

```
    socket.on('login', function(username) {
      socket.set('username', username, function(err) {
        if (err) { throw err; }
        socket.emit('serverMessage', 'Currently logged in as ' + username);
        socket.broadcast.emit('serverMessage', 'User ' + username +
          ' logged in');
      });
    });

    socket.on('disconnect', function() {
      socket.get('username', function(err, username) {
        if (! username) {
          username = socket.id;
        }
        socket.broadcast.emit('serverMessage', 'User ' + username +
          ' disconnected');
      });
    });

    socket.emit('login');

  });
```

You can test this by saving the changes to `app.js`, restarting your Node server, and then opening several browser windows into the chat app. If you close one of those windows, the other ones should be informed.

Separating Users into Rooms

You can also provide several chatrooms that users can join, limiting the chat messages to only the users who have joined that room. You could implement this by keeping track of which sockets are in which room, but fortunately Socket.IO supports this exact functionality.

But first, the client has to allow a user to join a room. For that, the browser command line has to be able to accept some commands like in the iRC protocol, where the user can enter a command that starts with the character /, followed by a verb and some arguments. Listing 22-9 has the client code that allows that.

LISTING 22-9: A Socket.IO chat client that accepts the /j <room> command.

```
  <html>
    <head>
      <title>Node.js WebSocket chat</title>
      <style type="text/css">
        #input {
          width: 200px;
        }
        #messages {
          position: fixed;
          top: 40px;
          bottom: 8px;
```

continues

LISTING 22-9 *(continued)*

```
      left: 8px;
      right: 8px;
      border: 1px solid #EEEEEE;
      padding: 8px;
    }
  </style>
</head>

<body>

  Your message:
  <input type="text" id="input">

  <div id="messages"></div>

  <script src="http://localhost:4000/socket.io/socket.io.js"></script>
  <script type="text/javascript">
    var messagesElement = document.getElementById('messages');
    var lastMessageElement = null;

    function addMessage(message) {
      var newMessageElement = document.createElement('div');
      var newMessageText = document.createTextNode(message);

      newMessageElement.appendChild(newMessageText);
      messagesElement.insertBefore(newMessageElement,
        lastMessageElement);
      lastMessageElement = newMessageElement;
    }

    var socket = io.connect('http://localhost:4000');
    socket.on('serverMessage', function(content) {
      addMessage(content);
    });

    socket.on('login', function() {
      var username = prompt('What username would you like to use?');
      socket.emit('login', username);
    });

    function sendCommand(command, args) {
      if (command === 'j') {
        socket.emit('join', args);
      } else {
        alert('unknown command: ' + command);
      }
    }

    function sendMessage(message) {
      var commandMatch = message.match(/^\/(\w*)(.*)/);
      if (commandMatch) {
        sendCommand(commandMatch[1], commandMatch[2].trim());
      } else {
```

```
          socket.emit('clientMessage', message);
        }
      }

      var inputElement = document.getElementById('input');

      inputElement.onkeydown = function(keyboardEvent) {
        if (keyboardEvent.keyCode === 13) {
          sendMessage(inputElement.value);
          inputElement.value = '';
          return false;
        } else {
          return true;
        }
      };
    </script>

  </body>
</html>
```

Here the function `sendMessage` is applied to the user input, and if it matches a command, the `sendCommand` function is invoked; otherwise a normal text message is sent to the server. In turn, the `sendCommand` function parses the command and invokes the proper server message. In this example, you only support the `/j <room>` command, which makes the user join a given room.

Then, the server has to interpret the `join` command, inserting the user into the room. When joining a room, that user may already be in another room, in which case the user needs to leave. Also, you store which room the user is currently in by associating the room name with the socket object. Listing 22-10 has the modified server code that allows this process.

LISTING 22-10: A Socket.IO chat server that allows users to join a room.

```
var httpd = require('http').createServer(handler);
var io = require('socket.io').listen(httpd);
var fs = require('fs');

httpd.listen(4000);

function handler(req, res) {
  fs.readFile(__dirname + '/index.html',
    function(err, data) {
      if (err) {
       res.writeHead(500);
       return res.end('Error loading index.html');
      }

      res.writeHead(200);
      res.end(data);
    }
  );
}

io.sockets.on('connection', function (socket) {
```

continues

LISTING 22-10 *(continued)*

```
socket.on('clientMessage', function(content) {
  socket.emit('serverMessage', 'You said: ' + content);

  socket.get('username', function(err, username) {
    if (! username) {
      username = socket.id;
    }
    socket.get('room', function(err, room) {
      if (err) { throw err; }
      var broadcast = socket.broadcast;
      var message = content;
      if (room) {
        broadcast.to(room);
      }
      broadcast.emit('serverMessage', username + ' said: ' + message);
    });
  });
});

socket.on('login', function(username) {
  socket.set('username', username, function(err) {
    if (err) { throw err; }
    socket.emit('serverMessage', 'Currently logged in as ' + username);
    socket.broadcast.emit('serverMessage', 'User ' + username +
      ' logged in');
  });
});

socket.on('disconnect', function() {
  socket.get('username', function(err, username) {
    if (! username) {
      username = socket.id;
    }
    socket.broadcast.emit('serverMessage', 'User ' + username +
      ' disconnected');
  });
});

socket.on('join', function(room) {
  socket.get('room', function(err, oldRoom) {
    if (err) { throw err; }

    socket.set('room', room, function(err) {
      if (err) { throw err; }
      socket.join(room);
      if (oldRoom) {
        socket.leave(oldRoom);
      }
      socket.get('username', function(err, username) {
        if (! username) {
          username = socket.id;
        }
      });
```

```
          socket.emit('serverMessage', 'You joined room ' + room);
          socket.get('username', function(err, username) {
            if (! username) {
              username = socket.id;
            }
            socket.broadcast.to(room).emit('serverMessage', 'User ' +
              username + ' joined this room');
          });
        });
      });
    });

    socket.emit('login');

  });
```

Here, when receiving a message, the server checks if the user has joined a room. If so, the server modifies the `broadcast` object to scope it to a given room by using the `broadcast.to(room)` modifier. If the user has not checked into a room yet, the message is broadcast to all users who have not yet joined a room.

You can save these changes into the client and server files, restart your Node server, and reload the chat application windows you may have open. Now you can use commands like `/j chatroom1` to join chatrooms.

Using Namespaces

This simple chat application could be a part of a larger website. If that website provided some near-real-time interactions that used Socket.IO, you would need to be careful and separate all server and client event names so they don't clash.

Fortunately, Socket.IO allows you to use namespaces to separate different applications on the server and on the client. First you have to connect to a specific namespaced Socket.IO URL on the client:

```
var socket = io.connect('http://localhost:4000/chat');
```

And then the chat server has to scope the sockets to only those that use this namespace:

```
var chat = io.of('/chat');

chat.on('connection', function (socket) {
  socket.on('clientMessage', function(content) {
  // ...
```

Now you can easily add another application to the client and server using the same technique without having to worry about whether the event names clash.

Distributing the Server-Side Application Using Redis

By using Socket.IO you allow all users to be connected using this one Node process. But in real production applications, you might need to have more than one Node process serving your application. For redundancy and/or load distribution, you may have a cluster of machines running your application server behind a load balancer.

> **NOTE** *If you are running a load balancer in front of a set of Node.js processes that run Socket.IO servers, you need to use one that supports WebSockets.*
>
> *If you want to run a Node-based Socket.IO server, I recommend looking at the node-http-proxy module, which is very malleable and feature rich. You can find more about it at:*
>
> `https://github.com/nodejitsu/node-http-proxy`

The problem with having a distributed set of processes like this is that any user can connect to any given Node.js process at any given time. That user will only be able to communicate with the other users who are also connected to that server. Other users will be connected to different servers and will be unreachable.

Fortunately, Socket.IO has a pluggable store. By default it uses a memory store that uses local process memory, but you can set the store to anything that conforms to a given protocol. For instance, a popular choice is to use the Redis database as a store.

Redis is a powerful in-memory key-value database with some advanced features. One of these features is to support pub-sub, where clients can publish events and several subscribers are notified of these events. Socket.IO already comes with support for a Redis store baked in, but you need to install the `redis` module:

```
$ npm install redis
```

Now the only thing you need to install is the Redis server itself.

> **NOTE** *Installing a Redis server is out of the scope of this book, but heading to the official website documentation should get you started:*
>
> `http://redis.io/topics/quickstart`

Once you have a Redis server installed and running, you are ready to configure your Socket.IO server so that it uses a Redis store:

```
var redis = require('redis'),
    RedisStore = require('socket.io/lib/stores/redis'),
    pub    = redis.createClient(),
    sub    = redis.createClient(),
    client = redis.createClient();

io.set('store', new RedisStore({
  redisPub : pub,
  redisSub : sub,
  redisClient : client
}));
```

And that's it. Just restart your server, and you should be using Redis. If your setup requires more than one server, Redis will now act as a centralized server for your messages, but because the `redis` module connects to the local host by default, you need to configure the server name for the Redis server:

```
var redisPort = 6379;
var redisHostname = 'my.host.name';

var redis = require('redis'),
    RedisStore = require('socket.io/lib/stores/redis'),
    pub    = redis.createClient(redisPort, redisHostname),
    sub    = redis.createClient(redisPort, redisHostname),
    client = redis.createClient(redisPort, redisHostname);
```

If you replace `my.host.name` with the hostname of the server that is running Redis, Listing 22-11 would then be the complete server code.

LISTING 22-11: A Socket.IO chat server that uses a Redis store.

```
var httpd = require('http').createServer(handler);
var io = require('socket.io').listen(httpd);
var fs = require('fs');

var redisPort = 6379;
var redisHostname = 'my.host.name';

var redis = require('redis'),
    RedisStore = require('socket.io/lib/stores/redis'),
    pub    = redis.createClient(redisPort, redisHostname),
    sub    = redis.createClient(redisPort, redisHostname),
    client = redis.createClient(redisPort, redisHostname);

io.set('store', new RedisStore({
  redisPub : pub,
  redisSub : sub,
  redisClient : client
}));

httpd.listen(4000);

function handler(req, res) {
  fs.readFile(__dirname + '/index.html',
    function(err, data) {
      if (err) {
       res.writeHead(500);
       return res.end('Error loading index.html');
      }

      res.writeHead(200);
      res.end(data);
    }
  );
}
```

continues

LISTING 22-11 *(continued)*

```
var chat = io.of('/chat');

chat.on('connection', function (socket) {
  socket.on('clientMessage', function(content) {
    socket.emit('serverMessage', 'You said: ' + content);

    socket.get('username', function(err, username) {
      if (! username) {
        username = socket.id;
      }
      socket.get('room', function(err, room) {
        if (err) { throw err; }
        var broadcast = socket.broadcast;
        var message = content;
        if (room) {
          broadcast.to(room);
        }
        broadcast.emit('serverMessage', username + ' said: ' + message);
      });
    });
  });

  socket.on('login', function(username) {
    socket.set('username', username, function(err) {
      if (err) { throw err; }
      socket.emit('serverMessage', 'Currently logged in as ' + username);
      socket.broadcast.emit('serverMessage', 'User ' + username +
        ' logged in');
    });
  });

  socket.on('disconnect', function() {
    socket.get('username', function(err, username) {
      if (! username) {
        username = socket.id;
      }
      socket.broadcast.emit('serverMessage', 'User ' + username +
        ' disconnected');
    });
  });

  socket.on('join', function(room) {
    socket.get('room', function(err, oldRoom) {
      if (err) { throw err; }

      socket.set('room', room, function(err) {
        if (err) { throw err; }
        socket.join(room);
        if (oldRoom) {
          socket.leave(oldRoom);
        }
        socket.get('username', function(err, username) {
```

```
          if (! username) {
            username = socket.id;
          }
        });
        socket.emit('serverMessage', 'You joined room ' + room);
        socket.get('username', function(err, username) {
          if (! username) {
            username = socket.id;
          }
          socket.broadcast.to(room).emit('serverMessage', 'User ' +
            username + ' joined this room');
        });
      });
    });
  });

  socket.emit('login');

});
```

SUMMARY

Socket.IO is a great cross-browser solution for providing near-real-time bi-directional communication between the browser and the server.

You can connect several clients to each other by broadcasting into all connected sockets, and you can also have the socket join and leave particular rooms and choose to broadcast to those rooms only.

By using namespaces you can also have several Socket.IO-based apps living safely together in the same client and server applications.

Also, you can distribute a Socket.IO application to many Node.js processes by using a Redis store that uses a Redis server as the central point of communication.

PART VI
Connecting to Databases

23

Connecting to MySQL Using node-mysql

WHAT'S IN THIS CHAPTER?

- Connecting to MySQL databases from Node
- Leveraging Node's asynchronous, non-blocking style when exchanging data with the database
- Avoiding security and performance pitfalls

As in many other programming environments, you will sooner or later want to persist certain types of data your application generates. This is especially true with multi-user server-client applications, in which information one user provides needs to be presented to one or many other users at a later point in time.

Although saving data in flat files or memory works in Node just as well as in other environments, it doesn't scale when structured access is needed for large amounts of data.

Relational databases like MySQL provide a reliable and fast solution to save and retrieve information in a structured manner by storing data on the hard drive and making it accessible through the standardized SQL language.

If your Node applications need to be able to communicate with MySQL databases and exchange data with them, the following sections on using the node-mysql library, reading from a MySQL database efficiently, and passing in data in a secure way will enable you to accomplish these tasks.

USING A LIBRARY TO CONNECT TO AND COMMUNICATE WITH A MYSQL DATABASE

As installing and setting up a MySQL database is not within the scope of this book, it's assumed that you have a working MySQL instance running on your localhost or on another reachable host.

To connect to your database, you must install the `node-mysql` package in your local directory with the following command:

```
$ npm install mysql
```

Once you have done this, write a simple application that connects to your server, as shown in Listing 23-1.

LISTING 23-1: Connecting and querying MySQL.

```
var mysql = require('mysql');

var client = mysql.createClient({
  host: 'localhost',
  user: 'root',
  password: 'root'
});

client.query(
  'SELECT "Hello, world!"',
  function (err, results, fields) {
    console.log(results);
    console.log(fields);
    client.end();
  }
);
```

Before saving and running this listing, you need to change lines 4, 5, and 6 to specify the host and credentials for accessing your MySQL server. If your installation is local, you may not need any credentials to connect to your MySQL server, in which case you can remove the user and password fields from the `createClient` options.

You can then save this code into a file named `hello_world.js` and run it:

```
$ node hello_world
[ { 'Hello, world!': 'Hello, world!' } ]
{ 'Hello, world!':
   { length: 35,
     received: 35,
     number: 2,
     type: 4,
     catalog: 'def',
     name: 'Hello, world!',
     charsetNumber: 192,
```

```
      fieldLength: 39,
      fieldType: 253,
      flags: 1,
      decimals: 31 } }
```

Even with this rudimentary example, you can see how the typical asynchronous callback flow is used once again to make the database request non-blocking. This is especially important in this context because — depending on the query and the size of the result set — database requests can be somewhat slow, putting the responsiveness of the application at risk if handled synchronously. Later in this chapter you'll look into an even more efficient way to retrieve results from the database.

When connecting to the database using `mysql.createClient()`, you can provide a set of options:

- `host`: The IP address or DNS name of the server that is to be connected. Defaults to localhost if omitted.
- `port`: The TCP port to connect to. Defaults to 3306 if omitted.
- `user`: The username used to authenticate against the server. Defaults to root if omitted.
- `password`: The password used to authenticate against the server. If omitted, a password-less connection is attempted.
- `database`: The database to be used upon successful connection. If omitted, no database is selected, and must be selected using a `SELECT` database query.
- `debug`: If set to `true`, *node-mysql* prints all incoming and outgoing data packets to the console. Defaults to `false`.
- `flags`: The MySQL connect protocol supports several flags that influence the low-level details of the connection handshake, such as which protocol version to use, whether to use compression or not, and so on. *node-mysql* ships with a sensible default, so unless your server is configured in a non-standard way, you don't need to set any of these flags. See `http://forge.mysql.com/wiki/MySQL_Internals_ClientServer_Protocol#Handshake_Initialization_Packet` for a list of available flags.

You have not yet queried for any real data. To do so, you need to create a database with a table and then add rows to the table:

```
client.query('CREATE DATABASE node', function(err) {
  if (err) {
    client.end();
    throw err;
  }
});
```

This shows how errors trigger the callback function. Here, you close the connection to the server if an error occurs. You can trigger an error case by running this script more than once. Because the database exists after the first run, it cannot be created again. Therefore, the second query fails.

ADDING DATA TO THE DATABASE WITH SECURITY CONCERNS IN MIND

Now, create a table and insert two rows of data:

```
client.query('USE node');

client.query('CREATE TABLE test ' +
             '(id INT(11) AUTO_INCREMENT, ' +
             ' content VARCHAR(255), ' +
             ' PRIMARY KEY(id))'
);

client.query('INSERT INTO test (content) VALUES ("Hello")');
client.query('INSERT INTO test (content) VALUES ("World")');

client.end();
```

This works well but has one problem. If queries are constructed this way and you have no direct control over the values used for the query (maybe because the value for `content` is provided by users inputting it through a form on a web page), your application becomes vulnerable to *SQL injection.* A malicious user can submit data to your application that, if passed on to the database unfiltered, breaks out of the intended SQL statement and allows the attacker to execute arbitrary statements that could cause harm.

Here is an example of SQL injection in action:

```
client.query('USE node');

var userInput = '"); DELETE FROM test WHERE id = 1; -- ';

client.query('INSERT INTO test (content) VALUES ("' + userInput + '")');

client.end();
```

It's a bit complicated to see what's actually going on, but this is what happens.

The code is written with the intent to supply a text string — entered by the user — to the query value for the `content` field. Of course, the actual user input is only simulated, but imagine that the value of `userInput` originates from a field of an HTTP form.

In this case, the attacker does not supply a simple text string, but instead prematurely closes the original query by closing the quotation mark and bracket with `");`. She then starts her own query that deletes the row with `id 1`. Because the second part of the original query — the closing quotation marks and the closing bracket — would result in invalid SQL, the attacker prefixes these with two dashes. This results in everything after these dashes being treated as a comment and therefore being ignored.

Thus, the complete statement received by the server is:

```
INSERT INTO test (content) VALUES (""); DELETE FROM test WHERE id = 1; -- ")
```

This results in one new row being inserted to the table, and the row with `id 1` being deleted.

You can, and should, protect your application against these kinds of attacks on several levels. The most important thing to do is to always treat incoming data as potentially harmful and reject any data that does not match a strict definition of "harmless" as early as possible.

At the point in your application where foreign data will make up parts of a database query, there is an additional precaution you can leverage to protect against certain attack scenarios. Using placeholders with value assignments, you can guarantee that any part of your query that is supposed to be treated as a value is indeed interpreted by the database as a value and can never be interpreted as, for example, a `DELETE` command.

Placeholders enable you to do this because, instead of concatenating your own commands together with user input into a final SQL statement (which allows an attacker to break out of the SQL structure), you write a SQL statement that only contains the commands you intend and doesn't contain any values. The placeholders denote the location of values, the values are provided separately, and the database combines both into a working statement.

This way, the query isn't digested as a whole but instead becomes semantically enriched — the database knows which parts of the query are to be treated as values and values only. Looking at the first example, the lack of this semantic allowed the attacker to execute a command instead of enter a value.

Here is how you can issue a statement with placeholders and value replacement:

```
client.query('USE node');

var userInput = '"); DELETE FROM test WHERE id = 1; -- ';

client.query('INSERT INTO test (content) VALUES (?)', [userInput]);

client.end();
```

Although the user input is still malicious, it cannot harm the database anymore. Because the server knows that anything in *`userInput`* is to be treated as the value for the `content` field, you don't end up with a deleted row 1 but with a new row whose content field has the value `"); DELETE FROM test WHERE id = 1; --`.

Although this is probably not the content you wished for, you have stopped the attack itself.

Value assignment in node-mysql works by writing a SQL statement with quotation marks as placeholders for values and by additionally supplying an array of values that replace each of the placeholders in sequence. Matching multiple placeholders with multiple values works by simply traversing the supplied array from lower to higher keys, thus the following statement will result in the same data being written.

```
var data = [100, "the content"];

client.query('INSERT INTO test (id, content) VALUES (?, ?)', data);
```

is equal to

```
var data = [];
data[1] = "the content";
data[0] = 100;

client.query('INSERT INTO test (id, content) VALUES (?, ?)', data);
```

Sometimes, you need to retrieve certain information when inserting or updating rows, like the ID of the last inserted record or the number of rows affected by a query. *node-mysql* provides this information to an optional callback:

```
client.query('INSERT INTO test (content) VALUES (?)', ['the content'],
  function(err, info) {
    if (err) {
      return handle_error(err);
    }
    console.log(info.insertId);
  }
);

client.query('UPDATE test SET content = ?', ['new content'], function(err, info) {
  if (err) {
    return handle_error(err);
  }
  console.log(info.affectedRows);
});
```

You can see here that the callback provides a first argument containing an error object in case of an error, as usual. If no error occurred, the second argument contains an object with the results of your query. If you insert into a table with an auto-incremented field, that object will contain an `insertId` property with the value of that field. If the query you performed deleted, updated, or removed rows, the property `affectedRows` will contain the number of affected rows.

READING DATA EFFICIENTLY

You can and should read from the database using placeholders, too. *node-mysql* provides the result set in two different ways. Providing a callback to the query call is the most straightforward way:

```
query = client.query(
  'SELECT id, content FROM test WHERE id IN (?, ?)',
  [1, 100],  function(err, results, fields) {
    if (err) {
      throw err;
    }
    console.log(results);
  }
);
```

The resulting output looks like this:

```
[ { id: 1, content: 'the content' },
  { id: 100, content: 'the content' } ]
```

As you can see, you receive the complete set of rows as an array of objects, in one go. When querying for large result sets, this can become problematic, because Node.js has to buffer the whole result set in memory.

To circumvent this, you can handle the result set row by row, by utilizing *node-mysql's* streaming API.

When sending a query to the server using `client.query`, a `Query` object is returned that emits several events to which you can listen: `error`, `field`, `row`, and `end`.

You can use these events as follows:

```
query = client.query('SELECT id, content FROM test WHERE id IN (?, ?)', [1, 100]);

query.on('error', function(err) {
  throw err;
});

query.on('field', function(field) {
  console.log('Received field:');
  console.log(field);
});

query.on('row', function(row) {
  console.log('Received row:');
  console.log(row);
});

query.on('end', function(result) {

  console.log('Finished retrieving results');

});
```

Which results in the following output:

```
Received field:
{ length: 38,
  received: 38,
  number: 2,
  type: 4,
  catalog: 'def',
  db: 'node',
  table: 'test',
  originalTable: 'test',
  name: 'id',
  originalName: 'id',
  charsetNumber: 63,
  fieldLength: 11,
  fieldType: 3,
  flags: 16899,
  decimals: 0 }
Received field:
{ length: 48,
  received: 48,
```

```
  number: 3,
  type: 4,
  catalog: 'def',
  db: 'node',
  table: 'test',
  originalTable: 'test',
  name: 'content',
  originalName: 'content',
  charsetNumber: 192,
  fieldLength: 765,
  fieldType: 253,
  flags: 0,
  decimals: 0 }
Received row:
{ id: 1, content: 'the content' }
Received row:
{ id: 100, content: 'the content' }
Finished retrieving results
```

Why is the `result` parameter passed to the `end` event callback? It's passed only if the query didn't yield any results and contains the content of the MySQL OK packet.

Having learned about the streaming query API and building queries with placeholders, you can put everything together into a simple yet complete application, as shown in Listing 23-2.

LISTING 23-2: A MySQL application.

```
var mysql = require('mysql');

var client = mysql.createClient({
  host: 'localhost',
  user: 'root',
  password: 'root',
});

client.query('DROP DATABASE IF EXISTS node');
client.query('CREATE DATABASE node');
client.query('USE node');

client.query('CREATE TABLE test ' +
             '(id INT(11) AUTO_INCREMENT, ' +
             ' content VARCHAR(255), ' +
             ' PRIMARY KEY(id))'
);

for (var i = 0; i < 10000; i++) {
  client.query('INSERT INTO test (content) VALUES (?)', ['content for row ' +
   (i + 1)]);
}

client.query('UPDATE test SET content = ? WHERE id >= ?', ['new content', 9000],
```

```
    function(err, info) {
      console.log('Changed content of ' + info.affectedRows + ' rows');
    }
  );

  query = client.query('SELECT id, content FROM test WHERE id >= ? AND id <= ?',
    [8990, 9010]);

  query.on('error', function(err) {
    throw err;
  });

  query.on('row', function(row) {
    console.log('Content of row #' + row.id + ' is: "' + row.content + '"');
  });

  query.on('end', function(result) {
    console.log('Finished retrieving results');
  });

  client.end();
```

Again, you probably need to change the hostname and credentials at the beginning of the file. Then, save this into a file named `app.js` and run it:

```
$ node app.js
```

Doing so results in the following output:

```
Content of row #8990 is: "content for row 8990"
Content of row #8991 is: "content for row 8991"
Content of row #8992 is: "content for row 8992"
Content of row #8993 is: "content for row 8993"
Content of row #8994 is: "content for row 8994"
Content of row #8995 is: "content for row 8995"
Content of row #8996 is: "content for row 8996"
Content of row #8997 is: "content for row 8997"
Content of row #8998 is: "content for row 8998"
Content of row #8999 is: "content for row 8999"
Content of row #9000 is: "new content"
Content of row #9001 is: "new content"
Content of row #9002 is: "new content"
Content of row #9003 is: "new content"
Content of row #9004 is: "new content"
Content of row #9005 is: "new content"
Content of row #9006 is: "new content"
Content of row #9007 is: "new content"
Content of row #9008 is: "new content"
Content of row #9009 is: "new content"
Content of row #9010 is: "new content"
Finished retrieving results
```

> **WARNING** *The MySQL protocol is sequential, which means that when using a connection you are executing each query in series. If you are building an application that performs many MySQL operations, having them all wait for each other is probably not a good solution.*
>
> *In that case you need to create more than one connection to MySQL. You can choose to have one connection per application user, but depending on the number of concurrent users and the capacity of your MySQL server, this might not work well.*
>
> *You can also choose to create a connection pool, whereby you have a number of connections to your MySQL server and distribute the queries to them.*

SUMMARY

Exchanging data with a MySQL database is straightforward and efficient, thanks to the *node-mysql* module. However, you must be careful and pay close attention when dealing with external and therefore potentially malicious data. By listening to asynchronous events, large result sets can be handled efficiently row by row.

24

Connecting to CouchDB Using Nano

WHAT'S IN THIS CHAPTER?

- Creating a CouchDB database
- Creating and updating a CouchDB view
- Inserting or updating a document
- Querying a view and presenting the results
- Attaching binary files to documents

In the last few years, a series of projects has tried to solve some relational database problems by providing a different approach to database management systems design. This movement has been named NoSQL. Not only does it reject a query language, it also rejects the relational model and, in most cases, simplifies that model and relaxes some of its assumptions.

> **NOTE** *For instance, in most relational databases, when making several modifications inside one transaction, it can be guaranteed that all the changes are done atomically, that is, that either all of them occur or they have no effect. In most NoSQL databases, when inserting or updating several documents, atomicity may not be guaranteed in exchange for a simpler and less problematic concurrency model.*

Right in the middle of the NoSQL "revolution" stands the successful poster child and Open Source project named CouchDB. CouchDB is a database that embraces web standards; it uses JSON for object storage and JavaScript for making queries.

> **NOTE** *Installing and learning how to fully operate a CouchDB database is out of the scope of this book. If you opt to use an Internet service that offers CouchDB hosting (like IrisCouch), you won't need to install CouchDB in your local machine.*
>
> *If you need to install it, though, head to* `http://couchdb.apache.org/` *and learn more about it.*

CouchDB also uses HTTP for client-server communication. In fact, when using CouchDB from Node, you need nothing more than the Node HTTP Client API even though, in the end, you will probably want to create some sort of library code to reduce code duplication.

Nano is just that — it's a third-party module that builds on top of Mikeal Rogers's `request` module (covered in Chapter 13, "Making HTTP Requests"), which has some helper functions for the most common CouchDB actions, minimizing abstraction in favor of simplicity.

This chapter builds on top of the Socket.IO-based chat application you developed in Chapter 22, "Making Universal Real-Time Web Applications Using Socket.IO," and provides message persistence and some other nice applications.

INSTALLING NANO

You can install Nano using the NPM install command, or you can add it to a `package.json` manifest like this:

```
{
  "name": "couch-socketio-chat",
  "version": "1.0.0",
  "dependencies": {
    "nano": "3.1.x",
    "socket.io": "0.9.x"
  }
}
```

In addition to the Nano module, you also have the Socket.IO dependency so you can build on top of the Socket.IO chat app.

You can now install the dependencies by running:

```
$ npm install
```

> **NOTE** *At the end of Chapter 22, you had a dependency on the Redis module, but now you can leave it out because you will only build using the memory store. If you want to use Redis later as a Socket.IO store, you can refer back to Chapter 22.*

You can get the code from Chapter 22 and copy the `index.html` file containing the client code and the `app.js file` containing the server code, which you'll build upon. Listing 24-1 shows the server example.

LISTING 24-1: The Socket.IO-based server example you'll build upon.

```
var httpd = require('http').createServer(handler);
var io = require('socket.io').listen(httpd);
var fs = require('fs');

httpd.listen(4000);

function handler(req, res) {
  fs.readFile(__dirname + '/index.html',
    function(err, data) {
      if (err) {
       res.writeHead(500);
       return res.end('Error loading index.html');
      }

      res.writeHead(200);
      res.end(data);
    }
  );
}

var chat = io.of('/chat');

chat.on('connection', function (socket) {
  socket.on('clientMessage', function(content) {
    socket.emit('serverMessage', 'You said: ' + content);

    socket.get('username', function(err, username) {
      if (! username) {
        username = socket.id;
      }
      socket.get('room', function(err, room) {
        if (err) { throw err; }
        var broadcast = socket.broadcast;
        var message = content;
        if (room) {
          broadcast.to(room);
        }
        broadcast.emit('serverMessage', username + ' said: ' + message);
      });
    });
  });

  socket.on('login', function(username) {
    socket.set('username', username, function(err) {
      if (err) { throw err; }
      socket.emit('serverMessage', 'Currently logged in as ' + username);
      socket.broadcast.emit('serverMessage', 'User ' +
```

continues

LISTING 24-1 *(continued)*

```
username + ' logged in');
    });
  });

  socket.on('disconnect', function() {
    socket.get('username', function(err, username) {
      if (! username) {
        username = socket.id;
      }
      socket.broadcast.emit('serverMessage', 'User ' +
        username + ' disconnected');
    });
  });

  socket.on('join', function(room) {
    socket.get('room', function(err, oldRoom) {
      if (err) { throw err; }

      socket.set('room', room, function(err) {
        if (err) { throw err; }
        socket.join(room);
        if (oldRoom) {
          socket.leave(oldRoom);
        }
        socket.get('username', function(err, username) {
          if (! username) {
            username = socket.id;
          }
        });
        socket.emit('serverMessage', 'You joined room ' + room);
        socket.get('username', function(err, username) {
          if (! username) {
            username = socket.id;
          }
          socket.broadcast.to(room).emit('serverMessage', 'User ' + username + '
           joined this room');
        });
      });
    });
  });

  socket.emit('login');

});
```

> **NOTE** *If you're having problems connecting from the client to the server, it may be because you need to make a small modification that I asked you to do by the end of Chapter 22, which was connect to* `http://localhost:4000/chat` *instead of* `http://localhost:4000/`:
>
> ```
> var socket = io.connect('http://localhost:4000/chat');
> ```

CONNECTING AND CREATING A DATABASE

Now you need to create a database connection. Unlike most database management servers, CouchDB clients don't use a connection-oriented protocol. Instead they use plain HTTP. HTTP is a stateless protocol, which means that each transaction is performed inside an independent HTTP request.

In this sense, there is no real "connection" to the database in Nano; there is only the reference to a CouchDB server and a database. This implies that any connectivity problems that arise happen only when an individual request is performed.

> **NOTE** *Installing and managing a CouchDB server is out of the scope of this book, but Internet services are available to provide a remote CouchDB server. One of these services is IrisCouch, which you can reach at* `www.iriscouch.com/`.
>
> *You can use IrisCouch to create and use a small database for free (if your usage is modest). When signing up, you will get a URL of the type:*
>
> ```
> http://myiriscouchserver.iriscouch.com
> ```

Once your CouchDB server is running, you need to import the `nano` module into the `app.js` file:

```
var nano = require('nano');
```

Then you need to create a database server reference:

```
var couchdb = nano('https://myiriscouchserver.iriscouch.com');
```

You should replace the default URL with the URL of your CouchDB database. If your database requires authentication to be able to create databases and insert or modify documents, you should add credentials to the URL like this:

```
var couchdb = nano('https://username:password@myiriscouchserver.iriscouch.com');
```

Next, make sure that a database named `chat` exists. For that you need to do the following:

```
couchdb.db.create('chat', function(err) {
  if (err) { console.error(err); }
  var db = couchdb.use('chat');
  // ...
});
```

Now, once the database is created, the callback is invoked. You can place the rest of the server initialization inside this callback.

Notice that you are just logging the error and proceeding anyway. This is because, if the database already exists, CouchDB will complain and yield an error, and you will get this error in the callback. You can try watching the error happen if you save Listing 24-2 into the file app.js and then stop and start your application twice. This will force your code to attempt to create a database that already exists, yielding the corresponding CouchDB error.

LISTING 24-2: The Socket.IO-based server that creates the CouchDB client when initializing.

```
var nano = require('nano');
var couchdb = nano('https://myiriscouchserver.iriscouch.com');

couchdb.db.create('chat', function(err) {
  if (err) { console.error(err); }
  var chatDB = couchdb.use('chat');

  var httpd = require('http').createServer(handler);
  var io = require('socket.io').listen(httpd);
  var fs = require('fs');

  httpd.listen(4000);

  function handler(req, res) {
    fs.readFile(__dirname + '/index.html',
      function(err, data) {
        if (err) {
         res.writeHead(500);
         return res.end('Error loading index.html');
        }

        res.writeHead(200);
        res.end(data);
      }
    );
  }

  var chat = io.of('/chat');

  chat.on('connection', function (socket) {
    socket.on('clientMessage', function(content) {
      socket.emit('serverMessage', 'You said: ' + content);

      socket.get('username', function(err, username) {
        if (! username) {
          username = socket.id;
        }
        socket.get('room', function(err, room) {
          if (err) { throw err; }
          var broadcast = socket.broadcast;
          var message = content;
          if (room) {
            broadcast.to(room);
          }
          broadcast.emit('serverMessage', username + ' said: ' + message);
        });
```

```
      });
    });

    socket.on('login', function(username) {
      socket.set('username', username, function(err) {
        if (err) { throw err; }
        socket.emit('serverMessage', 'Currently logged in as ' + username);
        socket.broadcast.emit('serverMessage', 'User ' + username + ' logged in');
      });
    });

    socket.on('disconnect', function() {
      socket.get('username', function(err, username) {
        if (! username) {
          username = socket.id;
        }
        socket.broadcast.emit('serverMessage', 'User ' + username +
          ' disconnected');
      });
    });

    socket.on('join', function(room) {
      socket.get('room', function(err, oldRoom) {
        if (err) { throw err; }

        socket.set('room', room, function(err) {
          if (err) { throw err; }
          socket.join(room);
          if (oldRoom) {
            socket.leave(oldRoom);
          }
          socket.get('username', function(err, username) {
            if (! username) {
              username = socket.id;
            }
          });
          socket.emit('serverMessage', 'You joined room ' + room);
          socket.get('username', function(err, username) {
            if (! username) {
              username = socket.id;
            }
            socket.broadcast.to(room).emit('serverMessage', 'User ' +
              username + ' joined this room');
          });
        });
      });
    });

    socket.emit('login');

  });

});
```

The second time you start your application, you will get an error like this one:

```
$ node app.js
{ [Error: Unspecified error]
  name: 'Error',
  scope: 'couch',
  status_code: 412,
  'status-code': 412,
  request:
   { method: 'PUT',
     headers:
      { 'content-type': 'application/json',
        accept: 'application/json' },
     uri: 'https://myiriscouchserver.iriscouch.com/chat',
     jar: false,
     callback: [Function] },
  headers:
   { date: 'Fri, 13 Jul 2012 14:21:55 GMT',
     'content-type': 'application/json',
     'cache-control': 'must-revalidate',
     'status-code': 412,
     uri: 'https://myiriscouchserver.iriscouch.com/chat' },
  errid: 'non_200',
  error: 'file_exists',
  reason: 'The database could not be created, the file already exists.',
  description: 'Unspecified error',
  stacktrace:
   [ 'Error: Unspecified error',
     '    at Request._callback (/Users/pedroteixeira/projects/wiley-node/code/24/no
de_modules/nano/nano.js:290:39)',
     '    at Request.callback (/Users/pedroteixeira/projects/wiley-node/code/24/nod
e_modules/nano/node_modules/request/main.js:120:22)',
     '    at Request.<anonymous> (native)',
     '    at Request.emit (events.js:70:17)',
     '    at Request.<anonymous> (/Users/pedroteixeira/projects/wiley-node/code/24/
node_modules/nano/node_modules/request/main.js:555:16)',
     '    at Request.emit (events.js:67:17)',
     '    at IncomingMessage.<anonymous> (/Users/pedroteixeira/projects/wiley-node/
code/24/node_modules/nano/node_modules/request/main.js:517:14)',
     '    at IncomingMessage.emit (events.js:88:20)',
     '    at HTTPParser.onMessageComplete (http.js:137:23)' ] }
```

You can see that this error has an HTTP status code of 412 and a sentence stating that `"The database could not be created, the file already exists."` You can then be more thorough and check that the error status code is the expected one:

```
if (err && err.status_code !== 412) {
  throw err;
}
```

Now you have a reference to the chat database that was sent in line 9:

```
var chatDB = couchdb.use('chat');
```

You can use this database reference to send queries and commands.

STORING DOCUMENTS

Next you will persist messages into the database. Every time a user sends a message, you need to store it in the chat database.

```
chat.on('connection', function (socket) {
    socket.on('clientMessage', function(content) {
      socket.emit('serverMessage', 'You said: ' + content);

      socket.get('username', function(err, username) {
        if (! username) {
          username = socket.id;
        }
        socket.get('room', function(err, room) {
          if (err) { throw err; }
          var broadcast = socket.broadcast;
          var message = content;
          if (room) {
            broadcast.to(room);
          }

          var messageDoc = {
            when: Date.now(),
            from: username,
            room: room,
            message: content
          };

          chatDB.insert(messageDoc, function(err) {
            if (err) { console.error(err); }
          });

          broadcast.emit('serverMessage', username + ' said: ' + message);
        });
      });
    });
```

Here, you are building a simple document that contains the message and some meta-data — when the message was emitted, who emitted it, and in which chat room.

> **NOTE** *Even though you are creating a simple flat document in this example, in CouchDB you can have documents as complex as you want, with as many nested levels as you need.*

CREATING AND USING COUCHDB VIEWS

Now that you have every message persisted, it would be nice if the users received the most recent messages every time they connect or join a room. CouchDB is just a simple key-value store. Given the correct ID, you could retrieve one single document by using the following:

```
chatDB.get(messageID, function(err, doc) {
  console.log('got document!', doc);
});
```

But that is of no use. You need to retrieve, say, the latest 10 messages for a given chat room, and for that you have to create a more complex query.

The way to create more complex queries is by creating indexes using `map-reduce` functions, which are JavaScript functions that reside in the CouchDB server. To create a mapping function, you need to think about which keys you'll be mapping each document to so that CouchDB can serve your queries. In this case, you want to index messages by room, so a mapping function like the following one works well:

```
function(doc) {
  emit([doc.room, doc.when], doc);
}
```

This mapping function will be invoked every time there is a new document or a document is changed, and every time it will emit the document indexed by a key containing the room identifier and the timestamp. This will allow CouchDB to order the index by room and creation time, allowing you not only to get all the messages pertaining to a certain room but also, in conjunction, to retrieve the messages created between two given dates.

Now you can wrap the server initialization to a function named `startServer`. This function will be called once the database initialization operations are finished. Then you can add some initialization code after you are sure that the `chat` database is created.

Now you need to insert this mapping function in a design document so that CouchDB creates the corresponding view.

```
couchdb.db.create('chat', function(err) {
  if (err && err.status_code !== 412) {
    throw err;
  }

  var designDoc = {
    language: "javascript",
    views: {
      by_room: {
        map: couchMapReduce.toString()
      }
    }
  };

  var chatDB = couchdb.use('chat');
```

```
    (function insertOrUpdateDesignDoc() {
      chatDB.insert(designDoc, '_design/designdoc', function(err) {
        if (err) {
          if (err.status_code === 409) {
            chatDB.get('_design/designdoc', function(err, ddoc) {
              if (err) { return console.error(err); }
              designDoc._rev = ddoc._rev;
              insertOrUpdateDesignDoc();
            });
          } else {
            return console.error(err);
          }
        }
        startServer();
      });
    }());
  });
```

Here you are building a design document. A design document is a special document type in CouchDB where you define, among other things, the views. Each view is composed of a mapping function (and an optional reducing function, which you don't need here). You then insert this design document into the `_design/designdoc` path. The path called `_design` is, in CouchDB, where all the design documents of a certain database go to live. The design document created here is simply called `designdoc`.

Beware that the insertion of the design document can fail, especially when a design document is already in CouchDB, in which case the error will indicate a `409 Conflict` HTTP response status code. In that case you need to update the design document revision so that there is no versioning conflict and try again.

> **NOTE** *Even though this book does not aim to teach you CouchDB inside and out, you need to understand some basic principles. One of them is the way CouchDB uses versioning.*
>
> *In CouchDB each document has a version number. To update a certain document, you need to pass in the latest version number. If you don't, CouchDB will return a* `409 Conflict` *HTTP response status code. This prevents two clients from updating the same document twice without each one knowing about the other.*
>
> *For instance, say that clients A and B have version 1 of document D. Clients A and B modify the document and order an update at the same time. Document D will have a* `._rev` *property with something like* `1-76e555f270676c7f20a73726875c50b8`.
>
> *The server processes A's request first and creates the second revision of the document, let's say* `2-676c7f20a73726875c50b876e555f270`. *When the edits from client B try to update document D, those edits still refer to version 1 (plus a checksum number). The database now has a revision number 2 for document D, so client B's update will be rejected with a* `409 Conflict` *status code.*

Listing 24-3 contains the full server code, which adds the necessary design documents for these views.

LISTING 24-3: The Socket.IO-based server that creates the database and the view you need.

```
var nano = require('nano');
var couchdb = nano('https://myiriscouchserver.iriscouch.com');

var couchMapReduce = function (doc) {
  emit([doc.room, doc.when], doc);
};

couchdb.db.create('chat', function(err) {
  if (err && err.status_code !== 412) {
    throw err;
  }

  var designDoc = {
    language: "javascript",
    views: {
      by_room: {
        map: couchMapReduce.toString()
      }
    }
  };

  var chatDB = couchdb.use('chat');

  (function insertOrUpdateDesignDoc() {
    chatDB.insert(designDoc, '_design/designdoc', function(err) {
      if (err) {
        if (err.status_code === 409) {
          chatDB.get('_design/designdoc', function(err, ddoc) {
            if (err) { return console.error(err); }
            designDoc._rev = ddoc._rev;
            insertOrUpdateDesignDoc();
          });
        } else {
          return console.error(err);
        }
      }
      startServer();
    });
  }());
});

function startServer() {
  var chatDB = couchdb.use('chat');

  var httpd = require('http').createServer(handler);
  var io = require('socket.io').listen(httpd);
  var fs = require('fs');
```

```
httpd.listen(4000);

function handler(req, res) {
  fs.readFile(__dirname + '/index.html',
    function(err, data) {
      if (err) {
       res.writeHead(500);
       return res.end('Error loading index.html');
      }

      res.writeHead(200);
      res.end(data);
    }
  );
}

var chat = io.of('/chat');

chat.on('connection', function (socket) {
  socket.on('clientMessage', function(content) {
    socket.emit('serverMessage', 'You said: ' + content);

    socket.get('username', function(err, username) {
      if (! username) {
        username = socket.id;
      }
      socket.get('room', function(err, room) {
        if (err) { throw err; }
        var broadcast = socket.broadcast;
        var message = content;
        if (room) {
          broadcast.to(room);
        }

        var messageDoc = {
          when: Date.now(),
          from: username,
          room: room,
          message: content
        };

        chatDB.insert(messageDoc, function(err) {
          if (err) { console.error(err); }
        });

        broadcast.emit('serverMessage', username + ' said: ' + message);
      });
    });
  });

  socket.on('login', function(username) {
    socket.set('username', username, function(err) {
      if (err) { throw err; }
      socket.emit('serverMessage', 'Currently logged in as ' + username);
      socket.broadcast.emit('serverMessage', 'User ' + username + ' logged in');
    });
```

continues

LISTING 24-3 *(continued)*

```
        });

        socket.on('disconnect', function() {
          socket.get('username', function(err, username) {
            if (! username) {
              username = socket.id;
            }
            socket.broadcast.emit('serverMessage', 'User ' + username +
              ' disconnected');
          });
        });

        socket.on('join', function(room) {
          socket.get('room', function(err, oldRoom) {
            if (err) { throw err; }

            socket.set('room', room, function(err) {
              if (err) { throw err; }
              socket.join(room);
              if (oldRoom) {
                socket.leave(oldRoom);
              }
              socket.get('username', function(err, username) {
                if (! username) {
                  username = socket.id;
                }
              });
              socket.emit('serverMessage', 'You joined room ' + room);
              socket.get('username', function(err, username) {
                if (! username) {
                  username = socket.id;
                }
                socket.broadcast.to(room).emit('serverMessage', 'User ' +
                  username + ' joined this room');
              });
            });
          });
        });

        socket.emit('login');

      });
    }
```

Now you can use the following URL to query the latest 10 messages on the chat room named `room1`:

```
/chat/_design/designdoc/_view/by_room?end_key=[%22room1%22,0]&start_key=
[%22room1%22,9999999999999]&limit=10&descending=true
```

This URL is querying CouchDB `by_room` view in the `chat` database. It gets all the objects with keys between `["room1", 0]` and `["room1", 9999999999999]` in ascending order, limited to 10 elements. This is a range query on the view, where you're getting every document with a key where the first place is `room1` and the second place can range from 0 (the beginning of time) to 9999999999999 (sometime in the future). You can place the call to this view inside a function named `sendBackLog`, which makes this query and sends it to a client socket:

```
function sendBackLog(socket, room) {
  var getOptions = {
    start_key: JSON.stringify([room, 9999999999999]),
    end_key: JSON.stringify([room, 0]),
    limit: 10,
    descending: true
  };

  chatDB.get('_design/designdoc/_view/by_room', getOptions,
   function(err, results) {
    var messages = results.rows.reverse().map(function(res) {
      return res.value;
    });
    socket.emit('backlog', messages);
  });
}
```

This function will then need to be invoked when the user logs in and enters a room. Once the response from CouchDB arrives, you get an object that contains the document count and the offset of the result. In this case you don't need these values. In the response object you also get the documents inside a `rows` property, which you collect and emit inside a `backlog` event sent to the socket.

You may have noticed that you are no longer emitting a string message. Instead you are emitting a message document that contains several attributes, including the message text and the author, room, and timestamp.

Next you need to change the front-end code to accept this document as the message format instead of a string. Using this, you can enhance the presentation of your messages by styling the message components differently. The front-end code for printing a message now is the following:

```
function addMessage(message) {
  var newMessageElement = document.createElement('div');

  newMessageElement.className = "message";

  if (message.when) {
    message.when = new Date(message.when);
  }

  ['when', 'from', 'message'].forEach(function(prop) {
    var newPart = document.createElement('span');
    newPart.className = prop;
    var messageText = message[prop];
    if (prop !== 'message') {
      messageText = '[' + messageText + ']';
      if (prop === 'from' && message[prop] === username) {
        newPart.className += ' self';
      }
```

```
      }
      messageText += ' ';
      var newPartText = document.createTextNode(messageText);
      newPart.appendChild(newPartText);
      newMessageElement.appendChild(newPart);
    });
```

Also, you need to add some CSS definitions for styling the content and use separate colors with each message component:

```
.message .when {
  color: grey;
}
.message .from {
  color: red;
}
.message .from.self {
  color: green;
}
```

Listing 24-4 now contains the complete front-end code.

LISTING 24-4: A new version of the Socket.IO-based chat client that formats the messages.

```
<html>
  <head>
    <title>Node.js WebSocket chat</title>
    <style type="text/css">
      #input {
        width: 200px;
      }
      #messages {
        position: fixed;
        top: 40px;
        bottom: 8px;
        left: 8px;
        right: 8px;
        border: 1px solid #EEEEEE;
        padding: 8px;
      }
      .message .when {
        color: grey;
      }
      .message .from {
        color: red;
      }
      .message .from.self {
        color: green;
      }

    </style>
  </head>
```

```
<body>

  Your message:
  <input type="text" id="input">

  <div id="messages"></div>

  <script src="http://localhost:4000/socket.io/socket.io.js"></script>
  <script type="text/javascript">
    var messagesElement = document.getElementById('messages');
    var lastMessageElement = null;
    var username;

    function addMessage(message) {
      var newMessageElement = document.createElement('div');

      newMessageElement.className = "message";

      if (message.when) {
        message.when = new Date(message.when);
      }

      ['when', 'from', 'message'].forEach(function(prop) {
        var newPart = document.createElement('span');
        newPart.className = prop;
        var messageText = message[prop];
        if (prop !== 'message') {
          messageText = '[' + messageText + ']';
          if (prop === 'from' && message[prop] === username) {
            newPart.className += ' self';
          }
        }
        messageText += ' ';
        var newPartText = document.createTextNode(messageText);
        newPart.appendChild(newPartText);
        newMessageElement.appendChild(newPart);
      });

      messagesElement.insertBefore(newMessageElement, lastMessageElement);
      lastMessageElement = newMessageElement;
    }

    var socket = io.connect('http://localhost:4000/chat');
    socket.on('serverMessage', function(content) {
      addMessage(content);
    });

    socket.on('login', function() {
      username = prompt('What username would you like to use?');
      socket.emit('login', username);
    });

    socket.on('backlog', function(messages) {
      messages.forEach(addMessage);
    });
```

continues

LISTING 24-4 *(continued)*

```
      function sendCommand(command, args) {
        if (command === 'j') {
          socket.emit('join', args);
        } else {
          alert('unknown command: ' + command);
        }
      }

      function sendMessage(message) {
        var commandMatch = message.match(/^\/(\w*)(.*)/);
        if (commandMatch) {
          sendCommand(commandMatch[1], commandMatch[2].trim());
        } else {
          socket.emit('clientMessage', message);
        }
      }

      var inputElement = document.getElementById('input');

      inputElement.onkeydown = function(keyboardEvent) {
        if (keyboardEvent.keyCode === 13) {
          sendMessage(inputElement.value);
          inputElement.value = '';
          return false;
        } else {
          return true;
        }
      };
    </script>

  </body>
</html>
```

Now you need to change the server to use this message format with every server-sent message. This means that you have to make subtle changes to every function that emits these messages, resulting in the server-side code shown in Listing 24-5.

LISTING 24-5: A new version of the Socket.IO-based chat server that sends structured message documents.

```
var nano = require('nano');
var couchdb = nano('https://myiriscouchserver.iriscouch.com');

var couchMapReduce = function (doc) {
  emit([doc.room, doc.when], doc);
};

couchdb.db.create('chat', function(err) {
  if (err && err.status_code !== 412) {
    throw err;
  }
```

```
    var designDoc = {
      language: "javascript",
      views: {
        by_room: {
          map: couchMapReduce.toString()
        }
      }
    };

    var chatDB = couchdb.use('chat');

    (function insertOrUpdateDesignDoc() {
      chatDB.insert(designDoc, '_design/designdoc', function(err) {
        if (err) {
          if (err.status_code === 409) {
            chatDB.get('_design/designdoc', function(err, ddoc) {
              if (err) { return console.error(err); }
              designDoc._rev = ddoc._rev;
              insertOrUpdateDesignDoc();
            });
          } else {
            return console.error(err);
          }
        }
        startServer();
      });
    }());
  });

  function startServer() {
    var chatDB = couchdb.use('chat');

    var httpd = require('http').createServer(handler);
    var io = require('socket.io').listen(httpd);
    var fs = require('fs');

    httpd.listen(4000);

    function handler(req, res) {
      fs.readFile(__dirname + '/index.html',
        function(err, data) {
          if (err) {
           res.writeHead(500);
           return res.end('Error loading index.html');
          }

          res.writeHead(200);
          res.end(data);
        }
      );
    }


    function sendBackLog(socket, room) {
      var getOptions = {
        start_key: JSON.stringify([room, 9999999999999]),
```

continues

LISTING 24-5 *(continued)*

```
      end_key: JSON.stringify([room, 0]),
      limit: 10,
      descending: true
    };

    chatDB.get('_design/designdoc/_view/by_room', getOptions,
      function(err, results) {
        var messages = results.rows.reverse().map(function(res) {
          return res.value;
        });
        socket.emit('backlog', messages);
      });
  }

  var chat = io.of('/chat');

  chat.on('connection', function (socket) {
    socket.on('clientMessage', function(content) {

      socket.get('username', function(err, username) {
        if (! username) {
          username = socket.id;
        }
        socket.get('room', function(err, room) {
          if (err) { throw err; }
          var broadcast = socket.broadcast;
          var message = content;
          if (room) {
            broadcast.to(room);
          }

          var messageDoc = {
            when: Date.now(),
            from: username,
            room: room,
            message: content
          };

          socket.emit('serverMessage', messageDoc);

          chatDB.insert(messageDoc, function(err) {
            if (err) { console.error(err); }
          });

          broadcast.emit('serverMessage', messageDoc);
        });
      });
    });

    socket.on('login', function(username) {
      socket.set('username', username, function(err) {
        if (err) { throw err; }
        var message = {
          from: username,
```

```
          message: 'Logged in',
          when: Date.now()
        };
        socket.emit('serverMessage', message);
        socket.broadcast.emit('serverMessage', message);

        sendBackLog(socket, null);

      });
    });

    socket.on('disconnect', function() {
      socket.get('username', function(err, username) {
        if (! username) {
          username = socket.id;
        }
        var message = {
          from: username,
          message: 'disconnected',
          when: Date.now()
        };
        socket.broadcast.emit('serverMessage', message);
      });
    });

    socket.on('join', function(room) {
      socket.get('room', function(err, oldRoom) {
        if (err) { throw err; }

        socket.set('room', room, function(err) {
          if (err) { throw err; }
          socket.join(room);
          if (oldRoom) {
            socket.leave(oldRoom);
          }
          socket.get('username', function(err, username) {
            if (! username) {
              username = socket.id;
            }
            var message = {
              from: username,
              message: 'joined room ' + room + '. Fetching backlog...',
              when: Date.now()
            };
            socket.emit('serverMessage', message);
            socket.broadcast.to(room).emit('serverMessage', message);
          });

          sendBackLog(socket, room);
        });
      });
    });

    socket.emit('login');

  });
}
```

ATTACHING FILES TO A COUCHDB DOCUMENT

Imagine allowing each user to define an avatar picture to be presented in every message. The user, after logging in, uploads an image file using a simple web form and the server saves it into CouchDB.

The first change you need to make is to provide the user with a form for uploading a file. For simplicity, this form can be placed on the bottom of the screen. Listing 24-6 contains the modified front-end code.

LISTING 24-6: A new version of the Socket.IO-based chat client that presents avatars.

```
<html>
  <head>
    <title>Node.js WebSocket chat</title>
    <style type="text/css">
      #input {
        width: 200px;
      }
      #messages {
        position: fixed;
        top: 40px;
        bottom: 50px;
        left: 8px;
        right: 8px;
        border: 1px solid #EEEEEE;
        padding: 8px;
        overflow: hidden;
      }
      form {
        position: fixed;
        bottom: 0;
      }
      .message .when {
        color: grey;
      }
      .message .from {
        color: red;
      }
      .message .from.self {
        color: green;
      }
      .message .avatar {
        width: 80px;
      }

    </style>
  </head>

  <body>

    Your message:
```

```
<input type="text" id="input" />

<div id="messages"></div>

<form action="/avatar" enctype="multipart/form-data"
  method="POST" target="avatar-target" id="avatar-form">
  <label for="avatar">Set avatar:</label>
  <input type="file" id="avatar" name="avatar" />
  <input type="submit" />
</form>

<iframe style="width:0;height:0;visibility:hidden" id="avatar-target"></iframe>

<script src="http://localhost:4000/socket.io/socket.io.js"></script>
<script type="text/javascript">
  var messagesElement = document.getElementById('messages');
  var lastMessageElement = null;
  var username;

  function addMessage(message) {
    var newMessageElement = document.createElement('div');

    newMessageElement.className = "message";

    if (message.when) {
      message.when = new Date(message.when);
    }

    message.avatar = '/avatar?username=' + encodeURIComponent(message.from);

    ['avatar', 'when', 'from', 'message'].forEach(function(prop) {
      var newPart = document.createElement('span');
      newPart.className = prop;
      var messageText = message[prop];
      if (prop !== 'message') {
        messageText = '[' + messageText + ']';
        if (prop === 'from') {
          if (message[prop] === username) {
            newPart.className += ' self';
          }
        } else if (prop === 'avatar') {
          var avatarImage = document.createElement('img');
          avatarImage.src = message.avatar;
          avatarImage.className = 'avatar';
          newPart.appendChild(avatarImage);
          messageText = '';
        }
      }
      messageText += ' ';
      var newPartText = document.createTextNode(messageText);
      newPart.appendChild(newPartText);
      newMessageElement.appendChild(newPart);
    });

    messagesElement.insertBefore(newMessageElement, lastMessageElement);
```

continues

LISTING 24-6 *(continued)*

```
      lastMessageElement = newMessageElement;
    }

    var socket = io.connect('http://localhost:4000/chat');
    socket.on('serverMessage', function(content) {
      addMessage(content);
    });

    socket.on('login', function() {
      username = prompt('What username would you like to use?');
      socket.emit('login', username);
    });

    socket.on('backlog', function(messages) {
      messages.forEach(addMessage);
    });

    function sendCommand(command, args) {
      if (command === 'j') {
        socket.emit('join', args);
      } else {
        alert('unknown command: ' + command);
      }
    }

    function sendMessage(message) {
      var commandMatch = message.match(/^\/(\w*)(.*)/);
      if (commandMatch) {
        sendCommand(commandMatch[1], commandMatch[2].trim());
      } else {
        socket.emit('clientMessage', message);
      }
    }

    var inputElement = document.getElementById('input');

    inputElement.onkeydown = function(keyboardEvent) {
      if (keyboardEvent.keyCode === 13) {
        sendMessage(inputElement.value);
        inputElement.value = '';
        return false;
      } else {
        return true;
      }
    };
  </script>

  <script>
    var form = document.getElementById('avatar-form');
    form.onsubmit = function() {
      if (! username) {
        alert('You must first log in')
```

```
        } else {
          form.action = '/avatar?username=' + encodeURIComponent(username);
          form.submit();
          console.log('submitted form');
        }
        return false;
      }
    </script>

  </body>
</html>
```

Here you are creating a form that will submit the avatar file into a hidden iframe element inside the document. You can use this trick when you don't want to leave a page and want to submit multipart data (such as when there is a file or more to upload).

In the last part you have a script that changes the URL before the form is submitted to pass the username in the query string so that the server knows which user you are talking about.

> **NOTE** *Note that this form can be very easily hacked. A user could easily submit pictures for other users. Because the site is not password-protected, the security requirements are very lax.*
>
> *For a session-based authentication example, check out Chapter 21, "Making a Web Application Using Express.js."*

The server needs to accept this file upload and insert it in a user database in CouchDB. First, you need to ensure that the `users` database is created. You can do that like you did for the `chat` database:

```
couchdb.db.create('chat', function(err) {
  if (err && err.status_code !== 412) {
    throw err;
  }

  couchdb.db.create('users', function(err) {
    if (err && err.status_code !== 412) {
      throw err;
    }

  //...
});
```

Now you need to accept and parse form uploads. For that you will use the `formidable` third-party module by Felix Geisendörfer. Add it to the `package.json` manifest:

```
{
  "name": "couch-socketio-chat",
  "version": "1.0.0",
  "dependencies": {
```

```
      "nano": "3.1.x",
      "socket.io": "0.9.x",
      "formidable": "1.0.x",
      "bufferedstream": "1.0.x"
    }
  }
```

You will also need the bufferedstream module. This module buffers the request data and makes it available when you need it.

Now that you've made these changes to the package.json file, you can install these two missing modules by doing:

```
$ npm install
```

Now you need to change the handler function that processes new requests:

```
function handler(req, res) {
  var username;
  if (req.method === 'POST' && req.url.indexOf('/avatar') === 0) {

    var currentUserDocRev;

    console.log('got avatar');

    var bufferedRequest = new BufferedStream();
    bufferedRequest.headers = req.headers;
    bufferedRequest.pause();
    req.pipe(bufferedRequest);

    // parse username
    console.log(url.parse(req.url).query);
    username = url.parse(req.url, true).query.username;

    userDB.insert({username: username}, username, function(err, user) {
      if (err) {
        if (err.status_code === 409) {
          userDB.get(username, function(err, user) {
            if (err) {
              console.error(err);
              res.writeHead(500);
              return res.end(JSON.stringify(err));
            }
            currentUserDocRev = user._rev;
            bufferedRequest.resume();

          });
          return;
        } else {
          res.writeHead(500);
          return res.end(JSON.stringify(err));
        }
      }
      console.log('username inserted, rev = ', user.rev);
```

```
        currentUserDocRev = user.rev;
        console.log('currentUserDocRev:', currentUserDocRev);
        bufferedRequest.resume();

      });

      // handle avatar upload

      var form = new formidable.IncomingForm();
      form.encoding = 'utf8';
      form.parse(bufferedRequest);

      form.onPart = function(part) {
        if (part.name !== 'avatar') {
          return;
        }
        var attachment = userDB.attachment.insert(
            username, 'avatar', null, part.mime, {rev: currentUserDocRev});

        part.pipe(attachment);

        attachment.on('error', function(err) {
          console.error(err);
          res.writeHead(500);
          return res.end(JSON.stringify(err));
        });

        attachment.on('end', function() {
          res.end();
        });
      };

    } else if (req.url.indexOf('/avatar') === 0){
      // serve the avatar
      username = url.parse(req.url, true).query.username;
      userDB.attachment.get(username, 'avatar').pipe(res);
    } else {
      // serve the index page
      fs.readFile(__dirname + '/index.html',
        function(err, data) {
          if (err) {
           res.writeHead(500);
           return res.end('Error loading index.html');
          }

          res.writeHead(200);
          res.end(data);
        }
      );
    }
  }
```

When there is a `POST` request to the `/avatar` URL, you instantiate a `formidable` form to parse the content. But first you need to pause the request — that's where the `bufferedstream` module comes. You pipe the request data into a buffered stream, which you set in the paused state. This guarantees that the buffered stream will keep buffering data and will not emit any before you resume the stream.

Then, you make sure a CouchDB document is created for the username in the `users` database. If such a user already exists, you get a `409 Conflict` status code, and you must get the user document version number. Once you have that, you can resume the request data stream, which will activate the `formidable` handlers you have set up for the file upload part.

Once `formidable` starts parsing the part of the request that contains the avatar image, the following code is activated:

```
form.onPart = function(part) {
  if (part.name !== 'avatar') {
    return;
  }
  var attachment = userDB.attachment.insert(
      username, 'avatar', null, part.mime, {rev: currentUserDocRev});

  part.pipe(attachment);

  attachment.on('error', function(err) {
    console.error(err);
    res.writeHead(500);
    return res.end(JSON.stringify(err));
  });

  attachment.on('end', function() {
    res.end();
  });
};
```

Here, you create an attachment using nano `db.attachment.insert(documentID, attachment name, mime_type, options)`, but this statement doesn't really do anything yet. Instead, it returns a writable stream that you can pipe the file to by using the following:

```
part.pipe(attachment);
```

Once the attachment stream ends, the avatar attachment is uploaded, and you end the response.

Now the front-end code will construct avatar image URLs to your server in the form of `/avatar?username=abc`. The browser expects an image to be returned by URLs like this. What you need to do is simply pipe the image from CouchDB like so:

```
// serve the avatar
username = url.parse(req.url, true).query.username;
userDB.attachment.get(username, 'avatar').pipe(res);
```

Listing 24-7 contains the new version of the server code. You need to restart the server and refresh the chat page.

LISTING 24-7: A new version of the Socket.IO-based chat server that presents avatars.

```
var url = require('url');

var nano = require('nano');
var couchdb = nano('https://myiriscouchserver.iriscouch.com');

var formidable = require('formidable');
var BufferedStream = require('bufferedstream');

var couchMapReduce = function (doc) {
  emit([doc.room, doc.when], doc);
};

couchdb.db.create('chat', function(err) {
  if (err && err.status_code !== 412) {
    throw err;
  }

  couchdb.db.create('users', function(err) {
    if (err && err.status_code !== 412) {
      throw err;
    }

    var designDoc = {
      language: "javascript",
      views: {
        by_room: {
          map: couchMapReduce.toString()
        }
      }
    };

    var chatDB = couchdb.use('chat');

    (function insertOrUpdateDesignDoc() {
      chatDB.insert(designDoc, '_design/designdoc', function(err) {
        if (err) {
          if (err.status_code === 409) {
            chatDB.get('_design/designdoc', function(err, ddoc) {
              if (err) { return console.error(err); }
              designDoc._rev = ddoc._rev;
              insertOrUpdateDesignDoc();
            });
            return;
          } else {
            return console.error(err);
          }
        }
        startServer();
      });
    }());
  });
});
```

continues

LISTING 24-7 *(continued)*

```
function startServer() {
  console.log('starting server');
  var chatDB = couchdb.use('chat');
  var userDB = couchdb.use('users');

  var httpd = require('http').createServer(handler);
  var io = require('socket.io').listen(httpd);
  var fs = require('fs');

  httpd.listen(4000);

  function handler(req, res) {
    var username;
    if (req.method === 'POST' && req.url.indexOf('/avatar') === 0) {

      var currentUserDocRev;

      console.log('got avatar');

      var bufferedRequest = new BufferedStream();
      bufferedRequest.headers = req.headers;
      bufferedRequest.pause();
      req.pipe(bufferedRequest);

      // parse username
      console.log(url.parse(req.url).query);
      username = url.parse(req.url, true).query.username;

      userDB.insert({username: username}, username, function(err, user) {
        if (err) {
          if (err.status_code === 409) {
            userDB.get(username, function(err, user) {
              if (err) {
                console.error(err);
                res.writeHead(500);
                return res.end(JSON.stringify(err));
              }
              currentUserDocRev = user._rev;
              bufferedRequest.resume();

            });
            return;
          } else {
            res.writeHead(500);
            return res.end(JSON.stringify(err));
          }
        }
        console.log('username inserted, rev = ', user.rev);
        currentUserDocRev = user.rev;
        console.log('currentUserDocRev:', currentUserDocRev);
        bufferedRequest.resume();

      });
```

```
      // handle avatar upload

      var form = new formidable.IncomingForm();
      form.encoding = 'utf8';
      form.parse(bufferedRequest);

      form.onPart = function(part) {
        if (part.name !== 'avatar') {
          return;
        }
        var attachment = userDB.attachment.insert(
            username, 'avatar', null, part.mime, {rev: currentUserDocRev});

        part.pipe(attachment);

        attachment.on('error', function(err) {
          console.error(err);
          res.writeHead(500);
          return res.end(JSON.stringify(err));
        });

        attachment.on('end', function() {
          res.end();
        });
      };

    } else if (req.url.indexOf('/avatar') === 0){
      // serve the avatar
      username = url.parse(req.url, true).query.username;
      userDB.attachment.get(username, 'avatar').pipe(res);
    } else {
      // serve the index page
      fs.readFile(__dirname + '/index.html',
        function(err, data) {
          if (err) {
           res.writeHead(500);
           return res.end('Error loading index.html');
          }

          res.writeHead(200);
          res.end(data);
        }
      );
    }
  }

  function sendBackLog(socket, room) {
    var getOptions = {
      start_key: JSON.stringify([room, 9999999999999]),
      end_key: JSON.stringify([room, 0]),
      limit: 10,
      descending: true
    };
```

continues

LISTING 24-7 *(continued)*

```
    chatDB.get('_design/designdoc/_view/by_room', getOptions,
      function(err, results) {
        var messages = results.rows.reverse().map(function(res) {
          return res.value;
        });
        socket.emit('backlog', messages);
      });
  }

  var chat = io.of('/chat');

  chat.on('connection', function (socket) {
    socket.on('clientMessage', function(content) {

      socket.get('username', function(err, username) {
        if (! username) {
          username = socket.id;
        }
        socket.get('room', function(err, room) {
          if (err) { throw err; }
          var broadcast = socket.broadcast;
          var message = content;
          if (room) {
            broadcast.to(room);
          }

          var messageDoc = {
            when: Date.now(),
            from: username,
            room: room,
            message: content
          };

          socket.emit('serverMessage', messageDoc);

          chatDB.insert(messageDoc, function(err) {
            if (err) { console.error(err); }
          });

          broadcast.emit('serverMessage', messageDoc);
        });
      });
    });

    socket.on('login', function(username) {
      socket.set('username', username, function(err) {
        if (err) { throw err; }
        var message = {
          from: username,
          message: 'Logged in',
          when: Date.now()
        };
```

```
        socket.emit('serverMessage', message);
        socket.broadcast.emit('serverMessage', message);

        sendBackLog(socket, null);

      });
    });

    socket.on('disconnect', function() {
      socket.get('username', function(err, username) {
        if (! username) {
          username = socket.id;
        }
        var message = {
          from: username,
          message: 'disconnected',
          when: Date.now()
        };
        socket.broadcast.emit('serverMessage', message);
      });
    });

    socket.on('join', function(room) {
      socket.get('room', function(err, oldRoom) {
        if (err) { throw err; }

        socket.set('room', room, function(err) {
          if (err) { throw err; }
          socket.join(room);
          if (oldRoom) {
            socket.leave(oldRoom);
          }
          socket.get('username', function(err, username) {
            if (! username) {
              username = socket.id;
            }
            var message = {
              from: username,
              message: 'joined room ' + room + '. Fetching backlog...',
              when: Date.now()
            };
            socket.emit('serverMessage', message);
            socket.broadcast.to(room).emit('serverMessage', message);
          });

          sendBackLog(socket, room);
        });
      });
    });

    socket.emit('login');

  });
}
```

SUMMARY

You can connect to a CouchDB server using Nano, a third-party module installable via NPM.

Using Nano you can create a database and views on documents by inserting design documents that contain map and reduce functions.

You can also insert documents and query these documents by accessing the generated views.

CouchDB also allows documents to have binary file attachments, and Nano allows you to write and read them using streams.

25

Connecting to MongoDB Using Mongoose

WHAT'S IN THIS CHAPTER?

- Installing and using Mongoose
- Defining schemas and models
- Understanding Mongoose data types
- Using schema validation
- Searching, inserting, and updating documents
- Paginating query results
- Defining indexes
- Using getters, setters, and virtual attributes
- Referencing documents
- Enriching models and document objects with higher-level methods

Document-oriented databases have regained popularity in recent years, being at the front and center of the NoSQL movement. These types of databases, unlike relational ones, don't require you to specify the structure of your data ahead of time. Instead, you can change it organically as your project requires. Another important difference from a relational database is that the document is generally the atomic unit and can be as complete as needed, eliminating the need to make costly joins and transactions across tables.

MongoDB is a popular document-oriented database that enables you to perform rich dynamic queries using a powerful query language.

In MongoDB, data is organized such that one MongoDB database holds a series of collections. Each collection has a series of documents, and each document comprises a set of fields. A field is a key-value pair, where the key is a string and the value can be a basic type (like a string, integer, float, timestamp, binary, and so on), an embedded document, or a collection of any of these.

A MongoDB query can be described using a JavaScript document literal. For instance, say you have a collection of users and want to find all the users with the first name "John" and the last name "Doe," you could apply the following query:

```
{name: {first: 'John', last: 'Doe'}}
```

You could also find all users with "Doe" as the last name by using this query:

```
{'name.last': 'Doe'}
```

You can also use regular expressions instead of static values. For instance, to find all users whose last name starts with a "D," you can use:

```
{'name.last': /^D/}
```

This also works for array values. For instance, if you are searching in a collection of articles for those that have the keyword `node.js`, you can use the query:

```
{keywords: 'node.js'}
```

You could also match all the documents with at least one of a set of keywords by using the following:

```
{keywords: {'$in' : ['node.js', 'javascript']}
```

There are several operators like this that you can use inside queries, such as to find all documents where the field `count` has a value that is greater than 10 and less than or equal to 100:

```
{count: {'$gt' : 10, '&lte': 100}
```

> **NOTE** *This book does not aim to make you proficient in installing and querying MongoDB; that would be the subject of a whole other book.*
>
> *If you don't have MongoDB installed in your system and you want to install it, use the information provided on the MongoDB home page at* `http://www.mongodb.org/`.
>
> *As an alternative, you can try using a MongoDB external service like the one provided by MongoHQ at* `https://mongohq.com/`.

INSTALLING MONGOOSE

In this chapter you create code that accesses a MongoDB server. To do this in Node, you will use the Mongoose third-party module. Mongoose allows you to access MongoDB using an object model.

In Chapter 21, "Making a Web Application Using Express.js," you had several route listeners for managing users, which were the public interface for managing a user database. This database was a fake in-memory object, making it obviously non-persistent and only suited for a prototype. However, now that you can use a MongoDB database using Mongoose, you can replace it with a real persisted data access layer.

Start by copying the final application code from Chapter 21 into the new project directory and start from there. Now you need to change the application manifest `package.json` file and add the Mongoose dependency, as shown in Listing 25-1.

LISTING 25-1: The application package.json manifest file.

```
{
    "name": "application-name"
  , "version": "0.0.1"
  , "private": true
  , "dependencies": {
      "express": "2.5.11"
    , "jade": ">= 0.0.1"
    , "mongoose": ">=2.7.0"
  }
}
```

This file notes that the scripts you are building require any version of Mongoose greater or equal to 2.7.0. Now you can actually install Mongoose by:

```
$ npm install
...
mongoose@2.7.1 ./node_modules/mongoose
├── hooks@0.2.1
└── mongodb@1.0.2 (bson@0.0.6)
```

UNDERSTANDING HOW MONGOOSE USES MODELS TO ENCAPSULATE DATABASE ACCESS

Mongoose is a tool for modeling objects that interact with the database. A database has many collections, and a collection has many documents. Nothing requires two documents in the same collection to have a similar structure, but, for instance, if a "user" collection contains user records, all documents in that collection will be similar.

In Mongoose you define document schemas. Each schema can contain a list of fields and their constraints. Each field can have a type and some type-specific constraints, like a minimum value, for example, if the presence of a value is required, if the value should be unique throughout the other documents in the collection, if a validation rule is required, and so on.

A model represents a database connection to a collection that uses a schema.

CONNECTING TO MONGODB

First you need to connect to your MongoDB server, whether you installed it locally or subscribed to an external service over the Internet. For this you need to specify a MongoDB database URL with the scheme:

```
mongodb://username:password@hostname:port/database
```

If you are connecting to MongoDB on your local machine, the server probably doesn't need a password, in which case you can simply use the following:

```
mongodb://localhost/database
```

Then you need to tell Mongoose to connect to the database, and you can do so in the `app.js` file:

```
var dbURL = 'mongodb://localhost/database';
var db = require('mongoose').connect(dbURL);
```

If you haven't created a MongoDB database for this application, you need to do so now.

DEFINING A SCHEMA

You now need to create a schema module to define what a user document will look like. You'll use the data/schemas directory to host the schema modules, where you will create a file named `user.js`, as shown in Listing 25-2.

LISTING 25-2: The user schema in data/schemas/user.js.

```
var mongoose = require('mongoose');

var UserSchema = new mongoose.Schema({
  username: String,
  name: String,
  password: String
});

module.exports = UserSchema;
```

Here you are defining a basic schema with three fields, all of them strings. Later in this chapter, you'll learn how you can evolve this schema to be more helpful and to support more complex documents.

DEFINING A MODEL

Now you need to define a model that will map into the user collection in the database. You will also define this as a module under `data/models/user.js`, as shown in Listing 25-3.

LISTING 25-3: The user model in data/models/user.js.

```
var mongoose = require('mongoose');
var UserSchema = require('../schemas/user');

var User = mongoose.model('User', UserSchema);

module.exports = User;
```

Now you need to use this model in your route listeners. But first you need to update some routing middleware to support the new user document model. First, create a module located in `routes/middleware/load_user.js` that defines a piece of middleware used to load users, as shown in Listing 25-4.

LISTING 25-4: The load user route middleware using the user model.

```
var User = require('../../data/models/user');

function loadUser(req, res, next) {
  User.findOne({username: req.params.name}, function(err, user) {
    if (err) {
      return next(err);
    }
    if (! user) {
      return res.send('Not found', 404);
    }
    req.user = user;
    next();
  });
}

module.exports = loadUser;
```

Here you are using the `findOne` method provided in the user model object. The first argument to it is the query parameters, which in this case is an exact match with the `name` request parameter. The second argument is a callback function that is invoked when there is an error or the find operation has terminated. If there is an error, it is forwarded to the next callback. If no such user is found in the user collection, you reply with a `404 Not Found` status code and stop execution. Otherwise, if the user is found, you assign it to the `req.user` property so other route listeners can use it later.

Now you can modify the user's route behavior, as shown in Listing 25-5.

LISTING 25-5: The user routes now using the user Mongoose model.

```
/*
 * User Routes
 */

var User = require('../data/models/user');
var notLoggedIn = require('./middleware/not_logged_in');
var loadUser = require('./middleware/load_user');
var restrictUserToSelf = require('./middleware/restrict_user_to_self');


module.exports = function(app) {

  app.get('/users', function(req, res,next){
    User.find({}, function(err, users) {
      if (err) {
        return next(err);
      }
      res.render('users/index', {title: 'Users', users: users});
    });
  });

  app.get('/users/new', notLoggedIn, function(req, res) {
    res.render('users/new', {title: "New User"});
  });

  app.get('/users/:name', loadUser, function(req, res, next){
    res.render('users/profile', {title: 'User profile', user: req.user});
  });

  app.post('/users', notLoggedIn, function(req, res, next) {
    User.findOne({username: req.body.username}, function(err, user) {
      if (err) {
        return next(err);
      }
      if (user) {
        return res.send('Conflict', 409);
      }
      User.create(req.body, function(err) {
        if (err) {
          return next(err);
        }
        res.redirect('/users');
      });
    });
  });

  app.del('/users/:name', loadUser, restrictUserToSelf,
    function(req, res, next) {
      req.user.remove(function(err) {
        if (err) { return next(err); }
```

```
            res.redirect('/users');
          });

      });

    };
```

Now you'll analyze the changes done here, one route listener at a time. First is the route listener for listing users:

```
app.get('/users', function(req, res){
  User.find({}, function(err, users) {
    if (err) {
      return next(err);
    }
    res.render('users/index', {title: 'Users', users: users});
  });
});
```

Here you are using the `find` method on the model and passing an empty query object, which means that MongoDB should find every user and return him or her. There are at least two problems with this: First, you don't sort the results. By not specifying the sorting order, MongoDB will use the natural order, which is the order in which the documents are stored internally. This is most probably not what the user is expecting. You can sort the query results by doing this:

```
User.find({}).sort('name', 1).exec(function(err, users) {
  if (err) {
    return next(err);
  }
  res.render('users/index', {title: 'Users', users: users});
});
```

Here you are making use of the query chaining API, where you can define the constraints, specify the sort order, and then execute the query in separate builder method calls. Here you are specifying that the results should be sorted by the `name` property in ascending order (hence the 1 value). If you used −1 instead of 1, the results would be sorted in descending order.

You can additionally sort by any other fields; just add them to the query object before executing. If, for instance, you wanted to sort users by age (descending order) and then by name (ascending order), you would use the following code:

```
User.find({})
  .sort('age', -1)
  .sort('name', 1)
  .exec(function(err, users) { ...
```

The second problem with this listener code is that, because you are telling MongoDB to fetch every object in the collection, the time this query takes to execute will grow as the user collection grows.

The user interface list needs to be paginated, which means you present slices of the list of users. You can use the `skip` and `limit` options to retrieve only one page worth of data:

```
app.get('/users', function(req, res, next){
  var page = req.query.page && parseInt(req.query.page, 10) || 0;
  User.find({})
    .sort('name', 1)
    .skip(page * maxUsersPerPage)
    .limit(maxUsersPerPage)
    .exec(function(err, users) {
      if (err) {
        return next(err);
      }
      res.render('users/index', {title: 'Users', users: users, page: page});
    });
});
```

Here you are retrieving the current page from the query string in the request URL. If there is no such element in the query string, you use the default value of 0. Then you tell MongoDB to skip the first *x* elements — *x* being the number of users on the previous pages — and to limit the results to the maximum number of elements in the page you want.

> **NOTE** *For this code to work, you need to define the* `maxElementsPerPage` *configuration variable in the module scope with a value that suits your needs:*
>
> ```
> var maxUsersPerPage = 5;
> ```

Then you need to pass the current page to the rendering template so that the UI knows which page the user is at so it can craft the "previous" and "next" page links. Now you need to change the `views/users/index.jade` template to accommodate the paging, as shown in Listing 25-6.

LISTING 25-6: Users list with paging in views/users/index.jade.

```
h1 Users

p
  a(href="/users/new") Create new profile

ul
  - for(var username in users) {
    li
      a(href="/users/" + encodeURIComponent(username))= users[username].name
  - };

- if (page > 0) {
  a(href="?page=" + (page - 1)) Previous
   
- }

a(href="?page=" + (page + 1)) Next
```

There is still a small problem with this code — the "Next" page link appears even when there are no more users on the next page. You can fix this by counting all the user records in the collection and figuring out how many pages are left. This can be done in the route listener in `routes/users.js`:

```
app.get('/users', function(req, res, next){
  var page = req.query.page  && parseInt(req.query.page, 10) || 0;
  User.count(function(err, count) {
    if (err) {
      return next(err);
    }

    var lastPage = (page + 1) * maxUsersPerPage >= count;

    User.find({})
      .sort('name', 1)
      .skip(page * maxUsersPerPage)
      .limit(maxUsersPerPage)
      .exec(function(err, users) {
        if (err) {
          return next(err);
        }
        res.render('users/index', {
          title: 'Users',
          users: users,
          page: page,
          lastPage: lastPage
        });
      });

  });
});
```

Here you are requesting a document count using the model `count` method. Once this operation is finished, you determine whether there are more pages and then pass that indication into the template.

The user index view template needs to be changed to the example shown in Listing 25-7.

LISTING 25-7: New version of the users list with paging in views/users/index.jade.

```
h1 Users

p
  a(href="/users/new") Create new profile

ul
  - users.forEach(function(user) {
    li
      a(href="/users/" + encodeURIComponent(user.username))= user.name
  - });
```

continues

LISTING 25-7 *(continued)*

```
- if (page > 0) {
  a(href="?page=" + (page - 1)) Previous
   
- }

- if (! lastPage) {
  a(href="?page=" + (page + 1)) Next
- }
```

There is still one situation in the route listener code that you can avoid — there is no reason why both queries (the count and the user fetch) be executed in series. You could execute them in parallel, reducing the average time it takes to respond to the user request.

> **NOTE** *One of the many advantages of using Node is that you can easily make parallel I/O requests. Take advantage of it!*

For this you can use the `async` module you learned about in Chapter 19, "Controlling the Callback Flow." First you need to add it to the `package.json` manifest, as shown in Listing 25-8.

LISTING 25-8: New version of the package.json manifest containing the async dependency.

```
{
    "name": "application-name"
  , "version": "0.0.1"
  , "private": true
  , "dependencies": {
      "express": "2.5.11"
    , "jade": ">= 0.0.1"
    , "mongoose": ">=2.7.0"
    , "async": "0.1.22"
  }
}
```

Then, install the missing dependencies:

```
$ npm install
async@0.1.22 ./node_modules/async
```

You are ready to import the module and use it in the route listener. Place the module importing at the top of `routes/users.js`:

```
var async = require('async');
```

Now you can parallelize the requests using `async.parallel` like this:

```
app.get('/users', function(req, res, next){
  var page = req.query.page  && parseInt(req.query.page, 10) || 0;
  async.parallel([
```

```
        function(next) {
          User.count(next);
        },

        function(next) {
          User.find({})
            .sort('name', 1)
            .skip(page * maxUsersPerPage)
            .limit(maxUsersPerPage)
            .exec(next);
        }
      ],

      // final callback
      function(err, results) {

        if (err) {
          return next(err);
        }

        var count = results[0];
        var users = results[1];

        var lastPage = (page + 1) * maxUsersPerPage >= count;

        res.render('users/index', {
          title: 'Users',
          users: users,
          page: page,
          lastPage: lastPage
        });

      }
    );
  });
```

The final callback (the last argument to `async.parallel`) is called when both operations are finished or when an error happens, and you get the results as an array, one for each operation. If no error happens, the first element in this array will contain the user count and the second one will contain the user list.

Next you are going to take a look at the user creation route listener:

```
app.post('/users', notLoggedIn, function(req, res, next) {
  User.findOne({username: req.body.username}, function(err, user) {
    if (err) {
      return next(err);
    }
    if (user) {
      return res.send('Conflict', 409);
    }
    User.create(req.body, function(err) {
```

```
        if (err) {
          return next(err);
        }
        res.redirect('/users');
      });
    });
  });
```

Here you are checking if a username is taken and, if it's not, you create the user using the `create` method on the user model. This code has at least one problem — another request can create a user with the same username between the time that you check whether a given username exists and the time that the database actually creates the user. This would result in more than one user with the same username inserted in the database, which cannot happen because you are looking up users based on that value.

You can avoid this problem entirely by adding an option to the user schema where you say that the `username` field is unique, as shown in Listing 25-9.

LISTING 25-9: New version of the user schema with a unique index in data/schemas/user.js.

```
var mongoose = require('mongoose');

var UserSchema = new mongoose.Schema({
  username: {type: String, unique: true},
  name: String,
  password: String
});

module.exports = UserSchema;
```

When you use this option, Mongoose will ensure that a unique index is created on that field. Now you can remove the code that checks whether that username already exists and simply rely on MongoDB returning you an error in `file routes/user.js`:

```
app.post('/users', notLoggedIn, function(req, res, next) {
  User.create(req.body, function(err) {
    if (err) {
      if (err.code === 11000) {
        res.send('Conflict', 409);
      } else {
        next(err);
      }
      return;
    }
    res.redirect('/users');
  });
});
```

When MongoDB yields an error, Mongoose captures the error code and passes it inside the error object. Here you are interpreting that error code, presenting a `409 Conflict` HTTP status code when that code signifies a `Duplicate Key Error`.

> **NOTE** *You can find out more about the MongoDB error codes at the documentation at the* `mongodb.org` *website.*

For the login to work you have to integrate it with Mongoose. To do so, change the file in `routes/session.js` to the following:

```
/*
 * Session Routes
 */

var User = require('../data/models/user');
var notLoggedIn = require('./middleware/not_logged_in');

module.exports = function(app) {

  app.dynamicHelpers({
    session: function(req, res) {
      return req.session;
    }
  });

  app.get('/session/new', notLoggedIn, function(req, res) {
    res.render('session/new', {title: "Log in"});
  });

  app.post('/session', notLoggedIn, function(req, res) {
    User.findOne({username: req.body.username, password: req.body.password},
      function(err, user) {
        if (err) {
          return next(err);
        }

        if (user) {
          req.session.user = user;
          res.redirect('/users');
        } else {
          res.redirect('/session/new');
        }
      });
  });

  app.del('/session', function(req, res, next) {
    req.session.destroy();
    res.redirect('/users');
  });

};
```

Now that the user routes are working with MongoDB, you can continue evolving your user schema to embody validators, document nesting, and more.

Using Validators

When users register a new user account on the website, they can enter whatever data they want in these fields — Mongoose makes no validations. You can, however, introduce constraints into your user schema. For instance, you can introduce a new `email` field that is required and has to match a regular expression, as shown in Listing 25-10.

LISTING 25-10: New version of the user schema with a new validated e-mail field in data/schemas/user.js.

```
var mongoose = require('mongoose');

// simple but incomplete email regexp:
var emailRegexp = /.+\@.+\..+/;

var UserSchema = new mongoose.Schema({
  username: {type: String, unique: true},
  name: String,
  password: String,
  email: {
    type: String,
    required: true,
    match: emailRegexp

  }
});

module.exports = UserSchema;
```

Now, to see the validator in action, you need to add the `email` field to the user creation form in `views/users/new.jade`:

```
h1 New User

form(method="POST", action="/users")
  p
    label(for="username") Username<br />
    input#username(name="username")
  p
    label(for="name") Name<br />
    input#name(name="name")
  p
    label(for="email") Email<br />
    input#email(name="email")
  p
    label(for="password") Password<br />
    input#password(type="password", name="password")
  p
    label(for="bio") Bio<br />
    textarea#bio(name="bio")
  p
    input(type="submit", value="Create")
```

You can now test the web application by starting your server:

```
$ node app
```

Point your browser to `http://localhost:3000/users` and try to create user profiles with correct and incorrect e-mail addresses. You will see that a validation error will trigger the callback with an error. If you print a Mongoose error when a validation error occurs, it will look something like this:

```
{ message: 'Validation failed',
  name: 'ValidationError',
  errors:
   { email:
      { message: 'Validator "regexp" failed for path email',
        name: 'ValidatorError',
        path: 'email',
        type: 'regexp' } } }
```

You can test for this type of error and handle it in the `routes/users.js` file:

```
app.post('/users', notLoggedIn, function(req, res, next) {
  User.create(req.body, function(err) {
    if (err) {
      if (err.code === 11000) {
        res.send('Conflict', 409);
      } else {
        if (err.name === 'ValidationError') {
          return res.send(Object.keys(err.errors).map(function(errField) {
            return err.errors[errField].message;
          }).join('. '), 406);
        } else {
          next(err);
        }

      }
      return;
    }
    res.redirect('/users');
  });
});
```

This will present a crude message to the users, but you can easily evolve this code and present a proper in-context message instead.

You can also enumerate the allowed values for a certain field. For instance, if you wanted to store the user's gender in a `gender` field, you can make the changes shown in Listing 25-11 to the user schema.

LISTING 25-11: New version of the user schema with a new enumerated gender field in the data/schemas/user.js file.

```
var mongoose = require('mongoose');

var emailRegexp = /.+\@.+\..+/;

var UserSchema = new mongoose.Schema({
  username: {type: String, unique: true},
  name: String,
  password: String,
  email: {
    type: String,
    required: true,
    match: emailRegexp
  },
  gender: {
    type: String,
    required: true,
    uppercase: true,
    'enum': ['M', 'F']
  }
});

module.exports = UserSchema;
```

Here, you are defining that the `gender` field should be a required string value equal to `M` or `F`. Before validating the values, though, you are requesting that the value be transformed into uppercase, which makes the lowercase values `f` and `m` also valid.

To test this change you need restart your server and add the `gender` field to the user creation form, as shown in Listing 25-12.

LISTING 25-12: New version of the user creation form with the gender field in views/users/new.jade.

```
h1 New User

form(method="POST", action="/users")
  p
    label(for="username") Username<br />
    input#username(name="username")
  p
    label(for="name") Name<br />
    input#name(name="name")
  p
    label(for="email") Email<br />
    input#email(name="email")
  p
    label(for="password") Password<br />
    input#password(type="password", name="password")
  p
```

```
    label(for="gender") Gender<br />
    input#gender(name="gender")
  p
    label(for="bio") Bio<br />
    textarea#bio(name="bio")
  p
    input(type="submit", value="Create")
```

Besides enumerating the possible values or providing a regular expression, you can provide a custom function that will validate the field. For instance, you may want to add a birth date to the user profile and, for some reason, validate that the user is at least 18 years old.

First, because JavaScript stores dates in milliseconds, you need to convert 18 years to milliseconds. You should do this at the beginning of your users routes module in `data/schemas/user.js`:

```
var TIMESPAN_YEAR = 31536000000;
var TIMESPAN_18_YEARS = 18 * TIMESPAN_YEAR;
```

Then you need to provide the validation function, which you should also provide at the top of your user's schema module in `data/schemas/user.js`:

```
function validate_18_years_old_or_more(date) {

  return (Date.now() - date.getTime()) > TIMESPAN_18_YEARS;
}
```

This function takes a date and returns a boolean that notes whether the date is more than 18 years old.

These are the required schema changes:

```
var UserSchema = new mongoose.Schema({
  username: {type: String, unique: true},
  name: String,
  password: String,
  email: {
    type: String,
    required: true,
    match: emailRegexp
  },
  gender: {
    required: true,
    type: String,
    uppercase: true,
    'enum': ['M', 'F']
  },
  birthday: {
    type: Date,
    validate: [
      validate_18_years_old_or_more,
      'You must be 18 years old or more']
  }
});
```

Notice that, in the validate field option, you are passing an array that contains two positions — the validation function and a message. This is how you can specify a custom message that will override the one that is automatically generated by Mongoose.

To test this you must again restart your server and add a date field to the `views/users/new.jade` template, as shown in Listing 25-13.

LISTING 25-13: New version of the user creation form with the birthday field in the views/users/new.jade file.

```
h1 New User

form(method="POST", action="/users")
  p
    label(for="username") Username<br />
    input#username(name="username")
  p
    label(for="name") Name<br />
    input#name(name="name")
  p
    label(for="email") Email<br />
    input#email(name="email")
  p
    label(for="password") Password<br />
    input#password(type="password", name="password")
  p
    label(for="gender") Gender<br />
    input#gender(name="gender")
  p
    label(for="birthday") Birthday<br />
    input#birthday(name="birthday")
  p
    label(for="bio") Bio<br />
    textarea#bio(name="bio")
  p
    input(type="submit", value="Create")
```

> **NOTE** *Mongoose accepts any date format that is compatible with* `Date.parse()`*, which means that it accepts the standard RFC2822 format and the ISO 8601 syntax. This means that you can introduce the dates with many alternative formats but, to simplify your tests, you can use the generic YYYY/MM/DD format.*

You can also define asynchronous validators if your validation function needs to do I/O. For instance, you may want to contact an external service to make some kind of validation. To simplify, you will add a field to contain a Twitter handle, and you want to simply validate that this handle exists using the Twitter API.

For this, simply emit an HTTP request to the Twitter user page and then observe the response HTTP status. If the response status is a `404 Not Found`, you can conclude that the Twitter handle is invalid.

To simplify the way you do HTTP, use Mikeal Rogers's `request` third-party module (covered in Chapter 13, "Making HTTP Requests"), which you must include in the `package.json` manifest (see Listing 25-14).

LISTING 25-14: A new version of the package.json manifest containing the request dependency.

```
{
    "name": "application-name"
  , "version": "0.0.1"
  , "private": true
  , "dependencies": {
      "express": "2.5.11"
    , "jade": ">= 0.0.1"
    , "mongoose": ">=2.7.0"
    , "async": "0.1.22"
    , "request": "2.10.0"
  }
}
```

Install the missing package:

```
$ npm install
...
request@2.10.0 ./node_modules/request
```

Import the module at the top of the user schema file in `data/schemas/user.js`:

```
var request = require('request');
```

And then, in the same file, define the validation function that takes a value and a callback and then calls back with a boolean when a response from Twitter arrives:

```
function twitterHandleExists(handle, done) {
  request('http://twitter.com/' + encodeURIComponent(handle), function(err, res) {
    if (err) {
      console.error(err);
      return done(false);
    }
    if (res.statusCode > 299) {
      done(false);
    } else {
      done(true);
    }
  });
}
```

Here you are simply making an HTTP call to the `twitter.com` user URL. If there is an error or the HTTP status code is not `2xx OK`, you presume that the field's value is invalid. Here, when using an asynchronous validator, instead of returning the value you invoke a callback function with a boolean noting whether the field is valid.

Using Modifiers

Sometimes you want to change the value of a field before you validate and save a document. For instance, the `gender` field has a declared `uppercase` modifier that capitalizes the string before entering the validation and saving step.

For fields of the `String` type, you can use the `uppercase` modifier, the `lowercase` modifier, and the `trim` modifier. The last one removes the leading and trailing white space from a string using the `string.trim()` method.

You can also use a custom modifier by defining a function that transforms and returns the value. For instance, the user can prefix the Twitter handle with `@` or not:

```
var UserSchema = new mongoose.Schema({
  username: {type: String, unique: true},
  name: String,
  password: String,
  email: {
    type: String,
    required: true,
    match: emailRegexp
  },
  gender: {
    required: true,
    type: String,
    uppercase: true,
    'enum': ['M', 'F']
  },
  birthday: {
    type: Date,
    validate: [validate_18_years_old_or_more, 'You must be 18 years old or more']
  },
  twitter: {
    type: String,
    validate: [twitterHandleExists, 'Please provide a valid twitter handle'],
    set: function(handle) {
      if (! handle) {
        return;
      }

      handle = handle.trim();
      if (handle.indexOf('@') === 0) {
        handle = handle.substring(1);
      }
      return handle;
    }
  }
});
```

Here you are first trimming the handle (if the user hasn't already) and then removing the first character if it is an `@`. This way, users can input `@mytwitterhandle` or `mytwitterhandle` and both will map to `mytwitterhandle`.

Using Getters

You can also filter what is stored in the database after MongoDB hands it to Mongoose, but before the object is available, by defining getters. Use a getter to filter or transform the value any way you want by providing a custom function. This can be useful, for instance, when you are performing data migrations.

Say you once allowed users to store Twitter handles that were prefixed by the `@` character. At a later point, you decided that you would use a setter to filter them out. You have, in your user collection, some Twitter handles that are prefixed with `@` and others that are not. You could do a complete data migration, although depending on your user collection size, that could take a long while and would have an impact on service performance. You could also learn to live with this inconsistency by changing the view code to allow both variations, but that would place the data filtering code on the wrong part of the application.

You could then define a filtering function like this at the top of the user schema module in `data/schemas/user.js`:

```
function filterTwitterHandle(handle) {
  if (! handle) {
    return;
  }
  handle = handle.trim();
  if (handle.indexOf('@') === 0) {
    handle = handle.substring(1);
  }
  return handle;
}
```

This function can now be used as both the setter and the getter of the `twitter` field, like this:

```
var UserSchema = new mongoose.Schema({
  username: {type: String, unique: true},
  name: String,
  password: String,
  email: {
    type: String,
    required: true,
    match: emailRegexp
  },
  gender: {
    required: true,
    type: String,
    uppercase: true,
    'enum': ['M', 'F']
  },
  birthday: {
```

```
      type: Date,
      validate: [validate_18_years_old_or_more, 'You must be 18 years old or more']
    },
    twitter: {
      type: String,
      validate: [twitterHandleExists, 'Please provide a valid twitter handle'],
      set: filterTwitterHandle,
      get: filterTwitterHandle
    }
  });
```

Using Virtual Attributes

You can also have some attributes that are not present in the document, but are computed dynamically, as Mongoose loads the document. For instance, the front-end code has to build the Twitter URL string based on a Twitter handle, but the Twitter URL is an attribute of the user, and as such should belong in the user document. However, because this attribute can be easily computed based on the Twitter handle, you can create what is called a `virtual` attribute. You do this by adding the following to the user schema module in the file `data/schemas/user.js`, immediately before the module exports:

```
//...
UserSchema
  .virtual('twitter_url')
  .get(function() {
    if (this.twitter) {
      return 'http://twitter.com/' + encodeURIComponent(this.twitter);
    }
  });
```

> **NOTE** *Virtual attributes aren't saved into the document.*

Now you can change the user profile view template to use all the new attributes, as shown in Listing 25-15.

LISTING 25-15: New version of the user profile template using the twitter_url virtual attribute in views/users/profile.jade.

```
h1= user.name

h2 Bio
p= user.bio

h2 Email
p= user.email
```

```
h2 Gender
p= user.gender

h2 Birthday
p= user.birthday

- if (user.twitter) {
  h2 Twitter
  p
    a(href= user.twitter_url)="@" + user.twitter
- }


form(action="/users/" + encodeURIComponent(user.username), method="POST")
  input(name="_method", type="hidden", value="DELETE")
  input(type="submit", value="Delete")
```

You can also define a setter for a virtual attribute. For instance, you might want to split the users' first and last names in the document, but keep the names as a single field in the user interface. You can then redefine a part of the user schema in file `data/schemas/user.js` like this:

```
var UserSchema = new mongoose.Schema({
  username: {type: String, unique: true},
  name: {
    first: String,
    last: String
  },
  password: String,
  email: {
    type: String,
    required: true,
    match: emailRegexp
  },
  gender: {
    required: true,
    type: String,
    uppercase: true,
    'enum': ['M', 'F']
  },
  birthday: {
    type: Date,
    validate: [validate_18_years_old_or_more, 'You must be 18 years old or more']
  },
  twitter: {
    type: String,
    validate: [twitterHandleExists, 'Please provide a valid twitter handle'],
    set: filterTwitterHandle,
    get: filterTwitterHandle
  }
});
```

```
UserSchema
  .virtual('full_name')
  .get(function() {
    return [this.name.first, this.name.last].join(' ');
  })
  .set(function(fullName) {
    var nameComponents = fullName.split(' ');
    this.name.last = nameComponents.pop();
    this.name.first = nameComponents.join(' ');
  });

UserSchema
  .virtual('twitter_url')
  .get(function() {
    if (this.twitter) {
      return 'http://twitter.com/' + encodeURIComponent(this.twitter);
    }
  });
```

Here, you are defining that the user document has a `name` field with an embedded object containing the first and the last names. Then, later, you're defining that any user document has a virtual attribute called `full_name` that is both of these values joined by a space character. This attribute can also be set, and the reverse operation is performed in the setter, splitting the name into the first and last names.

Now you need to make a slight modification in the view template, changing the attribute `name` to `full_name`, as shown in Listing 25-16.

LISTING 25-16: New version of the user creation form using the full_name virtual attribute in views/users/new.jade.

```
h1 New User

form(method="POST", action="/users")
  p
    label(for="username") Username<br />
    input#username(name="username")
  p
    label(for="full_name") Full name (first and last)<br />
    input#full_name(name="full_name")
  p
    label(for="email") Email<br />
    input#email(name="email")
  p
    label(for="password") Password<br />
    input#password(type="password", name="password")
  p
    label(for="gender") Gender<br />
```

```
    input#gender(name="gender")
  p
    label(for="birthday") Birthday<br />
    input#birthday(name="birthday")
  p
    label(for="twitter") Twitter Handle<br />
    input#twitter(name="twitter")
  p
    label(for="bio") Bio<br />
    textarea#bio(name="bio")
  p
    input(type="submit", value="Create")
```

You need to make the same change in the user profile view template, as shown in Listing 25-17.

LISTING 25-17: New version of the user profile template using the full_name virtual attribute in views/users/profile.jade.

```
h1= user.full_name

h2 Bio
p= user.bio

h2 Email
p= user.email

h2 Gender
p= user.gender

h2 Birthday
p= user.birthday

- if (user.twitter) {
  h2 Twitter
  p
    a(href= user.twitter_url)="@" + user.twitter
- }


form(action="/users/" + encodeURIComponent(user.username), method="POST")
  input(name="_method", type="hidden", value="DELETE")
  input(type="submit", value="Delete")
```

You also need to update the user list template in `views/users/index.jade`, where you can take the opportunity to transform the `for` cycle into a `foreach` iterator, as shown in Listing 25-18.

LISTING 25-18: New version of the user list template using the full_name virtual attribute.

```
h1 Users

p
  a(href="/users/new") Create new profile

ul
  - users.forEach(function(user) {
    li
      a(href="/users/" + encodeURIComponent(user.username))= user.full_name
  - });

- if (page > 0) {
  a(href="?page=" + (page - 1)) Previous
   
- }

- if (! lastPage) {
  a(href="?page=" + (page + 1)) Next
- }
```

You also have to change a view partial that shows the username at the top of the page when the user is logged in. Change the file `views/session/user.jade` to this:

```
- if (session.user) {

  p
    span Hello 
    span= session.user.name.first
    span !
  p
    form(method="POST", action="/session")
      input(type="hidden", name="_method", value="DELETE")
      input(type="submit", value="Log out")

- } else {

  p
    a(href="/session/new") Login
    span  or 
    a(href="/users/new") Register

- }
```

You might still have old documents in which the `name` field still has a string value instead of an embedded name document. Those documents will not have a `name.first` or a `name.last` attribute. Instead, the `name` attribute will contain a single string with the whole name.

To solve this inconsistency, you need to change three things. First, you need to declare that the `name` field is of `Mixed` type in the file `data/schemas/user.js`. This way, Mongoose allows you to sometimes have a string or an object (or any value, really):

```
var UserSchema = new mongoose.Schema({
  username: {type: String, unique: true},
  name: mongoose.Schema.Types.Mixed,
  password: String,
  email: {
    type: String,
    required: true,
    match: emailRegexp
  },
  gender: {
    required: true,
    type: String,
    uppercase: true,
    'enum': ['M', 'F']
  },
  birthday: {
    type: Date,
    validate: [validate_18_years_old_or_more, 'You must be 18 years old or more']
  },
  twitter: {
    type: String,
    validate: [twitterHandleExists, 'Please provide a valid twitter handle'],
    set: filterTwitterHandle,
    get: filterTwitterHandle
  }
});
```

You also have to change the `full_name` virtual attribute getter function to accommodate the old documents in which the name field still contains a string. In that case, you simply return the string:

```
UserSchema
  .virtual('full_name')
  .get(function() {
    if (typeof this.name === 'string') {
      return this.name;
    }
    return [this.name.first, this.name.last].join(' ');
  })
  .set(function(fullName) {
    var nameComponents = fullName.split(' ');
    this.name = {
      last: nameComponents.pop(),
      first: nameComponents.join(' ')
    };
  });
```

You also need to change the `full_name` virtual attribute setter to create the embedded name document when it is set. You have to do this because now Mongoose makes no assumptions — previously it knew that you had an embedded document, so it pre-populated the `name` attribute with an object. Now that the type is not defined, so you have to do it yourself.

You can now restart your application by pressing Ctrl+C and relaunching Node:

```
$ node app.js
```

You can now refresh the initial URL (`http://localhost:3000/users`) and try creating and showing the users' first names and watch the content of the database while you do so.

Using Default Values

You may want to track which date and time the user record was created. In this case, you can insert a `created_at` field of the `Date` type. This value should be automatic — you don't want the user to submit or even modify it. You can insert this field into the user document on the user creation route listener, but this is not the right place for this code. If you need to create a user somewhere else in your application, you would have to perform that again, which would lead to duplicate code and possibly some inconsistencies.

The right place for this is the user schema in file `data/schemas/user.js`, which would require some changes:

```
var UserSchema = new mongoose.Schema({
  username: {type: String, unique: true},
  name: mongoose.Schema.Types.Mixed,
  password: String,
  email: {
    type: String,
    required: true,
    match: emailRegexp
  },
  gender: {
    required: true,
    type: String,
    uppercase: true,
    'enum': ['M', 'F']
  },
  birthday: {
    type: Date,
    validate: [validate_18_years_old_or_more, 'You must be 18 years old or more']
  },
  twitter: {
    type: String,
    validate: [twitterHandleExists, 'Please provide a valid twitter handle'],
    set: filterTwitterHandle,
    get: filterTwitterHandle

  meta: {
    created_at: {
      type: Date,
      'default': Date.now
    },
    updated_at: {
      type: Date,
      'default': Date.now
    }
  }
});
```

Here you populate, by default, the `meta.created_at` and `meta.updated_at` fields with the current timestamp (which is cast into a proper date value before it's saved).

But this approach has one problem: If the user submits a form that changes the `meta.created_at` record, this value gets saved into the document, overriding the original value that you intended to be immutable. To prevent mutation of the value, you need to remove the `meta.created_at` and `meta.updated_at` values and insert the default values, all before the document is saved. To do so, add this snippet before the module exports at the end of the file `data/schemas/user.js`:

```
UserSchema.pre('save', function(next) {
  if (this.isNew) {
    this.meta.created_at = undefined;
  }

  this.meta.updated_at = undefined;
  next();
});
```

The user schema emits events before and after the object is saved or removed. In this case you are attaching a listener that is called before the object is saved. In this function, the `this` keyword is bound to the document.

You can also determine whether a document will be saved for the first time by observing the `isNew` property. In this case, you only want to remove the `meta.created_at` value when the object is created.

> **NOTE** *This code still doesn't work if the user somehow manages to override the* `meta.created_at` *value when the object is updated. To prevent this, you can create an attribute setter that doesn't allow any change in the value:*
>
> ```
> //...
>  meta: {
>    created_at: {
>      type: Date,
>      'default': Date.now,
>      set: function(val) {
>        return undefined;
>      }
>    },
>    updated_at: {
>      type: Date,
>      'default': Date.now
>    }
>  }
> ```

Defining Indexes

Unlike some other document-oriented databases, MongoDB lets you perform ad hoc queries, where the database creates a plan for running that query and tries to optimize it. To speed queries you can create indexes. You can index single fields or have compound indexes where you combine two or more fields.

An index can be unique or not. In the user schema, the username has the `unique` option set to `true`, which instructs Mongoose to ensure a unique index is created for that field before any queries run. It happens that you already have a unique index in the user's username property:

```
// ...
var UserSchema = new mongoose.Schema({
  username: {type: String, unique: true},
  name: mongoose.Schema.Types.Mixed,
// ...
```

As discussed, a unique index ensures that all documents have a different value for that field.

Also, an index can be sparse or not. If you define an index on a field, a normal index will contain an entry for all documents: those that contain the field and those that don't. But if you set the `sparse` option to `true` on a field, Mongoose will ensure an index is created that contains only the documents that contain the specified field.

Using sparse indexes has an impact on the result of queries that use this field. For instance, if you define a sparse index on the Twitter handle for the user schema, and then you order the results of a query by Twitter handle, the results will only contain documents for which the Twitter handle is defined. Try changing the user schema module in `data/schemas/user.js`, setting the `sparse` property to `true`:

```
  // ...
  twitter: {
    type: String,
    sparse: true,
    validate: [twitterHandleExists, 'Please provide a valid twitter handle'],
    set: filterTwitterHandle,
    get: filterTwitterHandle
  },
// ...
```

Running the following query will only fetch documents that contain the `twitter` field:

```
User.find({}).sort({twitter: 1}, callback);
```

You can combine sparse with unique indexes to create a unique constraint that ignores documents with a missing field. For instance, if you want the `email` field to be unique but not mandatory, you can create a sparse unique index, which uses that field by setting the following properties in the user schema in the file `data/schemas/user.js`:

```
// ...
email: {
  type: String,
  sparse: true,
  unique: true,
  match: emailRegexp
},
// ...
```

You can also define an index that combines the values of two or more fields at the schema level, by inserting it at the end of the file `data/users/schema.js`, before the module exports:

```
UserSchema.index({username: 1, 'meta.created_at': -1});
```

This creates an index that combines the values of `username` and `meta.created_at`, where the username is indexed in ascending order and the `meta.created_at` values are indexed in descending order. This index is useful for speeding up a query that uses these fields for filtering or sorting.

> **NOTE** *If you now try to restart your app, you may encounter the following problem:*
>
> ```
> MongoError: E11000 duplicate key error index: my_mongoose
> .users.$email_1  dup key: { : "myemail@mail.com" }
> ```
>
> *This will happen if you have more than one user with the same e-mail address in the database. To properly start the app, you have to change these duplicate records.*

Referencing Other Documents Using DB Refs

In Mongoose, a document can also contain a reference to another document. For instance, you may want to have an article collection that contains, among other fields, an author. This author can be a user. Instead of keeping the username, you can define that a field contains an object ID. Define the following schema under `data/schemas/article.js`, as shown in Listing 25-19.

LISTING 25-19: The article schema.

```
var Schema = require('mongoose').Schema;

var ArticleSchema = new Schema({
  title: {
    type: String,
    unique: true
  },
  body: String,
```

continues

LISTING 25-19 *(continued)*

```
    author: {
      type: Schema.ObjectId,
      ref: 'User',
      required: true
    },
    created_at: {
      type: Date,
      'default': Date.now
    }
  });

  module.exports = ArticleSchema;
```

Here you are defining a simple article schema that contains an author field that is of type `Schema.ObjectId` and references the model named `User`.

Define the model in Listing 25-20 under a file named `data/models/article.js`.

LISTING 25-20: The article model.

```
var mongoose = require('mongoose');
var ArticleSchema = require('../schemas/article');

var Article = mongoose.model('Article', ArticleSchema);

module.exports = Article;
```

Now you need to create a simple set of route listeners in the file `routes/articles.js` for responding to URLs under the `/articles` path (see Listing 25-21)

LISTING 25-21: The article route listeners.

```
/*
 * Article Routes
 */

var async = require('async');

var Article = require('../data/models/article');
var notLoggedIn = require('./middleware/not_logged_in');
var loadArticle = require('./middleware/load_article');
var loggedIn = require('./middleware/logged_in');

var maxArticlesPerPage = 5;
```

```
module.exports = function(app) {

  app.get('/articles', function(req, res, next){
    var page = req.query.page  && parseInt(req.query.page, 10) || 0;
    async.parallel([

        function(next) {
          Article.count(next);
        },

        function(next) {
          Article.find({})
            .sort('title', 1)
            .skip(page * maxArticlesPerPage)
            .limit(maxArticlesPerPage)
            .exec(next);
        }
      ],

      // final callback
      function(err, results) {

        if (err) {
          return next(err);
        }

        var count = results[0];
        var articles = results[1];

        var lastPage = (page + 1) * maxArticlesPerPage >= count;

        res.render('articles/index', {
          title: 'Articles',
          articles: articles,
          page: page,
          lastPage: lastPage
        });

      }
    );
  });

  app.get('/articles/new', loggedIn, function(req, res) {
    res.render('Articles/new', {title: "New Article"});
  });

  app.get('/articles/:title', loadArticle, function(req, res, next){
    res.render('articles/article', {title: req.article.title,
      article: req.article});
  });
```

continues

LISTING 25-21 *(continued)*

```
  app.post('/articles', loggedIn, function(req, res, next) {
    var article = req.body;
    article.author = req.session.user._id;
    Article.create(article, function(err) {
      if (err) {
        if (err.code === 11000) {
          res.send('Conflict', 409);
        } else {
          if (err.name === 'ValidationError') {
            return res.send(Object.keys(err.errors).map(function(errField) {
              return err.errors[errField].message;
            }).join('. '), 406);
          } else {
            next(err);
          }

        }
        return;
      }
      res.redirect('/articles');
    });
  });

  app.del('/articles/:title', loggedIn, loadArticle, function(req, res, next) {
    req.article.remove(function(err) {
      if (err) { return next(err); }
      res.redirect('/articles');
    });

  });

};
```

Because this is mainly a CRUD (Create, Remove, Update, and Delete) application (except that you didn't provide a method for updating, just for simplification), these route listeners are somewhat similar to the `User` ones, except that, when creating a new article, you assign it the author user ID by using the following code:

```
article.author = req.session.user._id;
```

> **NOTE** *Each object, after it's created in MongoDB, holds an* `_id` *field that contains a unique ID of the object inside that collection. Unlike some databases, this is not a sequential number; it's a random string.*

These route listeners use two new route middleware components — `loggedIn` and `loadArticle`. The last one loads the article that you can create under `routes/middleware/load_article.js`, as shown in Listing 25-22.

LISTING 25-22: A middleware component for loading an article in routes/middleware/load_article.js.

```
var Article = require('../../data/models/article');

function loadArticle(req, res, next) {
  Article.findOne({title: req.params.title})
    .populate('author')
    .exec(function(err, article) {
      if (err) {
        return next(err);
      }
      if (! article) {
        return res.send('Not found', 404);
      }
      req.article = article;
      next();
    });
}

module.exports = loadArticle;
```

This new route middleware component is similar to the `load_user.js` one, except that it instructs Mongoose to load the author using the following:

```
  Article.findOne({title: req.params.title})
    .populate('author')
    //...
```

This makes the corresponding user object available under the property `article.author`, which you can now use on the article-rendering template under `views/articles/article.jade`, as shown in Listing 25-23.

LISTING 25-23: The article detail view template in views/articles/article.jade.

```
h1= article.title

div!= article.body

hr

p
  span Author:
   
  a(href="/users/" + encodeURIComponent(article.author.username))=
   article.author.full_name

p
  a(href="/articles") Back to all articles
```

You also need to add the `loggedIn` middleware component under `routes/middleware/logged_in.js`, as shown in Listing 25-24.

LISTING 25-24: The article detail view template in views/articles/article.jade.

```
function loggedIn(req, res, next) {
  if (! req.session.user) {
    res.send('Forbidden. Please log in first.', 403);
  } else {
    next();
  }
}

module.exports = loggedIn;
```

For this to work you still need to add the new route listeners to the file `app.js`, as follows:

```
// Routes

require('./routes/session')(app);
require('./routes/index')(app);
require('./routes/users')(app);
require('./routes/articles')(app);
```

You need two new view templates as well:

- `views/articles/index.jade` contains the article list.
- `views/articles/new.jade` contains the article creation form.

See Listings 25-25 and 25-26.

LISTING 25-25: The article list template in views/articles/index.jade.

```
h1 Articles

p
  a(href="/articles/new") Create new article

ul
  - articles.forEach(function(article) {
    li
      a(href="/articles/" + encodeURIComponent(article.title))= article.title
  - });

- if (page > 0) {
  a(href="?page=" + (page - 1)) Previous
   
- }

- if (! lastPage) {
  a(href="?page=" + (page + 1)) Next
- }
```

LISTING 25-26: The article creation form in views/articles/new.jade.

```
h1 New Article

form(method="POST", action="/articles")
  p
    label(for="title") Title<br />
    input#title(name="title")
  p
    label(for="body") Body<br />
    textarea#body(name="body")
  p
    input(type="submit", value="Create")
```

Defining Instance Methods

Now you want to be able to list the most recent articles for a given user. To do this, you can create the query directly inside the user route listener, but that would not be the right place to do so. Instead, you'll create an instance method on the user object by attaching a method to the user schema before the module exports at the end of file `data/schemas/user.js`, like this:

```
UserSchema.methods.recentArticles = function(callback) {
  return this.model('Article')
    .find({author: this._id})
    .sort('created_at', 1)
    .limit(5)
    .exec(callback);
};
```

Now you can use this instance method to retrieve a list of the last five articles of a given user. Change the `GET '/users/:name'` route listener in file `routes/users.js` to retrieve the most recent user articles so you can list them:

```
app.get('/users/:name', loadUser, function(req, res, next){
  req.user.recentArticles(function(err, articles) {
    if (err) {
      return next(err);
    }
    res.render('users/profile', {
      title: 'User profile',
      user: req.user,
      recentArticles: articles
    });
  });

});
```

Now you need to change the `views/users/profile.jade` template and add this snippet right at the end:

```
h2 Recent Articles:
p!= partial('articles/list', {articles: recentArticles })
```

This makes use of the `views/articles/list.jade` partial template that you need to create, as shown in Listing 25-27.

LISTING 25-27: The article list partial template.

```
ul
  - articles.forEach(function(article) {
    li
      a(href="/articles/" + encodeURIComponent(article.title))= article.title
  - });
```

Because you already have this partial template for listing, you can replace the explicit listing in the `views/articles/index.jade` template with a call to this partial, as shown in Listing 25-28.

LISTING 25-28: A new version of the article list template that uses the article list partial.

```
h1 Articles

p
  a(href="/articles/new") Create new article

p!= partial('articles/list', {articles: articles})

- if (page > 0) {
  a(href="?page=" + (page - 1)) Previous
   
- }

- if (! lastPage) {
  a(href="?page=" + (page + 1)) Next
- }
```

Now is a good time to test the article creation and rendering by restarting your app and pointing your browser to `http://localhost:3000/articles`. Try logging in, creating articles, and browsing around.

Defining Static Methods

You can also expose methods on the model that provide higher-level operations or queries. For instance, you may want to provide a search function that returns articles with that string on the title or on the body. You can define it at the end of the article schema module in `data/schemas/article.js`, before the module exports:

```
ArticleSchema.statics.search = function(str, callback) {
  var regexp = new RegExp(str, 'i');
  return this.find({'$or': [{title: regexp}, {body: regexp}]}, callback);
};
```

Now you can create a route listener in file `routes/articles.js` to expose this functionality:

```
app.get('/articles/search', function(req, res, next) {
  console.log('searching for', req.query.q);
  Article.search(req.query.q, function(err, articles) {
    if (err) {
      return next(err);
    }
    res.render('articles/index', {
      title: 'Article search results',
      articles: articles,
      page: 0,
      lastPage: true
    });
  });
});
```

> **NOTE** *You should add this snippet before the* `app.get('/articles/:title')` *route so that it takes precedence.*

You can test this by restarting your server, logging in, creating some articles, and trying URLs like this, where *`somestring`* is replaced by a part of an existing article title or body.

```
http://localhost:3000/articles/search?q=somestring
```

SUMMARY

Mongoose is a database access library that allows you to map objects into collections and documents in a MongoDB database. Even though document-oriented databases allow unstructured data, Mongoose requires you to define a schema for each collection where you specify the data types, the indexes, default values, various validation functions, and other options.

You can then use these schemas in collection models that provide methods of searching, inserting, and modifying documents. Also, you can enrich these collection models and the returned document objects by defining new methods they provide that build on top of the existing ones.

You can also have references from one document into another document in the same or a different collection by using the `Schema.ObjectId` type and defining the target collection.

INDEX

INDEX

D

E

F

G

H

K

L

M

N

Q

R

S

T

U